Settling Scores

Settling Scores

A Life in the Margins of American Music

Joseph Franklin

Santa Fe

Sunstone books may be purchased for educational, business, or sales promotional use. For information please write: Special Markets Department, Sunstone Press, P.O. Box 2321, Santa Fe, New Mexico 87504-2321.

Library of Congress Cataloging-in-Publication Data:

Franklin, Joseph, 1944-
Settling scores : a life in the margins of American music / by Joseph Franklin.
p. cm.
ISBN 0-86534-478-7 (hardcover : alk. paper) -- ISBN 0-86534-477-9 (softcover : alk. paper)
1. Franklin, Joseph, 1944- 2. Musicians--United States--Biography. I. Title.

ML429.F736A3 2006
780.92--dc22
[B]

2006024701

WWW.SUNSTONEPRESS.COM
SUNSTONE PRESS / POST OFFICE BOX 2321 / SANTA FE, NM 87504-2321 /USA
(505) 988-4418 / ORDERS ONLY (800) 243-5644 / FAX (505) 988-1025

"I think the combination of age and a greater coming together is responsible for the speed of the passing time . . ."

—Sam Melville, excerpted from a letter written by the Attica inmate prior to his murder, and used as text by composer Frederick Rzewski for his composition "Coming Together."

"I don't worry about time.
You're here when you're here.
I worry about today and staying in tune."

—John Lee Hooker

CONTENTS

ACKNOWLEDGEMENTS

I am grateful to many people—friend and foe alike—who have influenced my life and served as inspiration for me to write this book. Among them is the late Grant Beglarian. At lunch in a very exclusive New York City restaurant, Grant, a respected educator, arts administrator and composer, confided in me that, at 70 years of age, he had become an "echo man." In response to my question of what or who is the echo man, Grant described the three stages of a man's life. "The first stage," he explained is "the initiate, when one learns his craft." "The second stage," he continued, "is the warrior stage where one, essentially, kicks ass." "The final stage," he concluded, "is the echo man, where one serves as an echo for everyone's questions." Somewhat remorsefully he concluded, "I guess I have become an echo man." He then looked me dead in the eye and said with a knowing smile, "Don't worry, Joseph, you're still a warrior."

I have carried that moment with me for over ten years as I traveled to, first, Montana, then Louisiana and, finally, New Mexico. Over those years I have hopefully maintained a warrior's stance, although to be honest, I do not stand as defiantly in front of my adversaries as I once did. As I age and gain wisdom I sometimes view Grant Beglarian's wizened image—the old warrior fading into eternity. And I suppose I view myself taking his place as an honored echo man. I only hope I can carry the title with the dignity that he and other warriors of his generation did.

This book could not have been written without the friendship and love of many people who have accompanied me on this crazy journey. Three of them edited the manuscript in various stages of its development: Maralyn Lois Polak (who encouraged me to write this book), Werner Strobel and Merilyn Jackson provided insight into our shared lives and suggested that I re-think certain aspects of my story, especially those important years with Relâche. Joe Kasinskas helped me re-live our trip to Lithuania and unearthed several of the photographs that appear in this book. Arthur Sabatini for continuing to talk and talk and...

This book is almost as much about discovering the southwest as it is about documenting a life in contemporary music. For that I thank John and Marjorie Wyckoff for giving me sanctuary when it was most needed. John and Rozella Kennedy in Santa Fe introduced me to James Clois Smith of Sunstone Press who accepted my proposal to publish this book and worked diligently to edit and help shape the final manuscript. Laurel Wyckoff has shared many of the stories that are told in this book. She has helped me remember the good times and the bad times and has supported me in my effort to affirm our lives lived in the margins of American music.

Finally, I dedicate this book to my mother and the memory of my father. Even in the most difficult of times they encouraged me to travel beyond the neighborhood and become who it is I have become.

PRELUDE
CRACKING THE CODES

Larry Tso speaks in code: "Believe one day back there...back in the eon time..." Canyon de Chelly appears like an apparition in the high dry desert, its outline resembling two giant slender hands elegantly conducting a warped tune, a surreal dance around the fires of antiquity. This is a mythical land trussed by steep sheer red rock walls that settle in deep canyons. Narrow rivulets flow slowly along the canyon floor fed in the summer by rainwater. In the winter melting snow seeps down the canyon walls to nourish the fertile farmland tended by small Navajo families who live on the canyon's floor.

For years I have traveled to Canyon de Chelly on my trips to the American southwest, pausing for one, two or three days on journeys throughout the Four Corners region of Arizona, New Mexico, Utah and Colorado. Each time I visit Canyon de Chelly I experience a spiritual transformation. I find myself strangely at ease and relaxed, open to new feelings. There is something about the landscape that caresses the soul and frees the body from tension that clings to the bones and muscles, residue of battles won and lost as an urban warrior and, as a reporter once described me as, "...a street fighter for New Music." In 1992 I traveled deep into the canyon with Larry Tso as my guide.

Prefacing his descriptions of rock formations, pictographs and ruins of cities built by the Anasazi, "the ancient ones," with the phrase "believe one day back there or "back in the eon time" Larry Tso transforms the majesty of the land into a personal account of his people's struggle to survive against natural and human forces of conquest. The Navajo people have survived because of their belief in "...one day back there"; a simpler time when people valued respect and honor, qualities sorely needed in much of the world today.

Larry Tso is a Navajo Indian guide on the Navajo Indian Reservation in northeastern Arizona, and Canyon de Chelly comprises two canyons, one named Canyon del Muerto, or Death Canyon, the other Canyon de Chelly, a Spanish mispronunciation of the Navajo word Tsegi, which means roughly Rock Canyon.

Larry Tso speaks in code. So do I: "...sonic traces; performative qualities; tonal language; timbral structure..." These are a few of the words that describe and encode the rhythms of the music I have heard over the past 30-plus years as a musician and director of Relâche, an ensemble for New Music that I co-founded in Philadelphia. Throughout those turbulent, complicated, satisfying years and during the past seven years since I left Philadelphia first for Montana, then Louisiana and New Mexico, I find myself asking time and again "who has broken the code?"

"One day back there," for me, is February 2000 I am sitting at my desk in Helena, Montana, wondering why I moved to that desolate mountain town away from the intellectual and artistic life that nurtured yet tortured me in Philadelphia, New York and points beyond. "One day back there" is June 2001 a year after the fires that ravaged the Montana landscape when I prepare to leave Montana for Baton Rouge, Louisiana and a tropical climate far removed from the numbing cold and despairing narrowness of many people who live among the high plains. Louisiana: Great Food! Diverse population! Singing and dancing! And rain. Lots of rain to lubricate the body and spirit. That day back there in February 2000 I began to write. That day back there in June 2001 I had completed nearly half this book. And now, today, satisfied and relieved I have completed this book, I still ask the question, "who has broken the code?"

I have written this book in an attempt to provide a historical context for musical activities and accomplishments by hundreds of talented people. Many of these people share with me a need to be part of a living musical culture, one that absorbs past cultural histories (...back in the eon time) and combines them with current experiences to create new musical forms and languages that settle on the ear and mind and body until they are forged—

ontologically—into a vernacular of time. Like me, many of these people value artistic integrity and intellectual curiosity in pursuit of a better understanding of our world. And many of these people share none of the qualities or values that shape my life; they pass through our shared space sometimes helping sometimes hindering the cause. But all of these people have contributed in one way or another to a life lived in the margins of American music.

My life began in the margins of Philadelphia, far from the gilded streets of Center City and even farther from the gilded and glossed streets of the Main Line. Kensington is a once proud neighborhood within a city of neighborhoods, now it's a part of Philadelphia that barely exists. It is a victim of greedy politicians and their developer friends who sold most of the neighborhoods down the river in order to resurrect Center City and line their pockets with money earned by the hard working folks living in the margins of urban post-WW II America.

From the early years in the 1950s to travels throughout the Pacific with the Navy in the 1960s then back to the city that nurtured and eventually rejected me, I celebrate my life in Philadelphia with stories and remembrances of "...the eon time...one day back there." These are the stories that shaped my life in the aesthetically emboldened world of new music, viewed through the collective eyes and ears of Relâche. Along the way I explore the history of the New Music America festivals that were presented throughout North America between 1979 and 1991. These were important events in late 20th century American music history yet little has been written about them. I discuss Music in Motion - The Virtualconcert, a national program designed to generate larger, better-informed audiences for new music and integrate early technologies developed for the World Wide Web into the process. And I tell the stories that shaped my life as an artist-administrator during the final years of the 20th century.

These stories are hopefully told in a language free of code, yet the codes permeate my life. I was trained by the United States Navy to intercept and decipher complex codes during the middle years of the Cold War. These experiences gave me insight to the codes that I would have to parse in order to gain access to immense wealth that had been deposited like an alluvial cone along the Byzantine corridors of American culture, money I can claim as my own if one dances a Hegelian jig, as I do. Like the Navajo Code Talkers who devised a unique code based on their concise aural language to confound the Japanese in the Pacific Theatre during World War II, I helped create a code to describe a musical language born from the marriage of multiple languages of musicians worldwide.

Since a code is intended only for the initiated, my hope is to give the reader sufficient narrative data in order to make him and her aware of a vital time in American music history, one that is described in an inclusive, broad narrative language. No doubt I have slipped into code from time to time. If so, I hope these lapses do not interfere with the reader's ability to parse the text and break the code. I hope by the time you have finished this book you will want to learn more about some of the music that shaped America in the late 20th century. And as a listener to the world's music you will begin to demand more from the music industry.

As I begin a new life in the American Southwest, I often think of Larry Tso. I wonder if Larry Tso is still alive and roaming among the ravines of Canyon de Chelly, explaining to adoring, albeit confused, tourists the meaning of the curious lines and shapes inscribed on the canyon walls depicting hunts, droughts and slaughters at the hands of enemies. And I wonder if Larry Tso tells his stories in a new code. I doubt it. Larry Tso appeared to be a man clearly of his time, and his awareness of time is shaped by "...the eon time."

If Larry Tso is still living the kind of life I observed in 1992, then I envy the apparent simplicity of his life as a guide in Canyon de Chelly. Larry Tso does not have to spend hours dreaming up schemes that will fit the politically correct agendas of agencies and institutions that govern much of early 21st century American life. Larry Tso does not have to wrestle with his conscience as elected and corporate officials plunder the American dream in the early years of the new millennium. No, Larry Tso has the time to dream, to continue speaking in codes and to "Believe one day back there...back in the eon time."

I have affixed to me the dirt and dust of countless ages. Who am I to disturb history?"
—Pig-Pen

BLUES AND ROOTS

If the first sounds one hears are from the womb then perhaps the first sound I heard was the elevated train as it rounded a sharp bend in the tracks as it headed toward center city Philadelphia, wheels screeching as they ground into the steel tracks that lay above the grit and gristle of busy Kensington Avenue. The piercing cry of the "El" would later waken me on warm summer mornings while on vacation from school; the serrated sound knifed through open windows on the second floor of our tiny row house, an alarm to hustle me out of bed to begin another long day of play in the city's streets and recreation centers. In the afternoon I went to work delivering The Evening Bulletin to the neighborhood houses along my enterprising paper route, taking care I folded the paper just right, so when I delivered it to each house on my route—threw it, actually—it would land intact at, or near, the front door away from the windows, while I simultaneously pedaled my bike up and down the curbs, from street to sidewalk—always a perilous journey.

The El passed through the working class neighborhoods of North Philadelphia coming and going from center city where it dispensed a cadre of sleepy women and men to secretarial and clerical jobs or to work on assembly lines in a variety of industries. Others found jobs in the public service sectors sitting for hours behind the steering wheels of trolley cars and busses, trucks and police cars or perhaps behind the rear turning wheel of a glistening red fire engine whose siren added its frightening sinuous wail to the rhythms of a working city as it sped through the streets. These folks returned in the early evening tired yet prepared for the rigors of household chores, caring for younger brothers and sisters or older mothers and fathers. Often they found relief in the company of friends for an hour or so at the corner taproom where glasses of locally brewed beers—Ortlieb and Schmidt the preferred ones—and shots of rough-edged whiskey would calm their fears and frustrations. It was a simple and, I suppose, somewhat satisfying life.

In the early 1950s, The El became more than an affordable mode of transportation. As a link to other and perhaps more exotic neighborhoods of Philadelphia, it allowed city kids a way to discover new worlds that were both fascinating and foreboding. During the mid-twentieth century Philadelphia was beginning a slow transformation from a city with dedicated neighborhoods—thriving "cities within the city" with localized economies and close-knit families—to a more culturally diverse urban megalopolis of scattered and shattered families living in fear and suspicion of "change." Those families who could afford it fled to the sprawling suburbs with their strip malls, wide streets and herbaceous green lawns with neatly trimmed hedges. Slowly, the character of the neighborhoods began to change as folks from cultures far removed from the Europeans who initially settled them began moving in. The soundscape changed as well; these new voices with their different accents and timbral shadings resounded along the narrow streets of brick row homes like screams or wails railing against a perceived or real authority. The history of the city's neighborhoods has been shaped by the diverse voices of people who strove to overcome the class distinctions that governed behavior and life-

Joseph Franklin Sr. circa 1940s

styles in Philadelphia throughout its history. In my neighborhood those distinctions were evident each day.

My mother and father were both the youngest of large families who endured the extreme hardships of inner city Depression-era life in Philadelphia. My father's family immigrated to New York from Wolverhampton, England, sometime in the early 20th century, eventually moving to Philadelphia in search of work in the textile industry. As a young man my father resembled the late film actor James Stewart, handsome and cocky, sure of his role in the street.

Well-dressed and meticulous, Joseph J. Franklin, Sr. stares out from a photograph taken in his early thirties, the look on his face fixed in a deceiving sneer to mask an insecurity born in childhood, the youngest and most troublesome in a family of four surviving boys. Undisciplined and combative, he clashed with the priests of St. Joan of Arc Parish, leading to his incarceration in reform school and eventually prison. After serving time for robbery and then a stint in the Merchant Marines working on cargo ships in the North Atlantic Sea during WW II, he drove trucks between Philadelphia and North Carolina supplementing his income by hanging wallpaper; a skill lost to time with the development of quick-to-rise homes and quicker-to-please decorator paints and acrylics. I would often assist him on these wallpapering jobs. My task was to help load the ladders, scaffolding and rolls of carefully selected paper onto the job site. Then after everything was set up I would hand him rollers and brushes as he slathered adhesive to the backs of the paper rolls before hefting them aloft and slapping them onto the walls of old homes in the hope that the fine raised patterns of the paper's design would bless the walls with an elegance that had been lost to the beast of time. I remember the smells of the work site: a gluey rubbery odor mixed with turpentine and tobacco smoke from my father's ever-present cigarette. Much later the horrors of tuberculosis and emphysema stapled him to home and hospital, his body—once powerful and proud—reduced to a barely recognizable form: 100 pounds of skin and bones.

As an adult my father presented the confident profile of a successful hard-working family man who one day might achieve, if not fame, then at least a semblance of wealth. That never happened, of course, but at least he would strive to look the part of a successful, financially secure man. Each day he would change from his denim or khaki truck driver's outfit into a stylish ensemble topped off by a gray felt hat cocked at just the right angle on his head to signal an apparent willingness to explore just about any and all potential deals that might appear. Without fail, those deals usually vaporized into the smelly air of our North Philadelphia neighborhood, too good to be true or, more often, not true enough to be good. My mom, in apparent opposition to my dad's outgoing confident manner, is quiet and a bit shy; she proved to be a more stabilizing presence in our small family.

Younger than my dad and without any pretense whatsoever, Edith Lutz endured a childhood of extreme poverty and a series of disappointments and traumas to live into her eighties, the past 30 years in Arizona. The youngest in a family of six girls—her eldest sister was 18 years her senior—born to parents and raised in Philadelphia and southern New Jersey, she was the quintessential American girl of her time and caste. She grew into a pretty woman, tall with long brown hair, a shy disposition and good sense of humor that no doubt helped her through some tough times. And there were indeed many tough times not only during her life in Philadelphia but also after moving to Phoenix in the late 1960s.

The author's parents circa 1943

After my father died in 1974, a new man in her life attempted to kill her; the gun misfired. She broke away from him and took refuge in a home for battered women. Several weeks later a police sharpshooter killed him after he walked into a bar and opened fire. It seems this man, gentle and caring at first, had been badly injured in WW II and required daily medication. After abandoning his family in Ohio he wound up in Phoenix and stopped taking the medication, telling no one about his condition. Over the course of six months or so he began to behave oddly, at first forgetting things then staring blankly for long periods of time. Then he became aggressive and abusive until he snapped. A year or so later my mother met and eventually married a local man named Leslie O'Connell, a big Westerner who had been in-and-out of the Army and Navy between Korea and Vietnam. A drifter of sorts, one of those rough-and-tumble guys who knew when and how to run a good con on some unsuspecting or slow-on-the-draw country boy, Les sort of met his match in my mother eventually settling with her, treating her lovingly while introducing her to a new life in Payson, Arizona where they moved after she retired from the Honeywell company. It was a good life for both of them until Les was diagnosed with cancer and died in 1995. Widowed three times, the woman is a survivor.

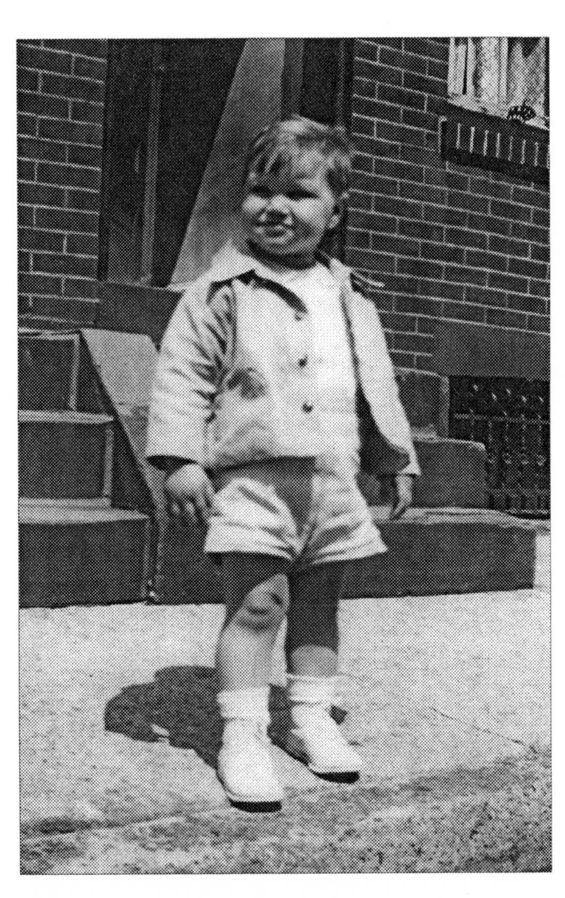

The author at 22 months in front of his Kensington home

Purposely and practically our family was relatively small. I have one younger brother who survived the lure of Philadelphia's bad streets to raise three kids and a brood of grandchildren. He lives in Arizona, better to keep his demons on the run as he hikes the trails of the Mogollon Rim country, disappearing for days into the desolate mountains. I have a large extended family as my numerous aunts and uncles honored the revered Catholic traditions so dominant in a city that evolved with the grand exodus from Europe by immigrants from Ireland, Italy, Poland and the Baltic states: their families were large. Over the years many left the neighborhood to join the exodus to the suburbs or fled Pennsylvania entirely to settle in New Jersey, Maryland and points south. Until their move west in the 1960s my parents remained rooted in the house where my mother was born, the Kensington I grew up in.

Unlike the affluent, immaculate section of London, from whom the name was evidently borrowed, the Kensington of Philadelphia was populated with working people. It consisted of neat, brick row houses, with spotless stoops, or steps that were daily scrubbed clean by the women. During the summer months a "huckster" drove through the neighborhood selling fresh fruits and vegetables from the back of a beat-up pick-up truck or station wagon. I still remember a horse-drawn wagon laden with large cubes of ice with wooden splinters sticking to the bottom of the cubes as they were seized by even larger tongs and delivered to our house, then placed in the freezer section of the refrigerator. In the winter, coal was delivered to the house by a dump truck. A metal chute was attached to the back of the truck angling down to a small basement window. Inside, another metal chute attached to the window to guide the flow of coal into a wooden bin, its sound skipping down the chute a rhythmic rattle of hard black rocks sliding over metal, shrill yet not too shrill. One of my jobs was to shovel the coal into a stove, close the metal grate and ignite old newspapers in the bottom of the stove to set the coals aflame, the heat rising throughout the small house. Another job was cleaning the furnace after removing the ashes and putting them outside at the curb for trash pickup.

Everyone in the neighborhood, it seemed, worked in one of the many factories or warehouses that were located throughout the area in the northern part of the city, stretching to the shores of the Delaware River. A network of railroad tracks running north and south, east and west connected the factories and warehouses. Freight trains carried raw and manufactured goods in and out of the city while passenger trains transported folks to Atlantic City, New York, Washington and beyond. All of the trains passed through the Frankford Junction, located just three blocks from our house.

The Frankford Junction—the "yard"—at the intersection of Frankford and Castor avenues was a busy place on most days. Empty coal cars and boxcars stood along sections of the yard until being connected to a train then routed to their destinations. A passenger station and ticket booth was located on the south side of the yard for those departing and arriving on the north or eastbound trains. A tunnel burrowed under the tracks led to the north side of the yard for those arriving or departing on the westbound train. I hated to go into that tunnel; the smell of urine and imagined danger forced me to hold my breath and run, the sound of my footsteps echoed off the dirty cement tiles lining the walls and floor. I couldn't wait to reach the end, bound up the stairs into daylight and release the air from my lungs. Once on the other side I would look back across 10 sets of rails at the activity on the station's platform, a feeling of accomplishment, of having defied the ghosts of the tunnel and successfully sped through the underground. The return trip to the station platform was much less troubling, but I still held my breath as I dashed back.

Back on the station platform I waited for a train to pull into the station or thunder by, powered by a huge black steam-powered locomotive. My friends and I would stand as close to the edge of the concrete platform as we could get, our bodies frozen in anticipation of the train's locomotive power. Looking to the west we could see the pilot light becoming larger, the gray steam from the engine becoming darker and the whistle's Doppler dance reverberating along the rails. If the train was not scheduled to stop at the station it zoomed by, wind churning out in its wake forcing us back as we turned our heads to the right, in the direction of the train. If it stopped at the station we searched for familiar faces departing the cars, offering to help neighbors carry their bags home.

For my friends and me the Frankford Junction served as a playground, one of many throughout the neighborhood. It was a dirty place, the surrounding area covered with black gravel, residue I suppose of coal used to power the early trains. The gravel left its mark on everything, from skin to sneakers. One particular patch of land was located alongside an embankment that separated the street from the railroad tracks. For some reason this area became an athletic field, used by kids from the surrounding neighborhoods. We called it the "black diamond."

I have many memories of baseball and football games on the black diamond, played to the accompaniment of trains going by (alongside of third base or at the goal line). Those memories often remind me of the pain I felt as the black cinders seared the skin of my leg or thigh as I slid into a base or was tackled. Why we played ball there while the local city-sponsored recreation center was located just three blocks away is still a mystery to me. I like to think it was because of the trains. With haunting sounds and majestic movement through the neighborhood the trains gave us a sense of place and purpose. One day we all knew that the train would take us to places we could then only dream about.

Kensington was one of the fabled "River Wards" that dominated the political history of Philadelphia for most of the 20th century. The factories primarily supported the textile industry. Some processed and cleaned raw cotton that was then transported to the assembly plants by a network of trucks always clogging the small streets of the neighborhoods. Small family-owned stores on every corner catered to the needs of a variety of families, many of whom communicated in their native language except of course at the corner grocery and candy stores where everyone spoke Philadelphia English.

Many of these voices sounded different from my parents and mine, tinged as they were with accents from Poland, Italy, and Ireland and later on *rapido* passages in Spanish sung by the Puerto Rican folks who eventually became a dominant group in the neighborhood. Growing up there I discovered an immediate attraction to the Latinas while—at the same time—I developed a tacit understanding of street-wise *machismo* to deal with the guys. Despite the colorful ambience of Latino culture I was continually drawn to the myth of Europe, expressed so dreamily by the older neighborhood *cognoscenti* who seemingly lived astride the two continents. When in high school I became friendly with several kids from other neighborhoods in and around North Philadelphia—who were actually *born* in Europe— the allure became even stronger. I vowed that someday I would move there; which country I wasn't certain but curiously Germany was at the top of the list. But first I had to grow up and decide which of the two major interests and talents I had would govern my life: athletics or music?

I was born with an acute and I suppose natural athletic ability that gave me an opportunity to participate and compete in any sport I chose and baseball was the first game to capture my imagination. Like most American boys of my generation, my dream was to be a baseball player. For me the dream became more than that as I grew and gained strength and skills while playing in citywide sandlot, American Legion and high school baseball leagues. I received excellent coaching by former professional players who had re-located to the city after their careers ended. In addition to baseball I competed in track and field excelling in the 100-Yard dash, 440-yard relay and the high and the long jumps. During these years I also developed a keen interest in boxing.

For an inner-city kid, especially in the 1950s, boxing was an essential skill to have. Eager and proficient teachers worked as volunteers with the Catholic Youth Organization and Police Athletic League to guide would-be boxers through the rudiments of the sport. I learned not only self-defense but self-esteem as well. I acquired the basic physical skills but never the killer instinct so essential to the sport. Although I competed locally during my teens I realized later when I was in military service that boxing wasn't for me, having been outclassed by more than one Marine who clearly had the killer instinct.

Although I continue to work out on the heavy bag and speed bag I've pretty much avoided confrontations that would recall the pain brought on by dull thumps to the head and even duller ones to the solar plexus. I'm content to wrap myself in the colorful metaphors of the "sweet science" while remembering the fights I've watched in dilapidated clubs smelling of wet leather, spilled beer and frying sausages. The Blue Horizon Auditorium in North Philadelphia makes frequent appearances in my nocturnal dreams, its smoky haze outlining the heroic figures of Gypsy Joe Harris and Eugene "Cyclone" Hart in Middleweight combat. But it has been the game of handball that has sustained my competitive life since I first began playing it in my mid-20s.

Handball is the damnedest game! At first glance it would appear to be quite simple. After all one needs only a ball and a wall to play it. And a pair of gloves, but that's only to keep the sweat off of the ball not to protect the hand from bruising. The goal is to strike a small hard rubber ball against a front wall after it bounces once off of the wood floor or cement ground to your opponent who, in turn, returns the ball to the front wall while attempting to keep you from returning it. This is accomplished by developing an arsenal of offensive and defensive shots that aim to keep the ball as close to the floor or ground as possible thus making it difficult for the other player to return the ball to the front wall. Each player attempts to "kill" the ball (a "kill shot") in order to prevent it from being returned back to the front wall and giving one's opponent another chance to put the ball away. It's a game of acute angles and speed, depending on how many walls one must use to maneuver the ball around the court.

There are three different types of handball games: one-wall; three-wall and the most popular, four-wall. One-wall is the purest of the games and is played on a court measuring 34 feet long by 20 feet wide with a front wall 16 feet high. Three-wall increases the height of the front wall to 20 feet and adds two parallel side walls also 20 feet high. Four-wall uses a 40 foot deep court and adds a 12 foot high back wall and a ceiling. The ways in which the ball bounces off of the various number of side and back walls or ceiling as it seeks the coveted front wall determines the type of game.

Handball was probably developed in 16th century Ireland both as a one-wall and three-wall game, often played next to or behind a favored pub. In the 19th century it was adapted to the inner city by Irish then Italian and Jewish immigrants mainly in New York City. It then fanned out to Boston, Philadelphia and other eastern cities before moving west to Chicago and points beyond. As YMCA facilities grew in number and popularity, four-wall handball courts with thick plaster walls and level hardwood floors were built as centerpieces to the "Y." Throughout the 20th century four-wall handball developed as a somewhat more sophisticated game although one-wall and three-wall are essentially more difficult to master. Of late, one-wall has made something of a come-back while three-wall remains elusive. I play four-wall handball.

Anyone who has played the game will tell you it's a humbling experience. Gifted athletes who might excel in baseball or football often find themselves being outclassed by lesser experienced athletes who have focused their energies on the interior psychology of the cloistered court. On the other hand, athletes experienced in expansive team sports often respond immediately to the singular challenges of one-on-one competition. It depends solely on the personality of the individual. Even though I participated in an individual sport like boxing, I was primarily an athlete steeped in the tradition of teamwork, so it took me a while to adapt to the single-minded tasks of individual athletic competition. Once immersed in the game, however, I—like so many others—succumbed to its cult-like mysteries of ball control and Zen-like strategies.

"Envision your kill shot. Have it etched in your mind even as you execute a defensive shot. You should know what kind of offensive shot you are going to take one or two volleys prior to the kill. If you develop that kind of mind-set, you'll win most of your games." Al Koff told me that one day after he humiliated me on the court. Of course he relished the notion of taking young cocky guys like me on the court and thumping us by placing the ball—time after time—exactly where he wanted to place it. Often he used an underhand fist shot that sent the ball off of the front wall to the ceiling then to the floor where it kissed the side wall before dropping softly into a back corner as we futilely reached for it. After about five or six similar shots I would stare at this guy in wonder. He was about 5'6" tall with knobby knees and a sort of sunken chest. He always wore a white tee-shirt, white gym shorts and white high-top Converse Chuck Taylor All-Stars sneakers. He was not the picture of a competitive athlete, especially when he walked into the gym with a bucket in one hand and a raggedy mop slung over his shoulder. He made his living washing windows in the commercial neighborhood that circled the Germantown YMCA. And he played handball just about every day. I guess I became a project for Al since he took the time to constantly criticize my game and tell me stories about his pals, many of whom had passed into handball heaven. After I shifted my club allegiance from the funky confines of the Germantown YMCA to the Downtown "Y," I really missed Al. I learned several years after I left that Al passed away joining, I hope, his old pals in a swirl of white shorts and tops as they pursued the perfect sweet kill shot.

Al Koff personified a certain type of handball player who reigned supreme during the early part of the 20th century. By the mid-sixties a new breed of player began to emerge, one who took advantage of better equipment and a sleeker ball construction to dramatically speed the game up. One reason for this was that a new type of handball court was being built. Instead of all of the walls being made of concrete and plaster, the new ones used wood. This made constructing the courts cheaper and quicker. It also provided a more flexible surface for the ball to react to. The elusive rubber handball that had always moved across and up-and-down the court like a shotgun pellet, now moved like a bullet. To successfully compete one had to not only learn all of the angles on the court but had to be in even better physical condition than earlier generations of players. The game required stamina, strength and a steel-like resolve to compete. It's a game that offers great rewards both physically and psychologically but it can also wear one down both physically and psychologically.

After about five years of steady play—and with Al Koff chirping in my ear—I began to develop a fairly strong game while beginning to ascend to the upper echelons of handball players. To achieve the exalted status of an "A" player, one had to win their club's "C" and "B" division championships. This was done on a yearly basis when the club hosted an in-house club tournament. Each year's division winner moved up to the next level. When one

The author circa 1985 resting following a handball match

arrived at the "A" division the competition was for club champion. There were also numerous other tournaments throughout the area that were open tournaments where one paid an entrance fee and competed in the appropriate division and age group. Whenever I had the time I would compete in these tournaments held throughout the Mid-Atlantic area. I enjoyed not only the competition and fellowship of the handball community but it provided me with an outlet from the world of the arts. For a few hours on the days I played handball I found myself talking about things that had nothing to do with being an artist and artist-administrator, I was, simply (almost) one of the guys.

I like to think my various experiences in athletic competitions prepared me for the life I've lived in the arts, a life that has proved to be more challenging than blocking a lethal left jab, hitting a hissing slider as it danced on the inside of home plate or wearing down a wily opponent on the handball court who continues to keep the ball in play.

I'm not at all certain what turned me to the study of music. I remember being attracted to my father's old collection of big band music on scratchy 78-RPM records, music from the thirties and forties, mainly Benny Goodman, Guy Lombardo and others from that generation. Although I listened carefully to these records the music was somewhat alien to me. I really didn't have a context for it although I suppose even at that early age I appreciated the complex sophisticated nature of the writing and playing. I remember not liking the loud brassy sections very much but really digging the winds— clarinets and saxophones—with their glossy cool sound. I succumbed more easily to the ballads, especially when sung by soft alluring female voices. The light and lilting timbre of the clarinet was nice but the more strident saxophone lines caught my attention. I decided this was my instrument: the saxophone.

Since my parents could afford to neither buy me a musical instrument nor pay for music lessons, I was fortunate that the school district of Philadelphia had at that time an excellent music education department to provide lessons and instruments—free of charge—to qualified students. Flutes and clarinets were then in abundance but saxophones were not, so the school issued me a clarinet and assigned one of many woodwind teachers who taught throughout the school system to guide me in the arcane practices of tone control and finger pressure while they danced across the keys of the instrument. If I were able to learn to play the clarinet well enough, I was told then I would be able to switch to saxophone later on, the fingering system being similar.

I remember the odd smell as I opened the battered black leather carrying case to assemble the clarinet, the instrument seated in five separate compartments covered in soft blue felt. The smell was a combination of stale saliva clinging to the cork underneath each note pad and fastening insert connecting each piece of the instrument together and the felt's peculiar mildew scent; this resulted in a distinctive and not particularly pleasant aroma. Sensitive to smells and smooth-textured cloths, I found this experience a double whammy: I couldn't get past the odor and hated to touch the felt cloth lining the inside of the case. It's no wonder that the clarinet and I did not forge a close bond. Despite these obstacles, I practiced hard, attended most of my lessons and acquired a reasonably decent tone. Most importantly I learned to read music and gained an understanding of ensemble playing that was to prove important to me later on. I had developed an appreciation for the mystery in meaning behind those little notes on the page.

Like most kids in the 1950s rock-and-roll commanded my attention, although I did question its rather simplistic musical structures, even at that age. The rebellious nature of the music and of the people who made it appealed to me more than many of the songs did, so it was inevitable that I would emulate in dress and actions some of the male teen idols of the day: Elvis, Jerry Lee Lewis and Buddy Holly. You'll notice that these guys are all white, from rural backgrounds, a long throw from Philadelphia. Guys like Frankie Avalon, Bobby Rydell, and Fabian—the city contingent from South Philly—were not my style at all.

I couldn't relate to their wholesome boy-next-door image fabricated by the record companies and agents after they picked them off the corner at 10th & Wolf streets and placed them on a rickety pedestal. Their ready-to-use good looks fit perfectly well on American Bandstand but I was looking for something else, something or somebody I couldn't find down the street or around the corner. Elvis and those other Southern boys, well when they came knocking on my door they carried with them more than a guitar slung over their shoulders and full pompadours plastered with Brylcreem. They brought a new way for me to view the world.

Elvis, Jerry Lee, Buddy Holly and others were "exotic," their southern accents alluring and their behavior rebellious. I could easily relate to their sneering images pasted in the pages of slick magazines lining the shelves of the local drug store and soda fountain, the collars of their black leather jackets, turned up just so to caress long menacing sideburns. Of course this was a fabricated image too concocted by *their* record companies and controlling agents. But these images worked for me, offering something different to us Philly boys of that era, many, like me, struggling to overcome the scripted boredom of the Eisenhower years.

I entered into an uneasy alliance with rock-and-roll while learning to "hang out" on the corner, at local weekend dances, comb my hair in a careful "Duck's Ass" style with just a twist of hair curling on the forehead. Overall I was trying my best to be a juvenile delinquent. But it wasn't working. I felt idiotic at times. I really got bored with the dumb fights that needed to be fought in order to maintain one's reputation. I became restless and decided to hang back a bit and focus once again on the clarinet while continuing to participate in athletics.

After graduating from high school I entertained thoughts of pursuing baseball as a career but soon discovered that I was not talented enough to compete at the higher professional levels. A baseball scout told me one time; "I can teach you to hit but not to run or throw." I could run like a deer and hit with reasonable power, but did not have a strong arm. Nor, it turns out, a strong will to compete, echoing my experience with boxing. Again the sounds that informed my youth began haunting me once again. I began my journey back to music, but not without one more detour—military service.

SIGNS AND SYSTEMS

I was raised with the expectation that I would serve in the military. Having grown up near a thriving waterfront, I was drawn to the Navy. I think it was the strange uniform with the bell-bottom pants and collared jersey, blue and white stripping. Less superficially, it was the image emblazoned on a recruiting poster that I passed nearly every day of my youth on the corner of Kensington and Allegheny Avenues: silhouetted against a crimson evening sky a young sailor in dress blues stood looking at a departing ship, sea bag at his side, lost in the reverie of exotic islands and the lure of beautiful women. I guess this romantic image worked. When the draft became an issue I resisted joining many of my friends who entered the Marine Corps and enlisted in the Navy.

My first stop was the ice-bound Great Lakes Naval Training Center for basic training where the authorities decided I would become a communications specialist—a Spy! This decision wasn't completely arbitrary since I had hoped to become a radioman or sonar man, preferably in the submarine service, having listed those intentions upon enlistment. At least I was on the right track. Communications and specifically the rating communications technician appeared to evolve from radioman, both required a command of communications codes, specifically, the Morse code that I had learned while serving— with little distinction—in the Cub Scouts and Boy Scouts, neither an easy fit for me.

For a city kid, scouting can be a strange experience, especially when taken on field trips into the countryside where the alien green environment clashes with the rubbed brown and gray tones of the streets. I couldn't garner much interest in hiking through the woods, learning to identify one plant or growth from another or learning the differences in shape and hue of a Maple tree or Oak tree. Camping was a problem as well. I just didn't enjoy the idea of sleeping on the ground in a tent when it rains. And forget about making a campfire! I did however enjoy learning the names of and how to tie an assortment of exotic knots, "slip knot," "double half-hitch" and "sheepshank" among my favorites. (Years later, I or a collaborator, would use some of these names as titles for or references in musical works, usually to infer an image of the piece or a way to play a passage in a piece.) But I liked learning methods of communications, especially the Morse code.

I learned the Morse code in the usual manner: tapping it out on a "key," a pulse sent over a thin electric wire to someone listening on a pair of inexpensive earphones, then listening over the earphones as the code is transmitted back. As each "dot-dit" (long-short) or "dit-dot" (short-long) pattern is learned one begins to listen for aural patterns so that the words and numbers become more easily identifiable within a syntactical context. Although these studies were elemental and would become infinitely more sophisticated later on, they imbued in me a unique sonic world or culture of sound that was similar to the world of music. Like reading music when one forms patterns of notes that define phrases, studying the Morse code requires that one learn aural patterns as a means of identifying word or number groups or phrases. Once learned, you can create games where the sound image becomes a real or imagined image and practice the code while simultaneously engaging in a variety of activities. I especially remember times playing baseball, standing in the field at either first base or center field during lulls in play I would silently spell out words and numbers in Morse code, holding a "virtual" conversation with myself—in code. Somehow I knew the Morse code would become an intimate part of my life.

Early in basic training I was given a battery of aptitude tests. One of the tests consisted of identifying by ear the Morse code. Since I already knew the code I did quite well—in fact I correctly dictated, or wrote down by hand, regardless of the speed of transmission—all of the letters and numbers that were sent via code over a wire connected to a pair of earphones. In the parlance of the times, I "aced it." The result of this test combined with my other test scores determined that, after basic training, I would undergo intense instruction to become a communications technician.

Basic training is an important component of the military experience, serving as a transition from youth into early manhood or adulthood. The training can be severe, characterized by mental and physical pressures that either propel a recruit forward or send him reeling back to civilian life. I loved the challenges. I concluded that if this experience was going to be a positive one I would have to learn how to work within the systems that the Navy constructed. I learned how to organize my time and possessions, to control my emotions and, essentially, how to develop my own systems that would prove helpful for the remainder of my military duty and beyond.

For example, every recruit is issued a small locker to store clothing in. The square metal locker measured two feet wide by three feet high and contained several compartments. Each of these compartments were allocated as "home" to various clothing items, like underpants, undershirts ("skivvies"), socks, work shirts and dungarees, etc. and, of course, blue and white uniforms. Each day the company commander of the recruit unit conducted an inspection to determine that each item of clothing was a) immaculately clean; b) folded precisely according to uniform standards; c) placed in the proper compartment. Infractions would cost points that would in turn determine extra duty assignments. I decided to organize my locker according to the regulations at the beginning of training with the intention of never wearing an article of clothing that I had carefully folded and stored. Each day I dusted them off. And each night I washed the same pair of underwear and socks, shirt and trousers and hung them in a "dry room" so that in the morning I could retrieve them, iron them and wear them. The system worked. At the conclusion of basic training I threw away the threadbare underwear, bought new ones and prepared for the next phase of training in Pensacola, Florida.

After completing basic training in February I boarded a train in Chicago with a dozen other graduates and headed to the Pensacola Naval Communications Training Command located next to the Naval Air Training Command where future fighter pilots learned to land and take-off from aircraft carriers, when they weren't crashing T-38 training jets into the Atlantic Ocean. Once again the train became a powerful force in my life. Only this time I was a passenger on the train beginning a journey that would transform my life.

The train ride south was memorable. It was the first time I had taken a long train ride anywhere. Previously the longest was from Philadelphia to Atlantic City and back again. This time the ride was more of an adventure as the train cut through flat farmlands of mid-America and ramshackle neigh-

The author as a young Navy recruit.

borhoods of the rural south. I observed for the first time just how dramatically different in landscape and demographics the United States is. This was 1964, only years into the civil rights movement and just years before the social revolution that was to change behavior and attitudes in the country. I was about to spend one year in the American South, where many of the events that caused these social changes were spawned.

The train pulled into Pensacola two days after leaving Chicago. Humid, steamy sunny Florida, my first visit; one of many I would eventually make over the years. As I stepped down from the train and onto a small railroad station platform I remembered all the times I stood at the Frankford Junction station, watching passengers depart or arrive. Then I dreamed of the day when I too would join the legions of world travelers. With their fancy initialed suitcases containing perfumed clothing and wing tipped shoes, these travelers might be on their way to some exotic city in a remote corner of a world that existed only in my imagination. Then again these travelers might have been and probably were doing the same thing I was doing: going to work. But they had to be more comfortable than my new shipmates and me on that early spring day in 1964 when we landed in Florida wearing flannel dress blue uniforms and carrying canvas sea bags full of government issued clothing. Although not necessarily a romantic image, it remains vivid.

I remember the smell as I stepped into the still air: a strange exotic combination of cotton candy and chocolate or cocoa with just a hint of vanilla. In reality it was the scents of palmetto palm trees and tropical flowers mixed into the humid air. I've never forgotten that smell. Years later, when I would spend much time in Central Florida, that same smell would be present every day often causing me to reflect back to that day in 1964.

Once enrolled in the training command, I began learning communications and electronic theories. I also learned to type. I had never before sat in front of a typewriter until that first day of training when those of us who did not type were given a crash course. We learned, fast. We were required to type—with accuracy—over 100 words per minute, essential since eventually we would be copying the Morse Code typing the characters as they sped over the line. We were being trained to intercept messages transmitted by the Soviet Navy, the code cracking over a wire using the Cyrillic Alphabet consisting of six more characters than the Roman one, necessitating that we learn a somewhat different keyboard in order to reach the extra characters with, if I remember correctly, the small fingers on each hand. During training the government conducted background checks on each of us to determine if we would be issued Top Secret Security Clearances. If approved we would then graduate to a more difficult phase of training. My clearance was approved and I was transferred to another program. In this one I would learn a totally new system of electronic intercept using more sophisticated equipment and technology.

This advanced phase of training proved difficult for me. Clearly, a natural musical ear eased the way for me to learn sophisticated codes. Now I was given reams of data and theory to read in preparation to learn this new system that intercepted special electronic transmissions from Soviet submarines, deciphered the codes and tracked the locations of the subs as they maneuvered around the Pacific Theatre. I studied diligently to piece these theories together. I had help from a new friend, Albert Davis, who tutored me in areas that were confusing. He had been trained as an electronics engineer at the University of South Carolina and was well versed in current methodologies. He patiently explained theories of electronics that, to me, were very new and somewhat arcane. Eventually, we were stationed together in Japan and developed an even closer relationship, one that has endured to this day.

After completing the training course I was assigned to the Seventh Fleet in Japan, disappointed at not being posted to one of the European locations like Bremerhaven, Germany or Port Leyote, Spain. Throughout the training in sub-tropical Florida I continued to dream of Europe, those fleeting images of living amid the romance of the carefree Europeans, sitting in dark mysterious coffee shops and bars, meeting exotic women while pursuing a bohemian lifestyle. But Japan? Little did I know at the time that these images would become more than that, they would become real experiences complete with dark mysterious coffee shops and bars and definitely exotic women.

Here I was, barely out of my teens, floating around Asia while all around me swirled scents and images from an exotic past, luring me into shadowy places soaked with intrigue and a hint of danger, meeting people whose features and body language revealed a history of ancient civilizations far from my experience and knowledge gleaned from books and films. I realized immediately how inexperienced and unprepared for life outside of America I really was. I became fascinated with these ancient cultures and dived into books, eager to learn more about their customs and arts. On liberty from military duties I explored temples, went to performances of music, dance, theatre and puppetry and engaged in conversation with young people who were eager to practice their English lessons on a "real" subject. I also explored the streets and alleyways of cities to engage other not so young people whose command of English was limited to the value of a dollar: the whores and hustlers who commanded the attention of young servicemen.

The author in Yokohama, Japan, kneeling far right in the first row

The languages I now heard spoken were seeded with indecipherable codes and undulating inflections that continually changed their meaning and intent; they were mesmerizing and utterly musical. As I was being educated in the real world, far from the sights and sounds of my neighborhood in Philadelphia, I was edging closer to a perception of the world in larger geo-political contexts where America was viewed with distrust or at least with skepticism by the local citizens. And I was beginning to forge an internal image of myself that would overshadow the external one.

The inner image was of a hip young guy, a hirsute bohemian in pursuit of knowledge and new alliances while the outer image of a clean-cut, short-haired white guy gave me away: Military! "Don't stray too far from your own kind," the commands read. "Be careful of who you talk to and how you look. Do not draw attention to yourself." I reacted to these restrictions by going to places that were off-limits to military personnel, sniffing around for the whiff of danger that, invariably, never lingered very long or never really existed other than in the narrow mind of a young officer whose mandate was to keep us young boys in line with "the program."

Despite doing a reasonably good job on duty I had difficulties with senior command officers who spent too much time trying to make career sailors out of the younger guys and not enough time developing strategies to improve the intelligence gathering. More than once, a senior officer reprimanded me, unhappy with my haircut or the way my belt buckle didn't glisten in the light, threatening me with disciplinary actions. When there were so many pressing important matters to deal with while on duty why these guys wasted their time inspecting the length of our hair or condition of uniforms was a mystery to me. Clearly I didn't fit their image of a good sailor.

During lulls in the spying game I would listen to stories told by old salts about their escapades in Europe. At this particular command many of the guys had done tours of duty in Germany, Turkey, Spain and Scotland—other strategic locations that intercepted and interpreted Soviet intelligence during the Cold War—and their memories of those experiences helped us all through some long and dark nights. Of course many of the stories were apocryphal, told as second-hand tales while others were no doubt remembered through a drunken scrim, the details probably twisted around for effect and affect. Most of the stories were based on incidents in Germany either at Bremerhaven or in Bavaria and most centered on alliances with statuesque blond blue-eyed German girls. Needless to say, for a young romantic bobbing somewhere in the middle of the Sea of Japan on a cold night these stories affirmed that I must one day visit this magical place to be seduced by women I knew only from my friends' stories and my dreams.

I spent my entire tour of duty with the Seventh Fleet protecting the homeland from real and imagined cold war desperados who sometimes slithered in the mercurial waters of the Pacific Ocean. Despite enticements from the career folks for assignments in Europe if only I would "re-up," I made certain that a priority for me was to become a "short-timer." No military career for this Leo! During my tour of duty I experienced something that would eventually change my life: I discovered jazz.

One night while I was off duty I went to the base library and selected a few LP albums. I was sitting alone listening to a Broadway musical—*The Flower Drum Song*, I think. I don't know why I selected that particular work but I found elegance in the lyrical quality of the songs, although admittedly I also found silliness or something else that didn't quite resonate with me. But I was not in the mood for rock-and-roll or country music, those being the musics of choice for most of my shipmates. After a few minutes a guy came in and sat down across from me. He looked at me and asked, "Say would you be interested in hearing something else, like maybe Miles Davis?" Since I wasn't exactly deep into *The Flower Drum Song* I agreed.

I had never heard of Miles Davis before so when he showed me the album cover with a photo of a gorgeous young black woman on it I was intrigued. The album was titled "Miles Ahead" and now years later and after hundreds of times of listening to it I still remember my reaction to the opening loud assertive statement. This was a far cry indeed from the music of my youth and it immediately caught my attention...in the gut. I said something to the effect like, "Whoa! What is that?" I also remember the guy smiling at me, as if he were sharing a mysterious language or code with me. This was quite appropriate since we were both in the business of intercepting and analyzing military codes at the time. I was hooked.

Mark, was from Philadelphia. In fact we attended rival high schools. His dad was Claude Herring, a well-known radio celebrity in Philadelphia and one of the on-air voices for the Philadelphia Phillies. We became friends and met whenever we were free to listen and learn about jazz, its history and personalities. He was one of those young guys who just devoured the music, imparting in me the same passion and curiosity that would later influence my behavior and life style. Not only did I begin a long journey to understand this music through intense listening but I also began reading books and, of course, *Downbeat Magazine*, then the most authoritative voice for jazz in America. On those days when I could get over to Tokyo I found small clubs and coffee shops that featured jazz, both records and live bands. USO tours often featured prominent artists like Dizzy Gillespie, Sonny Rollins and Miles. Discovering this music transformed my sensibilities and was the beginning of a long-standing interest in jazz. Most importantly it revealed an awareness of the social histories that shaped the music and lives of its creators and my eventual role as a working musician.

When my tour of duty was up I returned to the United States via Oakland where I was discharged. After spending a few weeks in San Francisco visiting some guys I had served with I bussed to Phoenix to spend some time with my parents, who, by then, had moved there so that my father might buy a few more years before losing his battle to emphysema. There I began the inevitable adjustment to civilian life.

Living in Phoenix during those early months proved cleansing. I knew nothing of the southwestern United States other than the seductive images scanned across numerous movie and television screens depicting the lonesome cowboy and fierce, proud Indian. What a joy to discover that real people lived there, worked in a variety of jobs—some even rode horses—and had a hundred stories to tell me about the "Old West." My interest in competitive athletics was rekindled when I began playing handball, a sport I've pursued ever since. I can't say that I fit into the culture of the southwest easily, but it was certainly refreshing when compared to the gritty street life that I knew as a kid in Philadelphia. Yet the lure of those streets proved too much. I returned to Philadelphia after only three months on the fringe of the southwest desert, and eased back into the shadows of a city that, for the next 25 years would nurture and, eventually, spit me out.

While overseas I had discovered a musical universe that was exotic and, at times, forbidden. In addition to jazz I encountered cultures of people for whom making music had nothing to do with making a living, but making a life. Music making was not commerce but an expression of the life force. The odd and, to my naive ears, out-of-tune, wailing of a variety of string and wind instruments and voices accompanied by drums and gongs speaking in languages from the depths of history provided an escape from the boredom and fears of military life. And those varied experiences set me apart from the guys and girls I had grown up with.

Visiting with my buddies from the old neighborhood proved difficult. We exchanged stories of our experiences; theirs of European encounters, mine of encounters in ports from Yokohama to Manila. A few fellows returning from Vietnam didn't say much. Listening to those who had returned from Europe brought back the earlier feelings I had about living there. In fact I found myself listing to starboard once again, feeling that old attraction; Europe beckoned! Although many of these guys had experienced deep trauma in their respective lives none had really changed that much. Their return to the neighborhood was nothing more than picking up where they had left off before entering the service: find a job, hang at a bar, make money, get married. I'm not certain what the priorities were. My conversations with them often ended in something like, "You're gonna do what? What kind of music is that? Damn, man, you've changed." I guess I had.

Time to leave the neighborhood once and for all! Not only was there a wealth of experiences to be had and new people to meet in Philadelphia, New York and, eventually, Europe but also I had to decide just what I was going to do now that I had achieved the venerable status of "adult." One thing became clear: I would return to study music, beginning again at the age of 22.

And so I immersed myself in musical studies. Rather than return to the clarinet or saxophone, I began studying percussion with an emphasis on keyboards: the marimba and vibraphone. I worked in construction during the day, practiced and attended private lessons in percussion, theory and eventually composition. Then, after saving enough money, I entered the Philadelphia Music Academy to pursue a degree in composition and theory, made possible by the GI Bill and scholarship monies. After graduating, I taught for a few years then entered Temple University's Graduate School of Music. For a few years I was enrolled in a doctoral program while teaching freshman courses in composition and history. All the while I was performing with jazz ensembles in the Philadelphia area and writing music for chamber ensembles, dance, theater and video projects. And I continued to dream of a life beyond America while remaining a citizen of America.

It had become clear to me that I was not a candidate to live a conventional life. The lure of the world of the arts proved irresistible, its freewheeling lifestyle and cast of attractive characters resonated easily with the displaced image I had of myself. One thing was certain: I had begun a journey that would eventually lead me into a world that I had only dreamed about. Now I was about to live that life.

"Thus it is not the singer who sings the song but the song who sings the singer, and therefore in performance it is the singer, not the song, that is the artistic artifact, the work of art."

—Greil Marcus from *Invisible Republic – Bob Dylan's Basement Tapes*

RELÂCHE

In the summer of 1977 I was living in the Germantown section of Philadelphia, a part of the city that had seen better days.

In the 19th and early 20th century, Germantown thrived. Located only 30 minutes or so from downtown Philadelphia, the area eventually developed as a residential community where land was abundant and green, a far cry from the concrete and steel of downtown Philadelphia and its tributary neighborhoods. Wealthy industrialists who could not or chose not to live in the class-conscious and, to some, insufferably snobbish Main Line built spacious mansions with guest homes and carriage houses on their large properties. Carefully manicured gardens adorned many of these mansions, providing a scenic and sensuous landscape that gave Germantown an aura of fine genteel living.

Working people who lived in Germantown often toiled in the busy mills and factories in bustling North Philadelphia and resided in row homes built on small narrow maze-like streets that formed more traditional neighborhoods so characteristic of Philadelphia. These small homes with even smaller back yards stood in stark contrast to the many large rambling homes surrounded by extravagantly foliated gardens. Merchants managed shops on gray cobblestone avenues fixed with trolley car tracks to guide the electric trolleys in-and-out of downtown and linking Germantown with other sections of the city. The serene countryside-within-the-city character of Germantown attracted people from other neighborhoods, especially on warm Sundays when entire families picnicked in nearby Fairmount Park—the largest city park in America—or walked along the Wissahickon Creek that snaked through the park for miles. For residents of the inner city, especially during the hot humid months of summer, Germantown provided a refuge from the noisy crowded streets, a brief respite from urban America. That is, until the mid 20th century when conditions there began to resemble other sections of the decaying city.

By the time I returned to Philadelphia from military service in the late 1960s Germantown had become an affordable but not necessarily inviting part of town. The mansions and guest homes had become apartment houses with the large rooms divided into small efficiency apartments ready-made for students, the elderly on fixed incomes— often with government support—and the descendants of the earlier working people who, sadly, no longer had the mills and factories to support their livelihood. Many of the utilitarian row homes had succumbed to urban decay and the perils of the ubiquitous urban underground economy: drugs. The carriage houses were prime locations for artists, many of whom built studios and small living quarters in them. Germantown was popular with students and faculty from Temple University, LaSalle College and several Quaker Schools— private institutions created as an alternative education to the public schools. It wasn't exactly hip to live in Germantown, but if you leaned towards the arts and thrived in a diverse cultural milieu then in this section of the city you could live comfortably.

I had moved to Germantown after a few years in a small center city apartment at 15th and Pine streets. I was living with the writer and poet, Maralyn Lois Polak. We had met just after Maralyn graduated from Temple University and, 18 months later, we got married. Although the marriage was brief, we shared a desire to learn and become working artists, she as a writer and I as a performing musician and composer. Over the decades, as our creative lives took shape we maintained a close personal relationship that survives today. Eventually, Maralyn moved back to Center City Philadelphia while I stayed in Germantown where I met a woman named Barbara Noska, subsequently moving in with her.

Barbara was a charismatic singer and eccentric beauty who floated in the stream of her Hungarian Gypsy ancestors: wild, unpredictable and utterly self-centered. Her flamboyant public profile contrasted dramatically with her private one, the residue of growing up in a large Catholic family: she cared deeply about the welfare of others, just as long as they did not pose a threat to her throne. Our relationship lasted 12 years, as we developed as musicians and collaborators.

Numerous composers, including me, wrote music specifically for Barbara's unique vocal and performance styles. Intrigued at her extended vocal techniques—derived from her daring and uninhibited experiments with any and all vocal sounds she could produce and an interest in European and African folk traditions—I developed several works using combinations of woodwinds and percussion and electronic sounds in support of these impossible to notate vocal articulations. Several of these works were odd, or at least, odd attempts to contextualize or serialize vocal sounds to create a referential language for future works. After several tries over a period of two or three years I exhausted my ability to find a working structure for these pieces and began collaborating once again with writer friends who developed poetic and narrative texts that I set to music for Barbara and the Relâche Ensemble. Despite sharing in musical successes and adventures, traveling together in Europe and the American southwest, our relationship proved difficult. We ended it in 1985 but continued to work together until the early 1990's.

The small third floor apartment we shared overlooked a rutted parking lot where Philadelphia shoppers searching for bargains or visiting the unemployment or welfare offices on Chelten and Germantown Avenues could stow their cars knowing that one of several over-the-hill cops working the lot would prevent packs of kids from breaking into their cars and stealing a cheap radio that, in the parlance of the street, would "Get them a nickel." From our windows I watched a parade of sad people wandering aimlessly around this once elegant shopping district. One person who wandered around those streets was far from sad. He was the young—very young—Aaron Jay Kernis, who would become a much celebrated composer by the time he reached middle age.

I was one of Aaron's first teachers. At fifteen, he rode the bus to Germantown from his Olney home to study composition, having been directed to me by a former teacher at the Philadelphia College of the Performing Arts. It seems Aaron sort of baffled the composition teachers at the school, probably by not paying close attention to their admonitions of what a tough life he faced as a composer in America. Aaron clearly was not listening, at least to those admonitions, and decided to try someone else. I was it.

For two years Aaron visited me once each week, bringing his dense but elegantly designed musical ideas in for my analysis and opinion. It was hard for me to really guide him as a composer since I discovered immediately that he had much more natural talent than me. I was able, however, to provide insight into the inner workings of traditional harmony and counterpoint. I like to think these descriptions and analysis of western music from the 19th and 20th centuries gave him a perspective that was of benefit to him later on in his studies. After a while it was clear to me that Aaron needed to move on, he needed someone with a larger musical vocabulary than I had to decipher all the notes he was committing to paper. One day I told him to leave, find someone else outside of Philadelphia. He was stunned at my directness, I think, but eager to accept the challenge. He found John Adams at the San Francisco Conservatory of Music and left Philadelphia for good, returning only to visit his parents and some old friends. For me it was time to move on to something else as well.

I had just completed three years of study and teaching at Temple University Graduate School of Music where I pursued a Doctor of Musical Arts while teaching undergraduate theory and history. Although I excelled at and enjoyed the challenge of musical scholarship, especially tackling the rigors of theoretical analysis using the strange yet satisfying teachings of the early 20th century Austrian theorist Heinrich Shanker, my passion was writing music while searching for a broader understanding of the musical universe—musics that integrated "popular" and "world music" forms. These I discovered in a variety of sources, from the early works of Philip Glass, Steve Reich and Terry Riley to the politically charged songs of the Jamaican singer-songwriter, Bob Marley and Nigeria's Fela Anikulapo-Kuti. During those years I was still reeling from the tumultuous sixties, especially the music of John Coltrane, Eric Dolphy and a generation of jazz artists with whom I identified closely in praxis and style. But in the context of the American university where music departments were immersed in the Euro-American "classical music" endgame, it was inevitable that I would lock horns with grainy gray professorial music teachers. Eventually I did.

By returning to graduate school and pursuing advanced music degrees I had bought into the concept of "serious music," studies of Western classical music in the context of an archaic intellectual arena that had little to do with actually making music. The music being composed and championed by faculty composers was either complex realizations of serial exercises or turgid attempts to revitalize the "Romantic Tradition" with little understanding of or appreciation for the emerging "minimalist" style evident in downtown New York City. Nor was there recognition of American popular music. Student and faculty recitals were deadly; played trance-like by technically adept musicians with little regard for their role in the diverse society they hid from. What a sad ceremony, and I had become a part of it. I began to react and challenge both faculty and students who were being sucked into this mindless ministry.

After a series of, yes, idiotic battles with composer-teachers on the faculty, I concluded that old Leo would growl sort of loudly if he were expected to roam within the halls of academe for any length of time. I resigned the university fellowship and hit the streets, not knowing just what exactly I'd do. But I was relieved.

At the time my companion Barbara Noska and I were struggling with part-time jobs both in and out of music. We barely made the rent but had enough resources to keep the parties going well into the night. We had become part of a group of artists—painters, writers, performance artists and musicians—striving mightily to create some semblance of a "bohemian" scene in Philadelphia. We tried to counter the bland conservative atmosphere that permeated the city during those years. Every gallery opening, musical performance, poetry reading or related "event" preceded a "hang." And this group was capable of "hanging out" with anyone; we raised some serious hell and collectively made some seriously good work while gracefully stepping into our thirties.

To pay the rent, we all had some type of "survival" jobs apart from the real work we were trained or desired to do. Some taught while some did journalism. Others had more traditional jobs. Barbara, for example, assisted a foot doctor by washing people's feet, cutting their toenails and scheduling their appointments. I was a bit more enterprising. Each week I wrote preview and review articles for an emerging "alternative" newspaper called the *Drummer*. In them I discussed issues that were then foreign to the music critics who wrote for the *Evening Bulletin* and *Philadelphia Inquirer*. I discussed upcoming concerts, interviewed artists who I would eventually become friendly with—like Robert Ashley—and reviewed performances. On the weekends I played around town with a variety of musicians; one job in particular is memorable: a fairly steady gig fronting a quartet of South Philly guys who couldn't decide if they wanted to cover Mowtown or Downtown. Philly, that is. During the day I worked in construction, specifically "road improvement."

One late-summer week I was working with a crew installing highway guard rails alongside a road in Bucks County. We carried those large gray ribbed barriers into position then bolted them to posts to keep errant cars and trucks from tumbling down steep embankments. They're big and heavy, a dead weight that is virtually impossible to balance properly. Lifting and moving these things invariably caused damage to your back if you were not careful. I was an experienced weight lifter, but carrying and hoisting these unbalanced slabs of steel was quite different from lifting well-tooled and balanced weights in a gym. Despite my carefully planning each lift of these guard rails, I still injured my back. The following morning it was so sore that I could barely stand up straight. Sciatic pains were coursing through my legs, a classic sign that my vertebrae was whacked out of alignment. On the advice of a friend I visited a chiropractor, thus beginning a lifelong curiosity and respect for the science of chiropractic medicine. Eventually the treatment and adjustments worked, but on that particular day I was hurting.

I entered our apartment and stared intently at the parking lot below, sharp pains knifing along my lower back. I suppose I was in a serious funk, too, probably feeling sorry for myself and ticked off that I had to work at a job that not only took time away from music production and study but was also causing serious damage to my body. I remember looking around the room and realizing that I had very little in the way of possessions: lots of books and records, some reasonably good audio equipment, a small console piano that barely fit in the tiny living room area—my percussion instruments did not fit, residing instead in the basement of the building where I had to continually put them up and take them down, a few pieces of furniture and one closet full of clothes. I had a growing stack of music—manuscripts, scores and parts—that I had been creating along with a collection of audio tapes containing a number of works made for dancers and dance companies in the electronic studio at the Philadelphia College of the Performing Arts using a vintage Moog Synthesizer. Aside from the electronic works on tape all these other compositions, ideas and sketches were either stuck in my head or written down on paper; music without a natural life.

Something was wrong.

I had to find a way to share these musical ideas and, most importantly, find an audience. Since an audience did not then exist I had to develop one. If I were going to work in the field of music then I had to create my own "milieu." I didn't fit easily into any of the boxes that were designed for people like me. I tried, but those boxes had some strange angles and overheads; they cramped me up something fierce. That day I vowed never again—regardless of the financial consequences—to work on a construction job, never again take work that was not related to the one thing I loved and had trained for: music. And I would concentrate on "new" and "experimental" music from throughout the world that I was in the process of discovering.

I suppose, in that small Philadelphia apartment overlooking that dilapidated parking lot, I experienced an epiphany of sorts. I knew I was made for better things in this life and now was the time to act. If I could not find a way to make a living as a practical musician then I would get out of the business and find something else to do. The journey began and with it a complete transformation from within. I decided to form a music group to play my music and the music of my friends. I would forge friendships and relationships with artists who shared my interests in New Music and related performance practices. I would do all of this in a city that had built its reputation for "brilliant musicianship" on the backs of dead European composers and symphony conductors who were treated royally by an adoring public and who generally rejected the music of their time. And I would do it from a perspective of a lapsed working-class kid whose caste was destined to labor in one of the many fading factories throughout Philadelphia. Thus began my long affair with the illogical worlds of concert production and presentation, content creation and, most illusory of all, arts administration.

From the beginning Relâche was an anomaly, especially in Philadelphia. At that time there were really no professional music ensembles in the city with an interest and expertise to perform music of the late 20th century. For several years an organization named "The Philadelphia Composers Forum" made an effort to develop a new audience for contemporary music. From a position aligned fairly closely with the University of Pennsylvania's music program, the Composers Forum commissioned and premiered many new works while raising just enough money to employ a core of excellent free-lance musicians. Later on, faculty members at Penn organized a group named the Penn Contemporary Players who essentially adapted the type of repertoire that the Composers Forum had championed. In the late 1980s the Penn Contemporary Players evolved into Orchestra 2001, a contemporary chamber music ensemble that continues to perform concerts in the Philadelphia area.

The Composers Forum was a small chamber orchestra that often sub-divided arranging the various instrumentalists into modular groups—

quartets, quintets, trios, etc.— to play works written for mixed instrumental combinations. The "Forum," as it was known, was under the direction of conductor Joel Thome who maintained a small core group of players with others coming and going depending upon the instruments needed for a specific work. Their concerts were often quite good but they projected an aura of precious institutional modernism; the audience consisting mainly of those with a lexicon for demanding marginalized music. Aspiring young composers, their teachers and academic musicians from area universities and colleges like Penn, Swarthmore, Princeton and Temple constituted a majority of the audience. Sometime around 1975 The Composers Forum relocated to New York City, changed their name to the Orchestra of Our Time and began presenting large-scale events in an effort to appeal to a broader audience. When Relâche entered the picture in 1977 it stepped into a deep resonant void.

Relâche gave its first performance at the Painted Bride Art Center, a former bridal shop located on South Street, then newly minted from the ashes of a downtrodden neighborhood just south of affluent Society Hill and north of the old working class neighborhood of Queen Village, settled in the 19th century by Italian, Polish and Irish immigrants who worked along the bustling Delaware Riverfront as stevedores and laborers. By the mid-1980s this entire area had become the darling of Philadelphia developers, with overly expensive apartment complexes scooped out of an old Abbots Milk dairy and equally over-expensive townhouses built on the ruins of old row houses attracting that much-despised species of eighties excess: the Yuppie. With trendy bars and restaurants to serve this new class of consumers, South Street eventually became a place sensible people avoided. It was Philadelphia's answer to San Francisco's Haight-Ashbury, only without the Bay and the Bridge. Or more directly, it was a concrete version of Wildwood, New Jersey's Boardwalk: where the vain and clueless vamped and vogued up and down South Street on weekends looking for urban action that played itself out on TV shows like Miami Vice. Somehow in the midst of this mindless excess the Painted Bride Art Center flourished.

The Painted Bride Art Center, known to the locals as "The Painted Bride," or simply "The Bride," hosted numerous exhibitions, poetry and stage readings and music performances, some very good and some very bad. There was little curatorial control over what appeared there, so one normally took their chances from night to night. Despite unevenness in the presentations, it remained the only place in the city where an emerging talent might find a forum and audience, the only place in town to nurture and encourage new experimental works in any medium. Over the years the Painted Bride grew exponentially. It now resides in an old warehouse in the Old City section of Philadelphia and is among the most respected performance venues in the country dedicated to presenting and nurturing new and controversial works in the visual, performing and literary arts. Although Relâche eventually outgrew the Bride's small spaces, it performed there numerous times over the years.

Early in 1977, shortly after making the decision to form a performing ensemble I organized a small group of composers and performers, culled from a larger group of people I had met at Temple University and the Philadelphia Musical Academy and asked if they would like to get together, rehearse some New Music and present a concert somewhere in Philadelphia. The musicians I asked were friends who I felt a kinship with. I did not select specific instruments for the group but rather specific individuals who I trusted and respected. There were six of us: pianist John Dulik, bassist/performance artist Annson Kenney, vocalist Barbara Noska; a flutist, oboist and me on percussion. Annson, John and I wrote a new piece for this combination of instruments and we began rehearsing these and a few others by, if memory serves me, Luciano Berio and John Cage.

I thought of giving the concert in the fabled historically revered Christ Church located at 2nd and Market streets. In previous years Annson Kenney had used that space for several performance works that, despite the irreverent nature of these performances, somehow intrigued the pastor, who was eager to open the church to new projects. Then Gerry Givnish, a co-founding director of the Painted Bride who knew of my interest in New Music, encouraged me to organize a series of concerts at the Painted Bride. After several invitations and seeing an opportunity to develop a long-term relationship with the Bride, I agreed. So, on a Sunday afternoon in May 1977 I presented my first concert of New Music. There was no formal name for the group or concert, just "New Music at the Painted Bride," produced by Joseph Franklin.

A few weeks following the performance I had lunch with my friend Romulus Franceschini who attended the concert. He informed me that another guy in town had also formed a small ensemble to play New Music. His name was Joseph Showalter, a trombone player and then aspiring conductor.

I vaguely remembered Joe from my undergraduate days at the Philadelphia Musical Academy. We were students at the same time but had never really met. Romulus and Joe were friends. Each had an interest in early and mid 20th century orchestral works, a by-product of Romulus's position as music editor at the Fleisher Collection of Orchestral Music where Joe spent many hours studying and researching scores. Romulus figured it would be easier for us to join forces rather than compete against one another for an audience, not to mention competing for the attention of those few players in town who had ears for New Music.

I called Joe and suggested we meet.

Joe and I shared a somewhat similar Philadelphia background: boys of working class families who were drawn to music through an inherent need to escape the caste that locked sons and daughters of the neighborhoods into meaningless jobs and lives lived in one of many bland Philadelphia suburbs with families and mortgages. Neither of us was especially "born" to music; we developed skills as average performers through sheer hard work, not through an innate natural gift. But we both had an ear and analytical mind for musical style, an ability to locate a style within defined historical contexts. As musical and social historians we were more fascinated by the behavior of certain individuals—in the ontology of their times—rather than being awed by the arcane matters of musical creation. For example, it was a lot more fun to read about, talk about and listen to the music of Erik Satie—as a social outcast and eccentric composer—than it was to read about, talk about and listen to the music of Arnold Schoenberg—as radical revolutionary composer and high priest of European Modernism. This shared interest in history and style along with our need to be part of something new forged an initial partnership. We joined forces and planned a concert for February 1978.

For the performance we selected the Old Pine Street Church, located in the heart of Olde City, just two blocks from the original Painted Bride Art Center. The denomination of the church is Presbyterian. At that time the pastor was a youngish guy with a somewhat "radical" reputation by sponsoring meetings and demonstrations to address social and political issues current in people's minds. The church hosted chamber music groups from throughout the area as well as a "jazz vespers" on Sundays. The acoustical character of the church is resonant and fairly even throughout. Although over the years the Relâche Ensemble would severely test the natural acoustical character of the church by presenting musical works using all manner of electronic enhancement and sound manipulation, for the inaugural concert Joe and I selected works that could be called chamber music.

Well, almost.

I don't recall the exact program but I do remember it was a mixed bag, to say the least. Essentially we combined each of our ensembles with Joe's larger group consisting of strings, winds and piano, motoring through works from the mid-20th century with him conducting. My group on the other hand presented all new works that included a piece of mine for singing actress interacting with sine-waves from an audio oscillator that severely tested the confines of the sanctified church. John Dulik performing his "Piano Sonata," a scorching virtuoso piece composed around dancing filigree lines that, at times, resembled a fugue caught in a wind tunnel. Only someone with John's steely percussive touch and massive technique could have brought it off. What I remember best about the event was just how audacious the whole thing was. Here we were in a church that had established its presence as a refuge for the disenfranchised and, well, "radical" segments of inter-racial inter-denominational Philadelphians, and here we were performing "new" music. It was perfect as was the name we gave the combined groups: Relâche, a gesture that was to prove fortuitous.

"*Relâche* is life, life as I love it, life without tomorrow, the life of today, everything for today, nothing for yesterday, nothing for tomorrow. Car lights, pearl necklaces, the delicate round contours of women, advertising, music, the car, a few men in evening dress, movement, noise, action, clear transparent water, laughter, that's *Relâche*...*Relâche* is movement without a direction, neither forward not back, neither to left nor right. *Relâche* doesn't turn and yet it doesn't go straight ahead; *Relâche* ambles through life with a great burst of laughter"

This, from the original 1926 Paris premiere program for Relâche, a collaborative work—a ballet, a theatre piece—by composer Erik Satie and artists Francis Picabia and Rene Clair. As a closing salvo to the Dada period, Relâche was perfect. In addition to a great score by Satie, Relâche contained a brilliant film titled Entr'acte by Rene Clair containing one of the first original soundtracks by Satie, of course, created in close collaboration with Clair and featuring the famed dancer Jean Borlin. Interestingly *Relâche* was also the expression that, on French theatre bills or shop windows, signifies, "the establishment is closed." Relâche was to signify that the old ideas were no longer usable . . . they were out of business.

When the original Paris premiere performance of *Relâche* was announced—amid great hype—an eager, curious audience showed, anticipating a unique event. But the performers did not show up. *Relâche!* They did show up the following evening and proceeded to give a raucous performance eliciting the usual reaction from Parisian audiences: laughter, derisive whistles, and finally clamorous protest. The artists were delighted; at the curtain call Satie and Picabia drove around the stage in a Citroen car waving to the audience. The painter Fernand Leger remarked, "it delivered a lot of kicks up a lot of bottoms, sacred or otherwise."

When Joe Showalter suggested the name Relâche for our group a half-century later, well, I just flipped out; it was perfect in ways that I'm not certain he really understood at the time. His intentions were pretty clear: he wanted to be a conductor and needed a group of musicians on whom he could practice and from whom he could learn the protocol for a successful conducting career.

I had other ideas.

My intention was to create an ensemble that would embrace all aspects of theatre, electronic and emerging computer technologies and musical performance; it would celebrate the works of the American experimental composers Henry Cowell and John Cage, et al. and the European avant-garde composers Karlheintz Stockhausen and Luciano Berio, et al. The ensemble I envisioned would work as a fully integrated democratic entity with each performer having input into the overall design or arc of a given work. Most importantly, the ensemble I envisioned would not be modeled on any current or previous group then active but rather would create a new type of musical ensemble: virtuosic and unpredictable, elegant and raucous, controlled yet uncontrollable. And this ensemble would not require a conductor. Eventually, over time, Joe's notion of ensemble clashed with mine and we drifted apart. But for the next five years we worked together as co-directors in a relationship that was at times less than graceful.

Early on I assumed most aspects of the administrative direction for the group. Joe and I were co-directors and therefore shared all of the responsibilities from programming to promotion to mailing. At the time the concept of "marketing" was alien to both of us, to be avoided at all costs if we were to lead as "revolutionary" a group as Relâche. Of necessity, this attitude changed dramatically as Relâche matured and grew. And then there was the simple matter of fundraising. How does one go about it and who would be in charge? This proved to be a deciding factor in Relâche's early history: fundraising. Relâche was operating out of my tiny apartment with the good intentions of a group of friends with little regard for the future. Behind the scenes I was maneuvering for something else: stability and long-term growth. That could only be achieved by developing a solid fundraising strategy. I dived into it without any training, connections or money, a decision that proved critical for the infant organization and for me.

The first matter of business was filing for not-for-profit status with the IRS. In those days the process was not nearly as long as it is today so, by early 1979 we had been approved. Our "Board of Directors" consisted solely of me, Joe and Romulus Franceschini, a circumstance that would change within the year. During the remainder of 1978 I began researching potential funding agencies where we could apply for support. Usually private foundations and government agencies require an organization be in existence for a two-year period before applying. With this in mind I targeted November 1979 as a deadline to submit initial grant proposals. This gave us ample time to develop new programs and secure venues and dates for performances. It also gave me time to organize a larger group of interested people to help administer the organization.

To manage the ensemble I determined that Relâche needed two separate entities: an administrative staff to formulate a business and fundraising plan and an artistic advisory committee to suggest repertoire, program content and evaluate the musicians recommending, when necessary, replacement and extra players. There was no money to pay anyone at that time so everyone worked as volunteers, each with their own agendas, or at least, their own intentions.

The administrative group—in addition to me—consisted of Joe Showalter and composers Tina Davidson and Neil Williams. The artistic advisory committee included the administrative group plus Romulus Franceschini, Annson Kenney and John Dulik, all composers and performers with little administrative experiences. Several months later, Neil Williams moved away from Philadelphia, eventually settling in Albuquerque, New Mexico where he lived under his birth name, Sean Williams, until his untimely death in 1995. Tina Davidson and I became more directly involved with the day-to-day business while Joe and the others provided assistance.

The meetings of the administrative and artistic advisory groups were often a bit testy, at times volatile. We strove for unity and a direction that would satisfy each individual's concept of the ensemble—and their roles in it—while trying to grasp the larger issues of organizational control and governance. By virtue of our dedication to the tasks at hand combined with having good organizational and secretarial skills, Tina and I gained control: I was appointed executive director and she associate director.

During this time we were meeting either in Tina's or my small apartment, neither of which proved very accommodating. It was clear that we had to find a small office space as the organization incrementally grew. Through a family contact Tina was able to secure a donated office space near the campus of the University of Pennsylvania in West Philadelphia that would serve as the Relâche office for the next nine years.

Dr. Britton Chance, a friend of Tina's family, was an internationally respected bio-physicist and director of the Johnson Research Center at the University of Pennsylvania. Dr. Chance owned a property at 40th and Pine streets, just blocks from his office in the Center. Like many of the structures in the area around University City, as the region is locally known, it was a spacious building converted from a large family dwelling into smaller apartments to accommodate students from Penn and Drexel Universities. On the first floor there was a large open space with a small guest apartment attached. This space was designated as a library to house overflow books and articles authored or commissioned by Dr. Chance. The space proved much too large for his papers so he offered it to Relâche, free of charge, as a favor to Tina Davidson. He asked only that we provide security and maintenance.

Beginning in 1979 Relâche occupied this office space *cum* library while scholars —some eccentric, some baffling, most exhausted—filtered in and out of the adjoining guest apartment. At times it was a bizarre scene: in one room a group of artists going about their business producing concerts and events, raising money and at times raising a little hell, while in the other room a brilliant physicist from Uganda writing a paper on a new discovery that only he and a few other equally brilliant souls at the Johnson Research Center could remotely comprehend. This arrangement ended in 1988 when Relâche outgrew the space, determined to move closer to downtown Philadelphia. We made the move after I found a location in Old City.

Relâche's first center city Philadelphia office was located on Market Street between Strawberry and Bank Streets, on the second floor above an electronics and appliance store operated by an affable Korean man whose real name we never learned, although he preferred that we call him by his adopted American name: Steve. From our second floor perch we could observe the action along Market Street through a full-length window, in which we installed the distinctive neon Relâche sign Annson Kenney had designed. At night the sign glowed, the low-level magenta light gave the impression that behind the window a mysterious or sinister activity was transpiring. To access the office space one had to climb a narrow stairway, dimly lit by a single light bulb hanging from the slanted ceiling. Bob Ashley and his wife Mimi Johnson commented when visiting me once that climbing those stairs reminded them of a scene from a vintage *film noir*, slowly cautiously climbing the dark stairs to visit a private investigator. I think they liked that part of the visit. The place had plenty of character but not a lot of square footage so I found a larger space around the corner and in 1992 Relâche moved to Strawberry Street.

Located between Market and Chestnut and Second and Bank streets, Strawberry Street was a picturesque commercial block tucked away from the noise and activity of busy Market Street. The office space was unique: two floors connected by a wrought iron circular stairway with ample room for desks and cabinets to house the large music library and archives accumulated over the preceding 14 years. In addition to having more space it had a curious controversial history.

During the early 1990s archeologists at the University of Pennsylvania discovered small rivulets located deep beneath the paved streets of Philadelphia in the areas emanating outward from the Delaware River in what was then the heart of the new city. These small underground rivers, it is surmised, connected with one another providing transportation for people and goods as they moved about, conducting their business and extending the city's boundaries. Apparently, according to studies on record, one of these rivulets ran below or very near what is now Strawberry Street.

Throughout the area warehouses and factories stored goods that were transported along these rivulets, including contraband stolen by pirates and other assorted bad guys. We found it especially ironic that the one truly "subversive" music organization in Philadelphia would find its way to a place where other subversives might have held forth. I have no idea when this facility was destroyed or taken over by the authorities or if indeed, the current structure is built on the original foundation, but something in the soil lends itself to nefarious deeds. Later on, the records tell us, it became a brothel, or something similar.

Over the years, small indiscreet nightclubs opened and closed with some regularity at addresses up and down Strawberry Street and adjacent Bank Street. Most of these establishments were designated as "after hours" clubs, meaning they could continue to do business after the 2 AM city-mandated closing time. The ladies and gentlemen who populated these clubs were not the kind of folks you were likely to find at PTA meetings; they did not necessarily advertise their presence nor did they encourage others to join in the festivities. So when a new business opened at 11 South Strawberry Street it appeared to fit nicely into the prevailing outré culture.

Sometime in the late 1960s a football player with the Philadelphia Eagles either purchased the building or allowed his name to be used in a new business. Well, actually an old business but at a new location. So 11 South Strawberry Street became a "gentleman's club" to entertain members of the Eagles—and their friends—as they strayed far from the nest. I doubt if this place were used by the players—and their friends—as a post game or after practice hangout to assess what might have gone wrong on the field. Whatever its use or mission, this gentleman's club survived for about five years until, one day (it is rumored) an arsonist torched the place. It is also rumored that the building was set ablaze by irate "Iggles" fans wearied of the team's lousy performance on the field. The place sat empty and rotting until, ten years later, a group of investors bought it, renovated it, and created an office space in the basement and first floor and offices and a living space on the second and third floors with a separate entrance. One of the investors was a friend of a friend who agreed to rent the basement and first floor to Relâche at a discounted price, claiming the discount as a tax deduction. It was perfect: large, uniquely designed, welcoming to visitors. Finally, Relâche had an office space that felt right, one that would nurture the coming years' growth.

Throughout the 1980s the Relâche Ensemble featured a mixture of instruments and voice: flute(s), clarinet(s), two saxophones (soprano, alto, tenor and baritone), bassoon, accordion, piano-synthesizer, percussion and voice. People often jokingly referred to Relâche as a New Music Klezmer band! At times there was one saxophone, not two or there were two saxophones, not clarinet. Or there were two saxophones, clarinet, flute and no bassoon. It varied depending on the situation or, at times, the availability of players. As accordionist Guy Klucesvek's professional and personal life became more centered on New York City, he did not perform with the group all the time, but with enough regularity and input to be considered a part of the "core" ensemble.

Early Relâche Ensemble – Left to right: Joseph Franklin, John Dulik, Flossie Ieardi (kneeling), Laurel Wyckoff, Steve Marcucci, Wesley Hall, Guy Klucevsek (seated), Robert Zollman, Barbara Noska, Chuck Holdeman, Tina Davidson

On average there were almost always eight performing members of the ensemble. The nature of performing ensembles in just about all areas of the music business is one of constant change brought on by a variety of causes like the musicians moving on to other interests; not being able to reconcile personality or artistic differences among the performing or administrative members; changing careers—leaving the profession entirely, etc. But the core Relâche Ensemble stayed together for long periods of time due, I think, to our having created a challenging collaborative environment in which to work. During my 22-year tenure with Relâche there were essentially three different ensembles, all of which sustained a musical cohesiveness because several of the players—especially since pianist John Dulik and flutist Laurel Wyckoff—stayed aboard during the changes; hence the consistency in sound and spirit of the group.

The Relâche Ensemble consisted of the same eight musicians between 1979 and 1983 adding replacements and extra players when needed for specific programs or projects. Between 1984 and 1989, with just a few changes in personnel, another group of eight performers stayed together, again adding extra players when needed. Then beginning in mid-1989 and continuing until 1991 Relâche began a shift that proved to be most dramatic in terms of sound and character.

Singer-actress Barbara Noska—so singular a presence during Relâche's first 12 years—began to ease away from the ensemble to pursue other musical and personal interests. She was not replaced.

Bassoonist Chuck Holdeman who added a distinct "French Bassoon" sound to the ensemble, moved to Seattle and was replaced by John Gaarder who plays the more familiar German bassoon. The French Bassoon is played by far fewer American musicians, the German instrument being the one most often used. The fingering is different with the French model delivering a lighter tone. When John Gaarder came on board there was concern that the heavier tonal quality of the German instrument would dramatically change the ensemble's sonic image. It did but in a very positive way as John added immeasurably to the new Relâche sound.

Helen Carnevale replaced Florence Ierardi as percussionist. Flossie and long-time friend Jerry Tanenbaum shared most of the playing during the early 1980s with Flossie taking over in the mid-eighties. A great player but reserved on stage, Flossie was always reliable and accurate. Helen was much more outgoing, her playing extravagant at times and always energetic.

Bassist Douglas Mapp overcame early skepticism to become one of the true believers in the group's mission while adding a strong, rock-solid foundation to the group.

Oboe-English Horn player Lloyd Shorter arrived with a great attitude. He is an excellent musician and audiophile who kept abreast of developments in audio-acoustical technologies, lending that expertise to the mix especially when recording new works. Saxophonist Ken Ulansey doubled on clarinet and, like Douglas and pianist John Dulik was an impressive improviser with roots in jazz and other world music traditions. Laurel Wyckoff remained as flutist and in addition to playing all of the flutes she assumed more and more administrative duties, serving as ensemble manager, librarian and tour facilitator.

When violist Kathleen Carroll joined the ensemble in 1992 it became—with due respect to each and every musician who contributed their talents to Relâche—the most versatile ensemble thus far and remained together until I left in 1998, participating in numerous projects, tours, recordings and related events. Sadly, Kathleen Carroll passed away in 2003 after a gutsy battle with Cancer.

The Relâche Ensemble circa 1996 – clockwise from lower left: Kathleen Carroll, Chuck Holdeman, Laurel Wyckoff, Douglas Mapp, John Dulik, Lloyd Shorter, Helen Carnevale, Ken Ulansey.

The instrumental complement of Relâche was problematic at times for composers, players and listeners alike. For example, finding the right balance for the viola when pitted against four woodwind instruments and percussion was often an issue. The same can be said for the alto flute. To compensate Relâche enhanced their performances electronically becoming in essence an "electric ensemble."

For all performances in Philadelphia microphones were placed strategically in front of and either below or above the wind instruments. The contrabass and viola had special microphones attached to the instruments' bodies and the electric bass and synthesizer were patched directly into the mix. Two microphones provided an even acoustic field for the piano while three and sometimes four microphones were positioned around an array of percussion instruments or directly below the vibraphone and marimba. In order to achieve a balanced sound—both for the ensemble on stage and the audience in the auditorium—the instruments were mixed their levels adjusted accordingly then sent back to the stage and into the auditorium via two separate mixes. This took time and patience, a condition carefully orchestrated by scheduling sound checks with detailed responsibilities for each player.

Around this time Werner Strobel, who had been Relâche's audio engineer and all-around technical advisor, informed me in his characteristically modest tone that, "Relâche needs a full-time sound engineer, one with better and up-to-date equipment, someone who spends all of their time dealing with sound enhancement. I just can't dedicate the time to it like I used to." He was right, of course but it was hard to accept. Werner had been with me from the very beginning of Relâche and was responsible for much of its early success. I had met Werner a few years earlier, when he took a course I taught on Twentieth Century Music at Temple University Extension Division. A brilliant engineer, who then worked for the U. S. Navy as a civilian instrumentation specialist, Werner was eager to learn the mystery of music production and practical theory. Although not formally trained as a sound engineer, Werner nevertheless became a very good one through years of dedicated service to a variety of situations, research into evolving sound enhancement hardware and methodologies, and listening with a keen ear to a variety of musics. During Relâche's first decade Werner was the technical director for all concerts in Philadelphia. To replace Werner I asked Chris Dietze if he were interested. He was, and we began a transition to a new style of sound enhancement.

Chris worked full-time for an audio firm in Philadelphia so, rather than hire Chris directly; we contracted with the company he worked for: Clear Sound, Inc. Our contract with them assured us that Chris would work all of the concerts using their equipment and assistants if necessary. Chris was one of the most experienced sound engineers on the scene. It was in his blood. His father had worked for RCA Victor in Camden, New Jersey as an engineer in the early glory days of that company. Chris inherited vintage microphones his dad helped develop, many of them used in Relâche concerts. His knowledge of current audio equipment and techniques was impressive. And he too has a great ear. He possesses a peculiar form of perfect pitch—unlike acoustically acute musicians, doesn't identify the precise pitch as a note in the tempered scale, rather its cycles per second. Often it was a point of humorous discourse between a player and Chris; each insisting the tuning was accurate. A player might say, "that C is out of tune." Chris would counter, "Yeah, it's two hundred twenty-two cycles per second." Chris, like Werner, is also a very nice guy, even-tempered, friendly, industrious—never a wasted gesture. With Chris at the mixing board Relâche was definitely in good hands. The same can be said for all other aspects of production, those details residing in the capable hands of our superb production coordinator: David Michael Kenney.

DMK. The initials stand for David Michael Kenney and DMK Productions. Most people in the performing arts business in Philadelphia who worked with him called him simply "DMK." I always called him David. He just isn't a "Dave" or "Davey" kind of guy. Highly organized, driven by details, smart, personable and honest, David was an essential member of the Relâche team beginning in 1985 and continuing until I left in 1998. In addition to a superb sense of business he was trained as an actor and theatre technician so he literally knows the stage inside out.

We had met several years back when he performed in Lanie Robertson's powerfully evocative play, "The Insanity of Mary Girard." I was so impressed with the piece that I would purchase the rights to create an operatic work based on the play, a work that I left unfinished when I finally made the decision to concentrate my energies on directing the Relâche organization. Meanwhile, in the original play, David played one of the seven Furies who taunted Mary Girard, trying to lure her into their madness and the "safe" confines of an institution. The story was based on the illustrious life of the Philadelphia financier and banker Stephen Girard who apparently had a penchant for taking in young girls, marrying them and, when he had used them up, dumped them in an insane asylum while he placed money in the hands of the asylum's director. This tactic proved successful until Mary resisted. Alas, the authorities eventually had their way and she accepted her fate. I can still see David's character, slender and sinewy as he traced circles around the resolute Mary, whispering in her ear encomiums of the historic ruling class of esteemed Philadelphians.

Sometime around 1985 David and his partner, Nan Gilbert, attended a Relâche concert and observed—accurately—that despite Werner Strobel's and my efforts, the production quality was not equal to the performance quality of the ensemble on stage. The sound was good, the lighting was good, the staging was good, but it was just that, good. David felt it could be excellent. His timing could not have been better since I was in the planning stage to present the New Music America '87—Philadelphia Festival. He made a proposal that outlined his role as production coordinator. In it he assumed all responsibilities to present Relâche in concert with full back-line and back-of-house support, including a ticketing service. DMK Productions would take care of all the details consuming so much of my time, freeing me up to manage the organization at a period when Relâche was beginning to expand.

What a relief!

Over the years David became a confidant of mine, helping me negotiate some tricky union relations, never, ever, misleading or misrepresenting Relâche or me. He was an invaluable ally in the quest to bring New Music and New Musical personalities to Philadelphia and showcase the Relâche Ensemble in ways that no other New Music ensemble then was being presented.

With a new ensemble starting to take shape and a new production crew in place I was able to dedicate far more of my time to essential tasks like raising money, building a board of directors, creating a commissioning program and developing performance opportunities worldwide. But there were problems brewing.

From the beginning Tina Davidson and I were to say the least, an odd couple, musically speaking. The daughter of a prominent American physicist, born in Sweden but raised in the U.S., educated in private schools and Bennington College, she viewed herself as destined for the role of "artiste." I had no such illusions.

We met, I remember, in early 1978 just as Relâche was beginning to become noticed around town. It was clear Tina had skills and smarts that partnered well with mine. Although our styles were radically different, each of us was very good at designing projects and building plans to support them while pursuing other interests, either professional or personal. Over the next couple of years we worked together on a variety of projects and fundraising plans so that by the mid-eighties Relâche was paying the musicians a reasonable fee for their services while paying the administrative staff yearly salaries. In addition to an expanded season in Philadelphia the ensemble was touring regionally while operating with a yearly budget of $200,000.

During those years Tina concentrated on finding performances for the Relâche Ensemble outside of Philadelphia while I concentrated on fundraising, concert production and personnel management. The programming was a result of our monthly meetings with the artistic advisory group that eventually included musicians from the ensemble who expressed an interest in learning more about repertoire or who wished to lobby for a particular work, usually one that featured them as a soloist or at least gave them a prominent role. I concentrated on developing contacts and relationships with local, state and federal funding agencies and philanthropies located primarily in Philadelphia.

I taught myself how to research and write detailed project descriptions and grant applications in support of a variety of projects, mainly our performing arts series. I established relationships with program officers at local foundations and corporations trying to make them more aware of "new" music and its role in contemporary life. Tina focused on building a network of presenters throughout the Mid-Atlantic States, arranging dates for the ensemble at regional festivals and college music programs throughout the region. Together we developed operating budgets and spreadsheets to track our finances and built a board of directors consisting of local musicians and a few business people. Overall the arrangement worked out to everyone's satisfaction.

As I began to concentrate more and more on other productions like New Music America Festivals and building a European network of presenters and composers, our relationship became strained, the result of our differing personal styles and professional expectations. But the thing that caused the most dissonance between us was wildly differing views on our respective roles with Relâche and as independent composers.

By this time I had begun to lose my enthusiasm to write music. I came to a realization that, although I had learned my lessons well and felt secure in my abilities to craft a coherent piece of music, I was not an original. Writing music did not come easily to me; in fact I often felt as if I were struggling to pull a musical idea out of some invisible or intangible object...like a rock or a wall. And once I pulled that idea free I struggled to place it in a context that was acceptable to me. Music should flow from the body and not be forged by the mind. I found myself *thinking* the music rather than *feeling* it and this just did not feel right.

At the same time I was rediscovering the pleasures derived from improvisation and began to question—once again—the notion of or validity for writing music down on paper. I was spending more and more time around musicians who played with such ease and conviction, who had the real gift to tell a convincing story in sound and not waste anyone's time with detailed extravagant scoring mechanisms. And I was learning more and more about the world's music while seriously questioning the role of "composer" in contemporary Western cultures. And so, in 1986 I decided not to write another piece of music for the Relâche Ensemble to play, but to dedicate my energy and talent to continue shaping the Relâche organization and grow it beyond its role as just a performing ensemble. Tina on the other hand had no such interest in questioning her role of composer. This is how she viewed herself, and she viewed herself with conviction. Tina Davidson was determined to be a successful composer. I suppose in the context of a contemporary life she has accomplished her goal by garnering commissions, gaining performances and achieving some semblance of national recognition. But I felt— fairly or unfairly—that she used her position with Relâche to build an independent career and we clashed over this issue on several occasions. Yet my problem was deeper than this. After all, many composers and performers work with music organizations so that they can better negotiate a role for their "creative" sides, to be acknowledged as "artists" and not simply "administrators." This is unfortunately a fact of life, one that causes unnecessary dissonance within an institutional context.

As Relâche evolved, it became harder and harder for me to accept music for performance by the ensemble that did not live up to my personal expectations, and those expectations did not embrace music that was ostensibly conceived according to the dated tenets of *modernism*; music without a connection to an event or perceived events which resonated with current political and/or social conditions or events. The notion of "art for art's sake" just didn't work for me any longer. And that is how I perceived Tina's music, no matter how engaging the title or the *raison d'etre* for making it, the music was not convincing to me and I believed that we—Relâche—had forged a unique sound for other types of music by virtue of the personalities of the ensemble members at that time, and Tina's music no longer fit well with Relâche.

During this time we both struggled with our relationship. I was as honest as I could be under the circumstances. And I think she was as well. Although disappointed and mad at the situation, Tina acknowledged our differences and we formed a pact of sorts: each season Relâche would program a new work by her while new staff members on the Relâche team assumed some of the responsibilities she had been carrying out. This worked for a while especially since Tina had recently given birth to a daughter and was dedicated to her new role in life. For the next few years, until 1993, we co-existed in this arrangement until she left to pursue a full-time life as a composer and create projects with other performing groups. I took this opportunity to re-tool Relâche both administratively and artistically.

Throughout the 1980s, the Relâche Ensemble developed a repertoire of musical works the way most similar music groups do: by renting or purchasing a score and instrumental/vocal parts from publishers like Peters and Universal International. These works usually specified the instruments required, although at times, and with permission from either the composer or publisher, an ensemble or soloist could switch an instrument or two as long is they were similar in timbre and range or had the same fundamental tone (i.e. soprano saxophone for trumpet or viola for violin). This the ensemble did quite often since the core instrumentation seldom fit with published works. Relâche forged relationships with composers who were intrigued by the odd instrumentation of the group and admired their collective spirit. These composers either offered or responded to a request to make a new work and in many instances that new work was created for a variable ensemble.

The variable ensemble is, essentially, a group of performers using any combination of instruments and voices to realize a work created by a composer who does not specify specific instrumentation. This type of work is often more "conceptual" and uses a variety of compositional tools such as graphic music notation—for example, straight and/or sinuous lines drawn within a relative time-frame axis to suggest pitch, timbre or duration—and explicit verbal instructions often interpolated within traditional notational sections to allow the performers wider interpretative latitude with the score or instrumental parts. Music constructed in this manner provides an opportunity for the performers and composer to collaboratively create a new work each time the piece is realized.

By necessity and temperament the Relâche Ensemble specialized in works for the variable ensemble, successfully building a reliable repertoire to highlight the distinctive sound of the group.

Performances of these variable works were in keeping with the spirit of democratization abundantly in evidence throughout the more "experimental" areas of the performing arts beginning in the mid 1960s and continuing into the early 1990s. Then in the early 1990s composers who wrote for ensembles other than their own once again began writing music for specific combinations of instruments with and without electronic and computer imaging. As the Relâche Ensemble transformed itself with new players coming in and others leaving, the repertoire required a change as well. To remake the sound of the ensemble with the complement of players and instruments then available, Relâche needed to commission a body of works and build a new identity for the group.

Throughout the 1990s Relâche commissioned over 100 new musical works from "The Fund for New Music" with grant money from philanthropic foundations in Philadelphia and music service organizations nationally. The Pew Charitable Trusts, William Penn Foundation, Stockton Rush Bartol Foundation and the Philadelphia Foundation were the principal sources in Philadelphia. Nationally agencies like the National Endowment for the Arts (before the dreaded "culture wars" eliminated direct grants to artists for the creation of new works), Meet The Composer and Chamber Music America have all championed the creation of new works and were usually generous to Relâche. Sometimes grants from Meet The Composer and Chamber Music America were awarded to a consortium of three different ensembles which shared in a commission. Under this arrangement, a composer would create a work to be performed by all three ensembles over a designated period of time with one of the ensembles—often Relâche—being the facilitator, responsible to pay the commissioning fee and ascertain that each ensemble performed the new work. To raise funds from any one of these agencies was a time-consuming effort which began with a detailed proposal.

Throughout my life in the arts I have learned to research, develop and write proposals, project descriptions and plans with authority. A proposal is most successful when it embraces multiple ideas of a creative team and then channels those ideas through an individual or organization's artistic vision.

First however it is essential that a close professional, or sometimes personal, relationship be developed among the foundation or agency officers and the artistic-executive leadership of the prospective grantee.

Carefully planned meetings are scheduled to gain a better understand of the funding priorities of the foundation or agency at that particular time; prove that the organization is fiscally sound and responsible; describe how the funds awarded will enhance the artistic mission of the organization; and prove how their funds will enable the organization to match monies from other funding sources and individuals, thus enabling the organization to grow. Once this information is gathered and analyzed, a business plan is created showing in precise detail how the goals of the project will be achieved, a detailed budget and a clear time-line for realizing those goals. All of this data is then crafted into a comprehensive proposal and submitted to the targeted agency. Usually it requires six months for them to evaluate the proposal, ask pertinent questions and either approve the proposal for funding or reject it. During these years Relâche raised substantial monies from philanthropic and service agencies for the commissioning fund.

The size of the commissions varied, from $2,000 to $15,000, depending on the reputation of the composer. For example young emerging composers received $2,000 - $3,000 for a new work while a more established composer received $5,000 - $10,000. Larger commissions were offered when possible to prominent well-known artists. Among those commissioned were Phillip Glass, Robert Ashley, George Russell, Fred Ho, Alvin Curran, Mary Ellen Childs, William Duckworth, Joseph Koykkar, Pauline Oliveros, Michael Nyman, Lois V Vierk, Stephen Montague, Eve Beglarian and Paul Epstein. All of the world premieres were given in Philadelphia and then performed on tour. Several have been recorded. Whenever possible the composer was invited to Philadelphia prior to beginning the work or during its development to spend a day or two with the ensemble, trying out some new ideas while getting to know the personalities and musical interests of the individual members in the ensemble. For the premiere performance the composer would once again be brought to Philadelphia to oversee the final rehearsals and be acknowledged as a featured or guest artist on the concert. Another source of monies for commissioning new works was large corporations. In this area, I believe, Relâche set a standard for New Music organizations nationwide, and the credit belongs to Drew Keegan.

Drew was born and raised in Upper Darby, Pennsylvania, a suburb known primarily as the end-of-the-line for the "Frankford El," or elevated train. Upper Darby is the southwest terminus for the El, arriving there after winding through Center City from the lower northeast section of Frankford. Although officially located in Chester County—outside the city limits—Upper Darby is really just another working class neighborhood in Philadelphia, primarily Irish-American, until in the 1970s when the area's demographic changed to Asian-American with a large influx of Koreans and then Vietnamese. Drew, like many who worked for Relâche during these times, escaped from the narrow confines of the neighborhood and began a career in sales and marketing for a large firm. For 12 years he was at the mercy of corporate America, bailing out finally after the company he worked for shipped him off to Alabama. That didn't work. Drew's a Philly kid through and through, smart and savvy, a student of the American political system. But for some reason I always had a difficult time understanding, he identified with the Republican Party, confusing the issue for me even more by referring to himself as a "Reagan Republican."

As the product of a feisty union family I could not remotely understand why anyone from grit-and-gristle blue collar Philadelphia could or would want to identify with the Republican Party in 1980s America and especially with Reagan whose conservative policies were alien to the traditional values of the underprivileged disenfranchised working classes. Somehow Drew absconded from his caste and embraced the issues so beloved of mainstream Republicans: smaller government and greater support for American business. During the eight years Drew and I worked together we formed a strange but strong partnership, one that began when he was hired to sell advertisements for New Music America '87. During our eight- year professional association each of us was transformed; he by an awareness of the role of the arts in contemporary life and I by a better understanding of and respect for certain business cultures. Our partnership resulted in several important projects.

Among these was Bell Atlantic's Evening of American Music. I suppose it was only fitting that Relâche opened this event in front of a glittering audience of Philadelphia officials, employees of Bell Atlantic Company and their assorted associates with one of the more innovative, and difficult to comprehend, works in the repertoire: *Critical Band* by James Tenney, a work discussed in detail later in this book. I sat next to Mayor Wilson Goode during the first half of the concert, trying my best not to radiate the tension I felt. Although I was, I admit, feeling a bit smug at having the audacity to program a work like this, I was also concerned I had indeed programmed *Critical Band* for an audience that probably was attending their first New Music concert ever, afraid they might walk out. There were plenty of confused looks on the majority of faces in the audience but nobody left. At the end of *Critical Band* as the pure dominant chord shimmered into silence, Mr.Goode turned to me and said, "that music must be very difficult for the musicians to play." Stunned, I shook my head yes.

In some ways *Critical Band* exemplifies the challenges New Music offers to many of the musicians who play it, as well as the audiences who listen to it. Neither is particularly prepared for these challenges, although the musicians are usually dealing with fundamental technical skills which apply to their particular instrument while the audience is asked to create a whole new context for listening. Those who attend a Relâche Ensemble performance—or a performance by almost any New Music ensemble—should listen directly to the music at it evolves with little regard for their prior knowledge of other "classical music" forms, or for that matter, music from any era or any part of the world. The reason? There are simply no codified ways in which much music from the late 20th century was organized. This is in contrast to earlier forms of Western music where the formal designs were predetermined and a set of "rules" applied to the musical language and syntax. It is to Wilson Goode's credit that he discerned something different was happening that night. And whatever it was, it was almost being created there on the spot by musicians in control of their element.

Later on, I noticed Drew Keegan nervously looking around the theatre no doubt thinking the same thing as I was thinking: *Critical Band*...here? We must be crazy. No, just resolute, like Drew and his quest to bring Big Business into the Relâche fold.

At the time Bell Atlantic was among the largest and wealthiest companies headquartered in Philadelphia. Somehow Drew met their vice president for marketing, Bob Hofsis. A former college football player and golf enthusiast, Bob and Drew shared an interest in sports; Drew as an ardent fan and Bob as a fan and golfer. They gained each others' trust and established a relationship that, to me, was more like father-son rather than just a couple of guys hanging out talking sports. After a while Drew felt he could approach Bob and explore how Bell Atlantic might support a project featuring the Relâche Ensemble.

Concurrently, Drew was becoming friendly with a woman named Judy Fay who, at that time, worked in public relations for the City of Philadelphia. Judy was a new fan of the Relâche Ensemble, attending concerts and socializing at after-concert gatherings. She and Drew envisioned a way that Relâche could become part of the huge fourth of July celebrations the city sponsored each year along Penn's Landing, an event that Bell Atlantic helped sponsor.

The Philadelphia Freedom Festival was created to celebrate Independence Day with concerts and events offered—free of charge—to residents and visitors alike at venues in and around the historic buildings and along the Delaware River at Penn's Landing. A major component of the Philadelphia Freedom Festival is the awarding of the Philadelphia Freedom Medal along with a $100,000 cash prize. Each year the Freedom Medal is bestowed upon a world leader who has championed the cause of freedom in their homeland. Among those who have received the medal are Nelson Mandela, Lech Walesa and Vaclav Havel. In keeping with the festival's theme, I along with Drew, Bob Hofsis and Judy Fay developed a proposal to honor four American composers who, in their own particular way, each celebrated freedom of thought and action in pursuit of their artistic visions. The proposal asked Bell Atlantic to support an evening of commissioned works for the Relâche Ensemble to premiere under the banner "Bell Atlantic's Evening of New American Music," with the performances scheduled to open the Philadelphia Freedom Festival celebrations. After lengthy negotiations with executives at Bell Atlantic, they agreed to contribute $60,000 to Relâche to commission two new works, the funds coming directly from the Bell Atlantic Foundation filtered through the marketing department. In consultation with Bell Atlantic, Relâche offered the commissions to George Russell and Alvin Curran.

Besides paying the commissioning fees, Bell Atlantic, in conjunction with the City of Philadelphia, co-sponsored a concert which opened the Philadelphia Freedom Festival with the world premieres of the two works plus two others by composers who had recently created new works for the Relâche Ensemble. Bell Atlantic's contribution would pay for the two commissions, plus honoraria and travel expenses for the other two composers to attend the performance. Relâche selected previously commissioned works by James Tenney and Stephen Montague to round out the program. To ensure the event received full coverage in the local and national media, Drew worked closely with Judy Fay and a marketing team from Bell Atlantic to generate a

Poster for Bell Atlantic's Evening of American Music

feature article in *The Wall Street Journal* describing the commissioning process and Relâche's role in developing new American musical works. Everyone appeared happy with the results. Relâche added two new works to their repertoire while performing before a large group of people who had never before heard a New Music concert. Bell Atlantic had their name on two New Musical works that eventually were performed in cities throughout the United States. The success of this endeavor led Drew to formulate a plan to enlist another corporate sponsor with a slightly different focus.

Philadelphia, then, as now, was in the midst of a successful restaurant renaissance. Small, elegant, and expensive new restaurants were opening all over the city with respected chefs creating varieties of cuisine aimed at well-heeled and discerning diners. Kobrand, Inc., a New York City based importer and distributor of fine wines and liquors whose best-known products in the early 1990s were Champagne Taittinger and Taylor Fladgate Port Wine, each among the finest in their class, supplied many of these restaurants as well as new nightclubs that added their luster to the entertainment culture of the city. Accordingly, Kobrand was interested in expanding their marketing campaign into the city. Drew Keegan saw an opening and, once again, Judy Fay provided assistance.

Kobrand's marketing and promotions departments were managed by two young women who targeted their products to well-educated professionals, men and women but with a bit more emphasis on women. They were interested in creating an identity for their products with consumers who attend high-profile arts events, similar to a successful strategy by Absolut Vodka which, during those years commissioned numerous artworks and performance events, especially at the Brooklyn Academy of Music, and created an advertising image in magazines and journals using the shape of the Absolut Vodka bottle in unique and humorous ways. Among those I remember from that time was the Absolut bottle painted on a canvas with a gilded frame around it and a caption that read, "Absolut Warhol." Kobrand wanted to have a similar connection with the arts by promoting Champagne Taittinger.

Judy Fay was just beginning to organize and market an event which has since become hugely successful in Philadelphia: "The Book and the Cook," a showcase for celebrity cookbook authors, and restaurateurs, to display their wares. Judy had started doing business with Kobrand and thought their young marketing officers might be interested in meeting Relâche. Using the corporate partnership-participation model we had created for Bell Atlantic, Drew and I devised a similar plan for Kobrand featuring New Music by women composers. Again, we requested funds to commission four new works, premiere them in New York followed by performances in Philadelphia and then record them. Kobrand liked the overall proposal and agreed to support two commissions plus concerts in New York and Philadelphia featuring, in addition to the new works, three others by women composers. Like Bell Atlantic, Kobrand paid a fee and expenses for all four participating composers. For the commissions Relâche selected Lois V Vierk and Mary Ellen Childs, with music by Tina Davidson, Janice Giteck and Eleanor Hovda rounding out the programs.

From an artistic perspective, the project was more than successful. The Relâche Ensemble gained five new works for the repertoire, all by women. Although Relâche had been performing music by women since its inception, this was the first time a project addressed the issue of women's music with such specificity. Mary Ellen Childs had already made a wonderful piece for Relâche titled *Parterre* that was performed worldwide and recorded on the Innova label (MN 108), produced by the Minnesota Composers Forum (now the American Composers Forum) and Tina, Eleanor and Janice had, or would in the future, make successful works for the Relâche Ensemble. Lois V Vierk's piece, *Timberline*, had the longest run of any of the works associated with the Kobrand project. Like *Parterre*, Timberline was performed worldwide and recorded (along with another work by Eleanor Hovda) on Relâche's CD "Outcome Inevitable" on OO Discs (OO Discs 17).

Despite the artistic achievement, and a focused well-managed marketing campaign, it is not clear if Relâche reached a substantial new audience with these works. Both the New York City and Philadelphia concerts were well attended, with elegant receptions following, but I remember taking note that the audience consisted of many folks I knew with women friends hosting small groups of their friends and friends of their friends. But something was missing in the manner or process of commissioning New Music, marketing and promoting the composer and the Relâche Ensemble. I pondered the conundrum, what more we could do. Here we had the prestige of an internationally acknowledged wine and spirits importer financially supporting New Music, the premieres in a respected New York City venue—Merkin Concert Hall—with an elaborate wine and cheese reception following the concert, a relatively substantial marketing and promotions campaign to subsidize the support of selected New York City media and yet the audience that night was moderate in size. They proved to be enthusiastic, to be sure, but by and large they were folks who would have attended most Relâche Ensemble concerts anyway. Following this project I began to seriously consider changing the way Relâche developed new works.

The goal to commission new works was one of seven objectives outlined in a comprehensive Five Year Plan developed along with Bill Terry Associates, a consulting firm based in Brooklyn. The fee to engage Bill's company came from the Pew Charitable Trust's Philadelphia Cultural Initiative project whose aims were to develop stronger administrative infrastructures among arts and cultural organizations in Philadelphia. Nineteen organizations including Relâche were selected to participate in this new program; each was awarded general operating grants after strengthening their administrations with the help of a consultant. One of the first things Bill did was suggest we formulate a stronger board of directors, one that would not only contribute directly to the organization but also be a liaison to other private donors in Philadelphia.

Few official governing bodies in American society are as unwieldy as the not-for-profit arts board of directors—a peculiar beast, to be sure. Mandated by state and federal government, the board is legally and fiscally responsible for the actions of the organization. Boards are usually the province of wealthy individuals who have attained their financial success in the empirical world of business or, sometimes, academia or the sciences. Successful boards have several factors in common: strong leadership and a vision to employ an executive director who can build an effective team with an often severely limited operating budget and individuals with strong connections to the local community who can rely on these individuals for contributions and business partnerships at a greatly reduced market value. All members must fully understand and believe in the mission of the organization. They are sufficiently confident to leave the day-to-day operations of the organization in the hands of the professional staff they have hired. Finally, and most importantly, their members—in the parlance of the times—raise money. Either they *"give, get or get off."*

Unfortunately only a few of the current board members gave.

Despite numerous attempts to form a board of directors which would connect Relâche to the kinds of people—ideally, a mix of wealthy socialites and corporate nouveaux riches types—who generously contributed their money and largesse to other arts and cultural organizations in Philadelphia, that never happened. In the minds of these folks, I suspect, Relâche simply did not seem to carry the same sort of social cachet of more traditional arts organizations' boards. And in a conservative musical culture like Philadelphia's, Relâche could not compete, initially, at least, with established orchestras and chamber groups for their attention. So, seeking out another echelon entirely, I organized a board of highly motivated individuals I knew would contribute their time and energies to a growing organization, one they believed in. As a first step I invited Anthony B. "Tony" Creamer to be on the board.

Tony is a rare breed in the button-down culture of corporate America. A financial consultant, he has established a successful career by advising clients worldwide. He works hard, as he once told me, so he would have the means to do what he really loves doing: listening to music, appreciating it, buying it. He's among the most literate consumers of music and all things musical I have ever known. With a huge collection of compact discs, LP records, tapes and books the man literally *lives* for music. And any style of music appeals to him: loud, soft, edgy, meditative, introspective or straight-ahead.

In 1985, Tony Creamer joined Relâche's board of directors that included financial advisor Ken Leith; Dr. Alfred Blatter, Dean of the College of Performing Arts at Drexel University and a composer, teacher and writer; architect Don Matzkin; artist-teacher Judith Vassalo; and marketing guru John Des Jardins. All these folks were friends who joined the board at my request. None were independently wealthy. All were dedicated to the success of Relâche and worked hard advising the staff in a variety of areas. Several contributed valuable in-kind services such as the use of office equipment and secretarial assistance. But they were not gifted at raising money.

Clearly raising and donating monies is the principal reason for sitting on a not-for-profit board of directors. In order to strengthen the fund-raising potential of the board I —with Tony Creamer's help—once again attempted to recruit a core of wealthy individuals who believed in the mission of Relâche, folks who possessed the same degree of passion for new concepts in music that those who played and worked for Relâche had. Despite our efforts we were not able to enlist wealthy contributors and Tony remained one of the few board members to contribute meaningful money to Relâche. After serving on the board for five years and providing invaluable assistance during the production of New Music America '87, Tony resigned to dedicate time to other interests, eventually accepting a seat on the board of directors of the Merce Cunningham Dance Company in Manhattan.

Around this time other board members left to pursue new interests. After their departure the board temporarily lost its focus. Essentially, Relâche did not have a working board of directors for about two years. In order to continue its appeals to large foundations for project support, Relâche had to demonstrate to these foundations that they had achieved more than artistic excellence; they demanded institutional stability with support and guidance from a working board of directors. To correct the situation I asked Tony to come back on board. He agreed. And I asked him to serve as president. He agreed to that request as well. Together we identified prospective board members, met with them to discuss their roles and slowly built a new board of directors that effectively functioned—more or less—like a board of directors of a not-for-profit arts organization should. Although more generous with contributions, the board still was not a major fundraising force.

In addition to board development and the creation of the New Works Fund, the Five Year Plan aimed to: expand concert productions in Philadelphia and on tour; record a new compact disc each year; create a new look for the Relâche Ensemble and a new marketing-promotions campaign; develop new education and community outreach programs and create an Internet presence and an expanded use of evolving information technologies. The plan called for each of these goals to develop concurrently, one supporting another as the ensemble and producing-presenting entity became more prominent in the eyes and ears of Philadelphians and audiences worldwide.

The makeover came first.

The general public often remarked that the Relâche Ensemble not only sounded good but looked good on stage as well. It was not by accident. Unlike some new music ensembles then active, members of the Relâche Ensemble were asked to dress neatly but casually and comfortably with matching clothing, primarily black or dark colors. And we asked that the ensemble develop a stage etiquette that was, essentially, missing from almost all new music performing ensembles at that time. To accomplish this we held sometimes discordant meetings to discuss how the ensemble was perceived by the audience. Several of the players dismissed the idea of developing a staged image feeling that the music alone should carry the message. I felt that the musical experience—from the audience's perspective—would be enhanced if the *mise en scene*; were attractive; the logic being that they would listen more easily if their eyes settled on an attractive colorful stage image especially when confronted with music that required a different listening discipline. A majority of the ensemble agreed with my position and, in response to one of the player's suggestion, we choreographed our entering and exiting the stage and rehearsed the bows so that everyone was responding to the audience's applause as an ensemble and not as eight individual performers. Further, everyone decided that the ensemble would project their sound better if everyone (except pianist John Dulik) stood while performing. This was a very dynamic aspect of the plan because it gave the players an opportunity to move—and groove—to the music in a very different way than if they were seated. It took a few concerts for the plan to settle in but eventually everyone became comfortable and the ensemble moved with more and more grace. With my knowledge of stage lighting I was able to design simple lighting plots using skin-tone colors to highlight the ensemble and individual players (when appropriate). Each piece on a program had a different quality of lighting that suited the mood or character of the music. To further enhance the overall ensemble appearance, we asked a local clothing designer to outfit the group. Yvonne Ogara, a young woman just beginning to create a name for herself in Philadelphia, designed individual vests for the players made of silk cloth from antique Japanese kimonos. The effect was terrific. The ensemble looked great on stage. Several years later we commissioned another design company named Enduo to create hand-painted jackets for everyone. These proved even more popular among the players and the audience. Having established a certain "look," the next challenge was to transfer this look onto promotional items and media documents. To accomplish this we hired a marketing-promotions firm in Philadelphia, a strategy that proved somewhat problematic.

Helen Schoenbrun and Associates was doing very well in the early 1990s representing a number of high-end clients. Helen was a smart, savvy dynamic woman who sought to be a player, a maker of images and a force in Philadelphia's business and artistic cultures. Helen and her associates' marketing and promotions strategies fit nicely into the changing character of center-city Philadelphia dominated as it was by two generations of arrogant self-serving disciples of the all mighty dollar: the desiccated Yuppie and the soon-to-be-anointed dukes and duchesses of the "dot.com" culture. Easily seduced by simplistic, synthetic slogans and images of unbridled wealth, these people were perfect foils for the audacious machinations of designers and wordsmiths whose collective knowledge of 20th century artistic matters was as insipid as the coffee confections available at their favorite Starbucks branch. Glitzy marketing concepts and Relâche should have been a good match. But it was not, despite each organization trying hard to adapt styles and methodologies to one another.

The Relâche logo designed by Lisa Torrieri

Take the Relâche logo. For me, few images from my time with Relâche are as enduring as the logo. Adapted from the original early Twentieth Century title inscribed by Erik Satie on the cover for the musical score to "Relâche," the calligraphic lines spelling out *"Re la che"* signify the musical entity Relâche.

To Helen, our logo was confusing; she thought it did not clearly identify or explain who or what Relâche is. I had heard that argument before in the past, with some consultants inferring that the French name itself was somehow pretentious, that the Relâche Ensemble should be renamed "The Joseph Franklin New Music Ensemble," or some other equally idiotic name. Needless to say, I resisted all previous and current efforts to change the name and the logo. After numerous attempts to persuade Helen, her design team and some of my own staff how important the logo is to the concept of Relâche, I gave in, agreeing to allow Helen's people to re-design the logo that would be used to drive the marketing-promotions campaign over the following two years. It was among the few decisions I made as Relâche's director that I truly regretted.

The new logo attempted to maintain the scripted character of the original, but without the action or movement across a page that handwriting produces. It was static. But worse it added the phrase: "Music Without Boundaries." What did that *mean*? Everything Relâche did, every piece of music that was programmed, indeed every concert program contained boundaries of some kind or another. The "boundaries" were the frames, the implied contexts for an array of stylistic, historic, philosophic references, implications, declarations of intent to inhabit. These delimited boundaries gave me points-of-reference to conceive music as an ongoing process of discovery, employing newly created and extant musical materials to develop and perform new works in the age-old context of the "concert." When I explained this to Helen and her team they seemed to respect my position but, correctly I guess, insisted that it doesn't translate to the average listener; the very people Relâche was aiming the marketing campaign at. "Relâche: Music Without Boundaries" in a muted magenta hue blazed from brochures, posters, print advertisements and stationery for the next two years, the heart and soul of the marketing-promotions campaign to make the Relâche Ensemble more user-friendly. I adapted to it, gracelessly no doubt; every time I saw it that still, small voice inside asked, "what boundaries?"

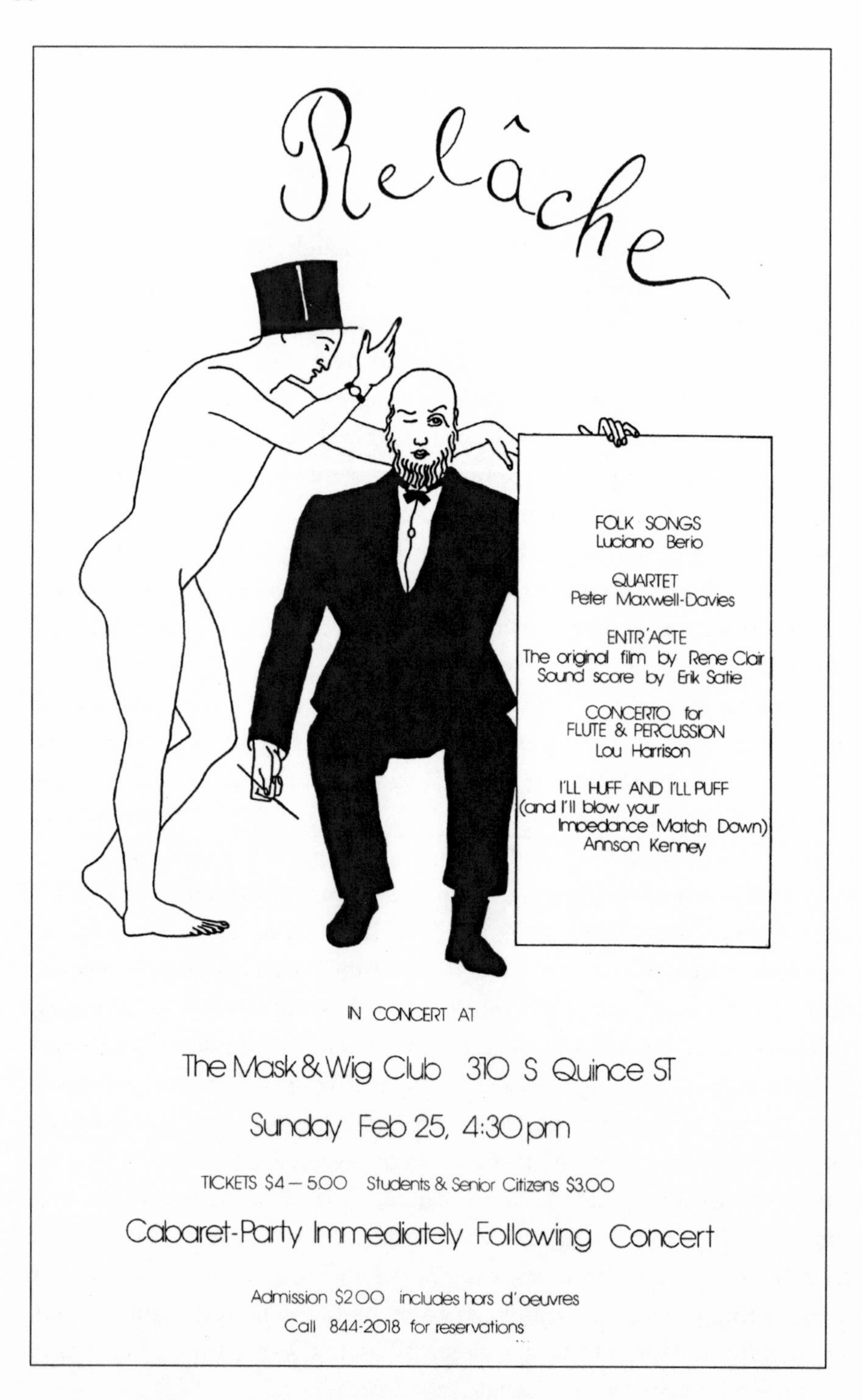

Original Relâche logo from Erik Satie's published score

New Relâche Logo

Two years later Relâche reverted to the older scripted logo once again leaving the concept of "boundaries" to be creatively interpreted.

In *The Poetics of Space*, philosopher Gaston Bachelard examines physical spaces and their reciprocal associations: how we shape them, and then how they shape us. Accordingly, for 12 years, between 1981 and 1993 the Relâche Ensemble performed at three venues in Philadelphia: the Painted Bride Art Center, The Ethical Society of Philadelphia and the Mandell Theatre at Drexel University. Each of these venues afforded me the opportunity to program distinctly different types of concerts.

The Painted Bride's cavernous space, although a sonic nightmare, was conducive to works that would not normally fit on a proscenium stage. If the players were required to move throughout the space, for example, there was ample room to do so in its black box-like configuration. More importantly the Painted Bride attracted people who expected something different, unusual or "experimental." Over the years those folks usually got what they were looking for.

The Ethical Society of Philadelphia, on the other hand, is not conducive to music that stretches the limits of the performance space. It is essentially a hall for chamber music. Located on Rittenhouse Square in downtown Philadelphia the Ethical Society has a recital-lecture hall seating 200. It has what is considered by many pianists in town the finest concert grand piano of any hall in the city. That factor and its center city location were the principal reasons the Relâche Ensemble performed there. It gave us the opportunity to program small intimate works, often using the spectacular piano as a centerpiece. Many works for piano solo or piano with flute, violin, cello, or various combinations of instruments combined with piano in addition to full ensemble works were performed in the context of 20th century chamber music concerts.

Both the Painted Bride Art Center and Ethical Society are far from ideal performance spaces for New Music. By necessity Relâche "made do," and, I believe, utilized these spaces in unique ways.

However, the Mandell Theatre was conducive to New Music. With complete theatre support systems at my disposal I was able to stage performances by the Relâche Ensemble in a manner that I had long wished to do. The years spent at the Mandell Theatre were highly important to Relâche's artistic development, due in large part to Dean Alfred Blatter who arrived in Philadelphia from the University of Illinois to become the head of performing arts at Drexel University.

Al Blatter is composer, performer, and producer of New Music events and author. His textbook, Instrumentation/Orchestration is widely used in college music departments. During his tenure as student then teacher at Illinois, Al collaborated with virtually everyone associate with New Music in America. Throughout the 1970s, the University of Illinois was acknowledged as having one of the most active and adventurous New Music programs of any large university in the United States. When he arrived at Drexel University to take over the performing arts program he inherited a department which did little outside of student productions. In Relâche he discovered kindred spirits and immediately invited the Relâche Ensemble to be ensemble-in-residence at Drexel.

Our residency required that we program and perform New Music in the 350-seat Mandell Theatre, make tickets available to students at a greatly discounted rate and be available to discuss with those interested students the history and praxis of the music. That was it! In addition, students in the theatre-performing arts department were assigned to assist the production team in preparing and presenting the concerts. Everyone involved benefited from the relationship; it was unquestionably one of the most important and productive associations that Relâche has had with any organization in Philadelphia.

By 1993 the situation began to change. The administration of Drexel University decided Mandell Theatre would no longer be available to outside interests and would become, essentially, a full-time teaching facility. By then the Relâche Ensemble was ready to move on. The Annenberg Center, just three blocks from Mandell, had been on my mind for several years as the next best performance space for the group, so I began the process to secure the Relâche Ensemble's Philadelphia series at the Annenberg Center.

In 1989 I approached Steve Goff, then managing director of the Annenberg Center, one of the premiere performing arts presenters in the region. Steve's background is in theatre, he had created a successful theatre series featuring touring productions from Europe and the United States, produced and presented a yearly children's theatre festival and hosted "Dance At The Annenberg Center." In the early years of the American Music Theatre Festival, they presented productions in the 1000-seat Annenberg Theatre or smaller 400-seat Harold Prince Theatre. From time-to-time Annenberg presented a well-known music group like the Philip Glass Ensemble or a touring

European chamber orchestra, but these were not part of an ongoing series. When I approached Steve my intention was two-fold: expand my presenting interests in Philadelphia, and produce and present concerts by the Relâche Ensemble in the Annenberg Center.

I proposed a six-part series to run through the season that I would program and co-present with Steve featuring jazz, New Music and world music artists in the Annenberg Theatre. The series would expand and diversify the audience base for the Annenberg Center while providing an opportunity for Philadelphians to hear world-class artists with superb technical and sound enhancement support. Steve and I would share the fundraising duties for this endeavor. In addition, Relâche would use the series to promote concerts by the Relâche Ensemble in the Harold Prince Theatre. Steve was eager to expand his audience base and accepted my proposal, beginning a rewarding and productive collaboration.

Over the next six years "New Music At Annenberg" presented a variety of artists to mainly large audiences. Among the artists who appeared were Steve Reich and Musicians, Ali Akbar Khan, the late Pakistani Qawwali singer Nusrat Fatah Ali Khan. The only appearance by Nusrat south of New York City attracted Pakistani devotees of Nusrat's from Baltimore and Washington, D.C. areas; the only problem was they didn't purchase tickets in advance. The concert sold out two days in advance. Those arriving without tickets were irate, refusing to accept management's apologies, threatening to barge into the theatre. The police were called in to settle things down. There were no further incidents. Nusrat and his musicians were extraordinary that night.

We also presented George Russell's Living Time Orchestra, John Zorn, Milton Nascimento and the Bulgarian Women's Choir who not only gave a scintillating performance but also charmed everyone in the theatre. I clearly remember entering the stage for dress rehearsal so I could introduce myself to the women of the choir and welcome them. I anticipated that they would be large Eastern European ladies with billowing and not particularly flattering costumes. Instead I walked into a group of young, extremely beautiful women dressed in form-fitting elaborately embroidered dresses. I was stunned and charmed. I later learned that many were on the lookout for a future American husband.

The promotional materials and concert playbills for the series cross-promoted the Relâche Ensemble's concerts with reduced ticket packages and other promotional schemes all in an attempt to create a cohesive package for those interested in an alternative musical experience, unique and utterly different from any other musical group or presenting series in Philadelphia. Did it work? Hard to say.

The attendance for the "New Music At Annenberg" series was excellent, many sold out, while attendance for the Relâche Ensemble increased, although audiences tended to be largest when well-known artists like Philip Glass or Michael Nyman were guest composer-performers with the ensemble. I remember being at a social event and, in the course of a conversation, learned that someone had attended a concert at Annenberg, one that I had produced. They had no idea that Relâche had been the presenting partner; in some cases they had never heard of Relâche. Despite having the name Relâche appear on every item of promotional literature, it still didn't register. This was frustrating. But overall the association with the Annenberg Center was an important one for Relâche. It gave the group a home that most people identified with, excellent institutional support and the potential to reach yet more people in Philadelphia.

"Why does the music always end in silence?" This question from a young student at a high school in Chester, Pennsylvania caught members of the Relâche Ensemble short, dead in their tracks; they did not have an answer. Chester, just a few miles south of Philadelphia, is one of the most depressed cities in the Mid-Atlantic region. Once a thriving ship-building center, Chester is now bereft of any industry. The powerful cranes that once lifted large slaps of formed steel to form a ship's hull now stood rusted and lifeless, slumped over the filthy still waters of the Delaware River. There Chester High School serves the children of the undervalued population of the city, its student body during the early 1990s consisted of African-American and Asian American children , like the young girl one who asked the question about silence. But, rather than being shy and uninterested, these students were among the more engaging that the Relâche Ensemble encountered while doing community outreach service around the Delaware Valley.

At one session we included Robert Ashley's extraordinary choral piece, "She Was A Visitor."

The band room at Chester High was like many band rooms at similarly designed high schools in the area. But on this particular day the sounds coming from that room were quite different than the usual sounds one hears: the diverse mix of students were hissing and humming, their accented voices converging around the haunting phrase, *She Was A Visitor...She Was A Visitor...She Was A Visitor*, articulated in hushed tones by a narrator—me—each voice wrapped around one of the phonemes of the phrase, *Sh-e-e-e-e—W-a(h)-s-s-s—A(h)-Vis-i-tor*, as per the performance instructions; the Muse making her brief appearance then fading away only to appear again later.

At another school across the state in Erie, Pennsylvania in a grade school auditorium a single voice chirps in *beep-beep* at the conclusion of John Zorn's "Roadrunner," a zany quick-paced piece constructed of short quirky musical fragments that start and stop, seemingly in a random order or without any order whatsoever. Like the Warner Brother's cartoon character, the "Roadrunner" zooms in-and-out of your consciousness or in-and-out of the accordion bellows that's squeezed so adroitly by Guy Klucevsek

In North Philadelphia's Hispanic neighborhood the voice of composer-singer Yadira Alborniz accompanied by Anglo musicians of the Relâche Ensemble conjoin with the sounds of Salsa blaring from car radios and open doors along *Calle Cinco* telling the story of "The Spanglish Aunt" to small bilingual children in the music school operated by the Association of Latin American Composers (AMLA), a steadying influence in that rough community. All these stories are part of the picture, one that gradually brought into focus the mystery of making music in a real-time environment free of the trappings of encrusted Euro-American notions about what is and what is not "music." And is the music ever over when it stops?

From the very beginning, Relâche has been committed to community outreach programs. As an antidote to under-funded and sometimes failed school music programs, professional music ensembles nationwide developed outreach programs to fill the gap and bring in some much-needed revenue for these ensembles that can never generate enough income by giving concerts. Sometimes these efforts were not always successful—either because the musicians were not really dedicated to education, viewing their roles as creative musicians as just that: creative musicians and not educators. Others of course understand their role in a larger context and eagerly dedicated their time and talents to education. Still other times the schools themselves can be a hindrance; overworked teachers reluctantly organize the students' schedules with the ensemble sometimes resulting in sessions that felt as if the musicians were intruding on valuable teachers' time. Then again, other teachers cannot get enough of these programs and work overtime to ensure that the programs meet everyone's goals. Early on, Relâche saw a need to develop a presence in the schools, creating a program called "New Music In The Schools."

After taking over Relâche's educational component from me in the early 1980s, Laurel Wyckoff, along with a contingent of players from the ensemble, created a unique and hugely effective program, one of the few in Pennsylvania to present New Music to students, and engage them in music and sonic experiences that would never normally have been a part of their lives. Laurel developed specific workshop themes using graphic notation or improvisation, discovering ways the students could participate in the creative process by writing short musical pieces or fragments that the ensemble would play, then critique, and having student musicians play along with the ensemble to learn to interpret a New Music score. Complete performances of works from the Relâche repertoire were played followed by a discussion of the work and a question and answer session. The aim to take New Musical ideas into the school systems throughout southeastern Pennsylvania was a priority with Relâche and proved to be one of many successful audience development efforts for the organization.

As part of the Five-Year Plan, Relâche evaluated each of the educational agencies and arts organizations to determine how we might continue our association and learn of other potential partnerships. The result was an expanded effort to reach yet more residents of the tri-state area. I then sought professional partnerships with specific organizations to share equally in the fundraising efforts and overall administration. This, I believed, would strengthen each of our positions with local and national funding sources. Over the coming years this proved to be a sound decision and resulted in several new initiatives including the development of the national program "Music in Motion," which in turn evolved into "Music in Motion - The Virtualconcert."

The Five-Year Plan outlined in specific detail a variety of goals and objectives aimed at strengthening the Relâche Ensemble's image on the national and international markets without losing touch with audiences and communities throughout the metropolitan Philadelphia area. The overarching goal of the plan was to elevate Relâche to a new level of awareness and operations, to create a forum for an exchange of ideas and information better suited to compete in a rapidly changing geo-political world. This plan guided me as I continued to lead Relâche into the final years of the 20th century.

Boxing is an art.
You can be the hammer or you can be the nail.
I wanted to be the hammer.
But if you don't have no paint brush
You can't be no artist.
—Gypsy Joe Harris, Middleweight Boxer

THE YELLOW SPRINGS INSTITUTE

A firefly traces a sinuous pattern through the moon's glare of a warm July night while observers move ceremoniously among the candles that outline the deitietic images of Rachel Fletcher's "Mandala," a site-specific art work placed in the outdoor earthwork at the Yellow Springs Institute. I was among those observers that night, one of many who were humbled by the simple power of the artist's installation, set in this elegant parcel of land that was conceived to gather the spirits and evoke the mysterious majesty of Stonehenge. Rachel's work was conceived as a palace for meditation, placed proportionately inside of the earthen circle surrounded by ancient maple and oak trees whose leaves transform and enhance the landscape during the Autumnal harvest, a long way from Gypsy Joe Harris' Philly streets that, sadly, no paintbrush can enhance or transform.

The Yellow Springs Institute, site of so many artistic collaborations and experimental endeavors over the final quarter of the 20th century is but a memory, a shadow that hovers over the history of Relâche. Without its support and spiritual guidance it's unlikely the ensemble would have gained the prominence it achieved. And I might not have become the person I am now.

Located twenty miles outside of Philadelphia in Chester County, Pennsylvania is the Village of Yellow Springs. Originally the village was a spa where affluent tourists, well-heeled Main Line residents and their friends, would gather to bathe and picnic in a luxuriant setting amidst numerous horse-breeding and training farms located throughout the area. Legend has it vocalist Jenny Lind (1820-1887), "the Swedish Nightingale," was one of many celebrants who came to "take the baths" at Yellow Springs. Abandoned sometime in the early 20th century, the village pretty much disintegrated, its once elegant baths and residences crumbled; forgotten as the area surrounding the village grew into yet another sprawling bedroom community adjoining metropolitan Philadelphia.

In the late 1960s a wealthy industrialist named Frederick Henry purchased the entire village and renovated one of the stately old mansions for his family to live in when they needed a respite from their permanent residence in Manhattan. Another building down the narrow road from his house was converted into an artist's' studio and gallery. A village commission was created whose principal aim was to attract painters and sculptors to the studio to take classes and organize exhibitions. Soon the Pennsylvania Academy of Fine Arts—located in downtown Philadelphia—assumed curatorial and managerial control of the studio and gallery, allowing some of the academy's students to spend valuable time away from the big city amid the quiet countryside. Soon a restaurant and bar re-opened in yet another one of the old buildings and took the name The Inn at Yellow Springs, eventually becoming a gathering spot, a place for social interaction for the people living in the area or those escaping from the heat and humidity of Philadelphia. The Village of Yellow Springs was a peaceful place to spend a spring and summer day.

Shortly after the village re-opened an architect named John Clauser became friendly with Fred Henry, eventually persuading him to subsidize an arts center or more specifically an arts and humanities residency facility in the village. The name he proposed was the Yellow Springs Institute for the Arts and Humanities, better known as the Yellow Springs Institute or, simply, Yellow Springs. Fred Henry liked the idea that John proposed and agreed to back this initial venture by commissioning John to design a black-box theatre over the shell of a big old barn located directly next to Fred's home. The barn had an interesting history. In 1958 a group of independent filmmakers used the facility to shoot scenes from what was to become a classic cult sci-fi horror film: "The Blob." I suppose some of the local residents would claim it was a natural segue from "The Blob" to new performance art, but the truth is that few of them knew of this historical fact. For those of us who were to work in the old barn however "The Blob" and its history was the basis for many jokes and irreverent references to failed performances.

Yellow Springs Institute Theater in the mid—1980s

Located next to the newly built theatre, John designed a small building to house the administrative offices and a conference room. Fred Henry agreed through his family foundation to support the staff and physical plant but John would be responsible to raise money for programs. Although John's initial plan called for a residency facility to house visiting artists and other participants, it was not until years later that a building was secured and renovated. For the first ten years of operations everyone stayed at a Holiday Inn located six miles away near Downingtown, PA. In 1978 the institute was about to open even though the theatre and administrative building were not yet completely ready. In anticipation of the opening John invited me to visit the grounds.

I arrived at Yellow Springs on a cool spring day and was immediately taken by its ambiance and physical design: the old barn housing the new theatre was set inside a high stone wall situated next to a grass terrace that ascended to a flat circular field with four concrete arches set at points around the circle, each one perfectly aligned with the movement of the sun's solstitial journey. Often, when standing in the field, the only sound one heard was a small private airplane or commercial jetliner, the air space overhead being part of the landing path into the Philadelphia International Airport for planes flying in from the west. This immaculate field was to serve as an outdoor performance site.

One of the arches at the Yellow Springs Institute's outdoor Earthwork

The theatre inside the old barn was equally attractive. The hard dark wood floors and interior wood walls created a soft resonant acoustically warm sound in the second floor performance space. Canvas and metal chairs were set on wood risers facing the rear terrace seen through a series of narrow windows, masked over with black theatre curtains for most performances so the sound would not refract off the glass. Overhead was a lighting grid with a requisite number of lighting instruments and a control booth for an engineer to operate the lighting and sound enhancement systems was located stage left overseeing the stage floor. On the first floor were several spaces used interchangeably as exhibition galleries, dressing rooms, meeting rooms and dining rooms, depending on the situation at hand. Overall it was a compact and efficient theatre environment.

John's concept for the facility— its mission— was simple: eventual year-round residencies between one week and one month would be created. Performing artists, musicians, composers, video artists, filmmakers and dancers were combined with writers, poets, scholars, researchers and lecturers to discover issues of shared interest and either chose to collaborate on a new work or chose not to. There was no real goal mandated by John and his staff for the participants to strive for, rather it was meant as an experience for everyone to determine how their individual work might or might not find resonance in the work of someone else with very different perspectives, personalities and styles of working. There might be a "theme" for the residency, or there might not. Clearly, it was a situation loosely defined. Except, that is, in John's mind. And so things sometimes became problematic.

John Clauser, who died in 2002, was a highly intelligent man with an extensive knowledge of primarily western classical and romantic music, architectural design and literary histories. He was a great conversationalist and teacher and fiercely debated anyone who did not agree with his position. He respected differing points-of-view, just as long as they did not run too counter to his. He spent a great deal of time and energy developing residency concepts, trying to determine who would or would not work well together, anticipating how a certain residency situation might play itself out essentially he wanted situations where ideas could be challenged and issues met head-on by dynamic accomplished outspoken people in pursuit of new ways of viewing the world through the arts and humanities. These attempts to create meaningful cultural and social discourses were admirable but sometimes the mix of personalities proved volatile, to say the least. But John always treated me as an equal and genuinely listened to my ideas and often acted on them. Our collaboration proved highly beneficial to me and to the future of the Relâche Ensemble.

I would say perhaps no other experiences played as significant a role in the history of Relâche—and in my own personal and professional life—as those occurring at the Yellow Springs Institute. For 15 years the institute offered a unique opportunity for musicians, dancers, writers, poets and performance artists to collaborate—or at least co-exist—with scholars and teachers in the context of multi-week residencies and daylong performance events. As I look back on my life with Relâche and evaluate how the organization matured and how I developed a broader awareness of and respect for historical and cultural contexts I must acknowledge the importance of the Yellow Springs Institute and its founder, John Clauser.

I first met John in 1975 while doing a column called "Earshot" for the alternative weekly arts and culture newspaper The Drummer, a precursor to the Philadelphia City Paper and other now familiar and often irreverent weeklies available in most large cities today. I was writing about an upcoming performance by Joel Thome and the Philadelphia Composers Forum featuring, I believe, the first-ever performance in the U.S. of Erik Satie's seldom performed masterwork, "Socrate." Joel was re-creating the premiere performance of this work along with a concert performance of "Four Saints In Three Acts," the enigmatic opera by Virgil Thompson and Gertrude Stein. He commissioned John Clauser to re-create a stage set based on the original one designed by Francis Picabia in Paris in the 1920s for "Socrate." A theatre stage designer and pianist as well as an architect, John was a perfect choice.

His re-design consisted of several metallic spheres of different bright colors that moved across the stage braced by a pair of pulleys (stage left-to-right) from positions suspended over the stage below the proscenium opening. Over the duration of "Socrate" the spheres moved slowly seeming to float over the quiet lyrical instrumental and vocal lines of the piece. It was an effective performance made even more memorable by the two contrasting theatres in which it was performed: the venerable, intimate Walnut Street Theatre in downtown Philadelphia and the cavernous Beacon Theatre in New York City. After interviewing John for the article I was writing we became lifelong friends.

During our initial meeting just prior to the official opening of the Yellow Springs Institute John asked me if I would serve as the technical director for the first summer's schedule. In those early years, as Relâche was taking shape, among the jobs I had was free-lance lighting designer-technician, a skill I learned in school and put to practice immediately upon graduation. I was working on regional opera, dance and theatre events designing and hanging lighting plots, building sets, hiring other required technicians. By virtue of my experience, John knew I could put together a good technical team which would help shape the Institute's physical plant and support future residencies and performances. And as a musician interested in New Music and a past collaborator with the Philadelphia Composers Forum John was impressed with the potential Relâche appeared to have at that time, and wanted Relâche to serve as the resident ensemble for the Institute. Having me as technical director who would manage the Relâche Ensemble during the initial year at Yellow Springs proved cost effective and added another dimension to the program's potential. I agreed to work for the Institute that summer, as did the members of Relâche. We stayed on for the following seven years.

My first decision was to enlist Werner Strobel as sound engineer for the institute. We then hired a young guy named Chris Lance who had worked in theatre at nearby West Chester University to run the lighting board and essentially maintain the physical space. He was eager to learn production and sound enhancement and proved to be a good addition to the new team. Chris stayed with Yellow Springs for about 10 years, eventually becoming technical director for the entire facility. With the technical support in place I began consulting with John to select and invite the musical artists who would collaborate with other artists and humanists over the course of the first year's schedule of events. For the first year John devised a program he called "Six Saturdays."

Six Saturdays was designed to explore a particular subject or theme. The invited participants arrived at the Institute on a Sunday then spent the following week in residence working alone or teaming up with others. Then on Saturday there was a daylong event featuring performances, installations, gallery displays, readings and discussions on the theme of the week. A paying audience arrived late in the morning, usually spending an hour or two walking around the village or having an early picnic lunch. The institute's events began at noon with appropriate breaks for lunch and dinner, and usually concluded at 9 PM.

Following the initial year of Six Saturdays and their attendant residencies, Arthur Sabatini came on board to work with John on future projects, providing an often different perspective to John's original vision. The three years that John and Arthur collaborated resulted in many extraordinary presentations and situations for everyone involved, especially me. During that time, there were many highlights.

Barbara Noska performing *La Testa d'Adriana* ***by R. Murray Schaffer at Yellow Springs Institute***

At dinner with John Clauser, Robert Bly and Joseph Campbell I watched and listened to Bly and Campbell recite—from memory—long passages of "Finnegan's Wake," each of their songs—songs, not recitations—flawless and musical, like jazz musicians in a small ensemble trading four-bar phrases, enunciating each line and spiking them with just the right type of shadings of pitch, timbre and dynamic; their deliveries giving shape and form to the work.

And there was a lighting plot created with the dancer-choreographer Kai Takei and her company "Moving Earth" for a new segment of her long work titled "Light." Day-in and day-out I observed how elegantly and seemingly flawlessly she sculpted gestures from the air invoking the simple act of seeding a rice field or climbing a mountain, an elegant example of minimal movement so powerful in its ability to tell a coherent story.

In addition, I hung out with musician and performance artist Jerry Hunt in the hotel room of the Holiday Inn during evening down times of his residency with the Relâche Ensemble as he explained in intimate glowing details how his cats always slept wrapped around his neck, their tails always finding a way to curl up his nose. All this while commenting on aspects of Dolly Parton's image—clothes, hair, shoes—as it blazed from the TV screen a cultural icon of the time. "Television," Jerry asserted, "is the only source of absolute truth."

During this time I stood transfixed with members of Relâche on the outdoor earthwork on a clear moonlit night as Rachel Fletcher's elegant fire-light Mandala lit the entire field as the moon rose directly between the white stone pillars. The silence was brilliant.

I also learned from media theorist Eugene Youngblood my job description: "metadesigner," *one who is trained in the arts, produces work of artistic and cultural merit and evolves into ...someone who creates broad contexts for projects and work(s) to occur in.*

And there was Angelika Wanke-Festa. I walked by her again and again all day long as she hung suspended at the head with cloth attached to a black cotton helmet covering her skull and neck, in turn affixed to a wooden frame. Her arms hanging limp as they swayed against gravity, in her left hand a smelly dead fish, its slimy body bent almost in a U-shape, while another person stood on a box in the corner of the gallery space continuously clapping oven mitts together. "Fishdance" might have been the strangest work presented during my tenure at Yellow Springs.

And yet, a single, even more dramatic incident stands out in sharp relief: the concluding event of a day that at first glance appeared to be a relatively benign combination of personalities and forces.

Clarence Glacken, a respected cultural geographer, was one of the invited participants for a residency and "Six Saturday" event whose theme that week was Place, how various cultures used their physical and spiritual place through history and time. Clarence Glacken, who died in 1989, was then head of the Department of Geography at the University of California at Berkeley and author of *Traces on the Rhodian Shore*, a highly respected text which explores our relationship to a changing Earth and how its physical configuration and climactic conditions help shape character and human nature.

A quiet and humble man, Glacken was then in his mid-seventies and clearly not accustomed to the spotlight in a theatre environment or being around performers. So, he was understandably nervous or perhaps reluctant to take center stage surrounded as he was by more outgoing personalities. As a performance component to the event, I programmed a work by Joseph Kasinskas performed by members of Relâche that was tailor made for the acoustical properties of the Yellow Springs Institute theatre, a work that was to throw everyone—including Clarence Glacken—into an altered state of awareness, or consciousness, or somewhere.

The piece, titled "Echoes In Palindromes," is among the more dynamic works ever performed by Relâche during its long history. Joe Kasinskas had studied with composer and installation artist Alvin Lucier and, like Alvin, was interested in creating performance situations which explore

A performance of** Echoes In Palindromes **at Yellow Springs Institute; left-to-right: Joseph Kasinskas, Romulus Franceschini and Karen Campbell

the psycho-acoustical phenomena of a given space or the sonic phenomenology of a situation or series of situations. In this case Joe's work was designed to explore the resonant frequency of a space, arrived at through a series of instrumental articulations realized while the performers follow a carefully choreographed schematic, their sounds captured and altered electronically. The piece is elegant in design and concept, its results often downright frightening.

Three woodwind players—flute, clarinet and oboe—enter the space and walk to a designated position: flute downstage center, clarinet upstage right and oboe upstage left. (These positions and instruments change according to the personalities and availability of the players used.) In front of each player is a large score containing musical palindromes notated in various sizes in order to denote the relative dynamic level to be played; the note heads determine how far the player moves away from the score. Composer Kasinskas chose this method of notation to imply choreographed movement for each player, using the original Greek meaning of palindrome to "walk backwards." As Joe informed me after the performance, "I wanted to highlight the elegance of seeing someone walk forward and away while playing a palindrome...that's part of the experience of the piece." In the middle of the stage located behind the flute position is a contrabass or cello player. For this performance it was a cellist. Behind the cellist upstage left and right are two microphonists holding microphones attached to long cables. The cables are connected to two analog reel-to-reel tape recorders, an audio amplifier and mixer to process the sounds and direct their sound back into the space via two (or four) speakers.

As the woodwind players articulate their parts, they move from position-to-position in a clockwise motion, walking slowly and deliberately, stopping at each position to play their particular musical palindrome. The two microphonists follow the players, alternating among the three while holding the microphones close to the floor to, essentially, capture their sounds as if the sounds were following each player in their wake. The sounds captured by the microphones are recorded by the recording heads on the first tape recorder then passed to the playback head of the second tape recorder, the take-up reel of the second recorder placed about six feet from the first recorder. The sounds from the playback heads are then mixed and amplified and sent to the speakers to direct the sound back into the performance space. This creates an audio delay between the live and recorded sounds that builds an aural scrim through which the players and microphonists pass, eventually defining the resonant frequency of the space. The cellist attempts to capture the resonant frequency, tuning and re-tuning the instrument accordingly until all of the articulated sound seems to be absorbed into the cello.

When and if the resonant frequency is achieved, the sound will cause the building to react, to vibrate in harmony with itself as the physical material holding the building together begins to find its natural place in the structure. You can imagine the effect this process has on a room with a rich resonant character. And the performance space in the Yellow Springs Institute had character, an ethereal reverberant quality that embraced the instrumental and processed sounds of Joe Kasinskas' piece and transformed them into what can only be described as a sort of meta-resonant frequency.

During the dress rehearsal for "Echoes In Palindromes" I sat next to Clarence Glacken, who, although intrigued, was somewhat confused about our intentions. He had a puzzled look that implied something like, *"this is very strange."* Of course it was. The man had never before seen or heard musical works that were intended to do anything other than represent a composer's intentions to speak in the language of the Common Practice Period from Western music history. If I remember correctly his favorite music was of the European Baroque. Clarence was a cultured man of his time and place but somehow neglected the power of sound in his studies of anthropomorphic space. I like to think that between the rehearsal and performance Clarence Glacken gave some serious thought to what he was about to experience. To this day I'm not quite certain what he was thinking.

For the performance that evening I once again sat next to Clarence. He had finished his presentation and appeared to be relaxed. Given what happened next I'm not certain that being relaxed was the right condition to be in. I'm not even sure I was prepared for what happened next.

Everything came together in the performance of "Echoes In Palindromes." The players, Laurel Wyckoff on flute, Wesley Hall on clarinet and Peter Ferris on oboe, interpreted their parts with precision while moving about the space as per their directions. The microphonists for this performance were Joe Kasinskas and Romulus Franceschini who moved about the space like police detectives searching for clues to a crime. The cellist, Lori Barnet, sat erect, eyes closed searching for the right tuning, which she eventually found. Overall it was great theater. As the sounds built and moved around the space searching for their place in the scheme of things the resonant frequency was achieved; it shook the building for about five seconds as the piece reached its climax. Laurel completed her turn first arriving back at her starting position. I vividly remember two things: watching Laurel standing erect, her flute cradled in her arms, trying not to grimace or show discomfort as the cumulative sounds built to an ear-piercing volume; and then feeling the vibrations in my feet as the chair bounced on the wooden riser almost as if an earthquake were causing it. It was an exhilarating and chilling experience. I looked over at Clarence. His face was ash white. He said to me in his now even softer voice, "I've never seen anything like that." I looked at Clarence and said, "Yeah, but what did you hear?" He didn't say anything, just looked away and stared before getting up and slowly leaving the theatre. I never spoke with Clarence Glacken again.

There was a stunned silence as the audience disappeared into the night, everyone, it seemed, was deeply touched by the performance of "Echoes in Palindromes." After helping Werner and the technical crew strike the equipment and securing the space I drove home with an image—sonic and visual—of "Echoes In Palindromes" competing with the monotonous sound of the car's engine and glare of oncoming headlights slipping past me on the Schuylkill Expressway leading back to Philadelphia early in the morning.

During the eight years the Relâche Ensemble was in residence at Yellow Springs the group came together in many ways. The weeklong residencies during which the ensemble worked closely with a variety of composers to shape a new work vividly changed the way each member related to one another. In essence, the weeks spent at Yellow Springs taught Relâche how to be an ensemble, how to communicate their ideas to one another and to the composers they were working with. These experiences paved the way for me to develop other residency programs like Music in Motion and helped broaden the Relâche Ensemble's reputation around the New Music community as a performing ensemble which genuinely wanted to collaborate on the creation of new works and not simply "play" works from the repertoire before moving on to another. Sure, we did that too, but the musical works which proved to be most successful and most often performed were those developed through collaboration. And none was more successful during Relâche's first decade than the residency with Pauline Oliveros.

Both John Clauser and I were eager to have Pauline Oliveros participate in a residency. John tendered the invitation to Pauline suggesting that she collaborate with Relâche. She countered by proposing dancer Deborah Hay participate by developing and performing a dance component for a new work created along with the instrumental sections. We all agreed.

This was truly an important collaboration for the Relâche Ensemble, coming at a time when the group was on the verge of a dramatic change. During the early years I was trying to find a way to build awareness within the group for collective improvisation among musicians with divergent skills and experiences. On the one hand there were spectacular players like Guy Klucevsek, John Dulik and Marshall Taylor who could improvise easily and there were some who had little or no experience in playing "off the page." It was up to Pauline and Deborah to find a way that their ideas could be translated to all of the musicians.

Both Pauline and Deborah had become recognized for their abilities to create performance situations in the context of interactive social environments. Pauline created musical works for groups of trained and untrained singers based on chant or some other form of musical articulation; their combined reactions to an event in situ forming the overall performance form or structure. Deborah, an influential member of the Judson Dance Theater in New York, was adept at combining movement and gesture with improvised music, creating a mobile flexible theatrical experience. In tandem Pauline and Deborah were set to challenge the Relâche Ensemble to re-think their roles as creative musicians in the context of a group culture.

As writer-theorist and long-time Relâche associate, Arthur Sabatini wrote so succinctly in his liner notes to the Hat-Art recording of the work eventually titled *The Well,* "For Pauline Oliveros, the processes involved in making music are as fundamental as the music itself...Oliveros desires to create, in her words, an inclusive and interdependent and unfolding world of relationships. A world in which the sound and the practices entailed in making music merge; become at once, source and atmosphere, energy and essence, presence and dynamic." That she and Relâche accomplished this in such a short period of time was somewhat remarkable and proved to me that indeed the future of the Relâche Ensemble resided in a still vague world whereby the ensemble would play a major role in musical composition through long-term collaborations with composers whose working methodologies were compatible. Not only were Pauline's and Deborah's methods compatible with Relâche, they proved prescient to this evolving group of relatively young musicians.

The story of the creation and evolution of the new work titled *The Well* originated as an image of "midnight well water" which appeared to Deborah Hay in a dream. The dream image led Pauline and Deborah to Hexagram 48 of the *I Ching*, the ancient Chinese Book of Changes so beloved by John Cage and others. The hexagram contains six broken and unbroken parallel lines and became the basis for creating movements for the dance and a non-traditional scale for the musicians to work from. Again, Arthur Sabatini's liner notes capture the scene: "The prevalent images in 'The Well' are wood, water and earth and the sign speaks of the 'inexhaustible dispensing of nourishment.' A well is also, literally, a fixed, natural source of replenishment and a meeting-place for members of a community. It is a rich metaphor for social and political notions, as well as for natural and creative processes."

Deborah created the dance by selecting certain images from a literal interpretation of *The Well*, transforming them into an elegant combination of energetic athletic movement contrasting those with slow dreamlike gestures. Pauline created a score or schematic comprising a five-note scale and five guidewords for the players to follow. These five guidewords are *listen, merge, match, support* and *soar* and are transmitted to the ensemble orally by Pauline. Each performance of *The Well* depends upon the abilities, personalities and imaginations and spirit of the players involved. "...Oliveros clearly wants performers to participate directly in the creation of the work," Sabatini's notes continue. "And she trusts them to work together. Although the instructions sound simple, in practice things can become complex and demanding. Players must make imaginative choices, focus and react to each other, take chances and intuit and discriminate from moment-to-moment during a performance. For Oliveros, this process allows the musicians the opportunity to *pass through stages of awakening to the possibilities* inherent in making music. For all those involved there is also a degree to which working together can lead *to the essence of what can shape musical impulses and individual freedom at the same time.*"

Throughout the residency week Relâche, Pauline and Deborah really hunkered down, working hard through the many passages that the basic musical materials provided —scale, dynamic shaping, combinations of instruments and rhythmic modes—and interpreting those in the context of the five guide-words. Initially there were several sections where Pauline played alone, solo renderings which stood somewhat apart from the ensemble sections. In later versions of *The Well*, Pauline and Guy played a dual role, combining their accordion voices to serve as relays or introductions to the other ensemble segments. As *The Well* evolved in concert Guy assumed a solo role in the introduction segment titled "The Awakening." When Relâche performed with Pauline—as they did on many occasions—Guy and Pauline played this section as a duo. Deborah's movement was designed to weave in-and-out of the physical setting for the musicians, allowing everyone a chance to respond to her gestures, and she to theirs.

The Well proved to be one of the most successful works in Relâche's repertoire. It was performed numerous times between 1983 and 1992 in concerts and radio broadcasts throughout the U.S., Europe and Japan. It was recorded by Werner Strobel for Hat-Art Records (Hart-Art 2020) at the Yellow Springs Institute in 1985, one of the first digital master recordings made in the days before the dawn of the compact disc.

The camaraderie and hard work in evidence throughout the weeklong residency pushed the Relâche Ensemble in a new direction. It was Pauline Oliveros and Deborah Hay and the Yellow Springs Institute that provided the opportunity. Without this and other residencies, Relâche might have gone in a very different direction. I doubt it would have become the kind of group it is now if it weren't for all the artists who collaborated with the ensemble at the Yellow Springs Institute.

John Clauser's vision to create a context where disparate, sometimes contrasting personalities engaged one another, communicated with one another, and worked towards a shared—or at least a commonly perceived—goal, was realized at the Yellow Springs Institute over a period of 20 years. John's legacy includes directing the institute at a complex time in America's cultural history when it served as an incubator for the creation of new works and new ways to look at the world.

PLACES AND PEOPLE, SOME AURAL HISTORIES

Erie, Pennsylvania is nicely situated in the far northwestern corner of the state on the southern edge of Lake Erie, a five-hour ride from Philadelphia through verdant Amish farmlands and staid old industrial towns with red brick buildings that glow with a burnished brilliance on clear days at sunset. A drive from the decaying, noisy streets of Philadelphia to Erie over narrow winding roads lined with lush green and brown foliage is absolution *in excelsis*; hours to be savored and remembered for the purity of an American landscape forever lost in then-late 20th century travels, or travails.

Like all former "rust belt" cities—the main industry for most of the 20th century was Bucyrus Erie, manufacturers of heavy-duty construction equipment—Erie is slowly transforming itself into a modern service oriented city serving as a gateway to Ohio and Western New York State. The aging factories and mills have been transformed into shopping arcades, restaurants and streamlined apartments populated by graduates from one of several small private colleges, regional universities or community colleges situated throughout the region; the children of a former working class citizenry who, along with small emerging companies have been responsible for Erie's new look. Among the civic leaders who have been instrumental in changing the city's face is the Erie Art Museum located downtown just blocks from the lake.

The museum has served as an "outpost," the only institution located in northwestern Pennsylvania to exhibit a variety of paintings, sculptures, ceramics, and photographs representing a diverse history of the region and nation. Since 1968, John Vanco, a specialist in early American arts and crafts, has guided the Erie Art Museum. He has organized major shows featuring works by artists renowned in these formal designs. But John is also a passionate listener to American folk music, jazz and New Musics in all their myriad forms. As part of his programming at the museum John has presented a yearly series of music performances featuring many of North America's finest musicians. Among the performers at the Erie Art Museum has been Relâche.

The Relâche Ensemble was, for a five-year period, the resident ensemble at the Erie Art Museum, giving performances and outreach activities in schools and colleges throughout the city and immediate vicinity sponsored, in part, by the Pennsylvania Council on the Arts. Over the years Relâche developed personal relationships with area residents—especially students and teachers—to affirm the vitality and accessibility of contemporary music forms. The performances by Relâche in the museum were always well attended, accompanied by receptions and after-dinner gatherings at a local restaurant to further discuss aspects of the music. Overall, the relationship between Relâche and Erie was rewarding for everyone, especially for a couple of local guys who, as you will learn later on, attempted to prove that "art" is indeed for everyone.

During the years Relâche visited, the Erie Art Museum was a small intimate facility. It is slowly evolving into a larger more diverse complex, one that in addition to the newly built children's museum will have a fully equipped performance space. During Relâche's residencies the performances were often given in the museum, sharing space with whichever exhibition was currently in place.

Usually the ensemble was seated in the center of the building directly beneath a dome rising about eight feet high, creating a full resonant sonic chamber as the instrumental and vocal sounds floated up then around the oval chamber searching for their natural blending and mixing before seeping back down to spread throughout the space. It was, overall, a warm nurturing sound, aided by acute electronic enhancement. The audience sat in chairs placed in front of the ensemble. To the right of this space were the galleries, configured differently to house a particular showing of paintings or sculptures, etc. On this particular night, in the early 1980s, with a cold wind swirling off Lake Erie, local artists selected from a jury process filled the galleries with a variety of their works.

For a concert performance at venues like the Erie Art Museum we normally reserved the afternoon for a full rehearsal, then a short break before having a technical rehearsal, concluding around 4 PM. After a dinner break the ensemble would reconvene around 7:30 for an 8 PM performance. Usually the ensemble would run through each piece scheduled for performance, with some needing more work than others. This provided ample time for everyone to tune their instruments to the space and to one another, go over specific ensemble details such as cueing and discuss potential "train wrecks"—those disastrous moments in a piece where one or more players run "off the track," or "into each other." During the run-throughs I would work with the sound engineer to balance and equalize each instrument and voice within the group in order to achieve the "Relâche sound" with respect to the sonic properties of the performance space. During breaks in the rehearsal we would browse around the museum to check out the current exhibition. Invariably there would be one or more works that elicited either an excited positive or negative response from someone in the group, thereby providing lively dinner conversation. In this exhibition there was one work that caught everyone's attention and absolutely ticked everyone off. For our purposes we'll call the piece the *Cat on the Books*.

In the middle of the exhibition gallery setting on a frayed Oriental rug stood a stack of old musty books, maybe 15 in all, precariously balanced against varying weights and sturdiness, and sort of pitched at a 10-degree tilt. These books, the chair and rug constituted part of an artwork. Lying on top of the books was the other part of this artwork: a cat. Or rather the carcass of a cat, its legs sticking out straight from the torso, its ribs beginning to peek through the dingy gray mat of hair which was slowly falling from the beast. It was truly an ugly sight. During one break in the rehearsal, or perhaps it was during the set-up of chairs and instruments, I remember the entire ensemble standing around this work, staring in awe or maybe in horror at the thing. Laurel Wyckoff, mumbling in her displaced Southern accent said something like, "God, what the...do you see this thing? Damn, it smells like a wet raccoon or something. Ugh!"

The members of Relâche were a diverse group. All had been trained in music conservatories or university music departments and, accordingly, were exposed to art history courses, humanities studies and, in general, issues that required a degree of aesthetic judgment within broad historical contexts. Some of the players were more insightful than others but, overall, each Relâche ensemble throughout its history was contained smart savvy professionals with attitude—'tood'—an endearing characteristic of anyone living in Philadelphia! And they were not at all averse to displaying this attitude by expressing their opinions—to anyone, wherever or whenever.

While viewing the *Cat on the Books* I, like everyone else, struggled to understand the intent of this piece, to give time and place to it within its proper "socio-historical context." But, like everyone else, this one really threw me. I stood for minutes on end staring at this thing, trying to figure out what the heck was going on, drawing absolutely nothing from my considerable database of, well, data, on art and other related issues. Looking at this dead creature, lying on top of a stack of old books, its eyes open, its hair falling off. Well, I was stumped.

I remained standing there when everyone else had moved away, silently induced into a trance or some other state of suspended animation. I felt a strange tingling sensation in my fingers, the result of images drawn from memory that seemingly appear between my conscious self and another distant affirmation of self. At times like this I'm aware of the psychology of time and place, but unable to manipulate or control its innate mechanisms: I can't move or react. As I stood there floating in a dream-like state staring at the *Cat on the Books* an image formed in my mind, a memory of an incident from a time in the early 1950s.

Christmas Day 1950, I was six years old living with my mother, father, younger brother and aunt (my mother's eldest sister who served as a legal guardian to my brother and me) in our small row house. It was a "White Christmas," one of only two I remember from my life in Philadelphia.

We had a dog, a small white terrier named Toy, not a particularly charismatic dog but friendly and, well, dumb. Actually, he was probably just about the same size as the dead cat in the artwork.

Because the house was only one block from the Frankford Elevated and two blocks from the Frankford Junction, it was not a good idea to let the dog run free. Toy was restricted to our back yard, if you can call it an actual yard, all eight square feet of concrete ending at a rickety old fence separating the house from an alley that ran between the rows of similar looking houses. During the winter months Toy had the run of the house, as well as the dank basement. Somehow, on Christmas Eve day Toy escaped into the dread of the neighborhood, just before it began to snow.

On Christmas Day we awoke to the sounds of my father's creation:

The Platform! It was a yearly construct, a ritual of creation that occupied my father's spare time between Thanksgiving and Christmas when he removed from musty storage all of the hardware and software of his one and only cultural diversion and assembled *The Platform*.

In essence it was a pretty simple design: a slab of plywood about three feet wide by six feet long painted green and set on two wooden saw horses. On top were arrayed small plastic houses and small plastic people placed at or near various civic institutions: a hospital, schools, churches, all of which were set along on the side of streets adorned with small plastic trees and benches and light posts. Running through the center of this fantastic village were plastic automobiles stapled onto a three-inch wide leather belt that ran over metal rollers placed in cut-out openings about three feet apart from one another and driven by two electric motors my father had built and placed beneath the platform behind red-and-white fake brick paper.

As the large wheels on the motor turned—pushing and pulling the leather conveyor belt—the plastic cars would appear to travel through the village, causing a distinct sound each time one appeared from beneath the platform to begin its journey along the "highway" before disappearing down into the bowels of the imaginary earth. Covering each of these "up" and "down" positions was a papier-mâché tunnel, or what appeared to be a tunnel opening. Each time the cars came up there would be a sound like a plastic "slap"; each time a car descended at the other end of the highway it would sound a slight plastic "thunk," depending on your state-of-mind at that most surreal moment. Surrounding the village, of course, was a set of Lionel trains, pulled by the black locomotive puffing out smoke from a valve located on its topside and a fairly well tuned whistle that could be sounded from the command post, a wood stand where the black transformer was located. Of course the train had the requisite milk can-dispensing car with a small mechanical figure of a man who, at the touch of a button on the transformer, would appear through an open door on the milk car with a miniature milk can and throw it, missing its target: a small magnetized platform located beside the village dairy. A mess of miniature milk cans amassed at some point next to the small platform along with some plastic people and trees lying on their backs and sides appearing as if a miniature earthquake had just rumbled under this fantastic village.

This wonderfully weird serene village was always placed to the right of the Christmas tree, which in turn set next to a window with a view into our concrete back yard. Just outside the window we kept the garbage can; one could barely see the garbage can lid with its distinctive metal handle appearing just above the windowsill. On this Christmas Day the garbage can lid was covered with about eight inches of pure white crystalline snow. Next to the garbage can on the windowsill sat a small white dog looking mournfully through the window at our joyous celebration, at the fantastic plastic village and the lighted Christmas tree with the angel on top. The dog was shivering and covered in blood.

My father and one of his brothers who was visiting us that Christmas day went outside to retrieve old Toy, gently picking him up in their large callused hands. They surmised that a car had probably hit the dog and left it to die in the snowy streets of North Philadelphia. If that were the case old Toy wasn't as dumb as we all thought since he was able to navigate himself to our/his house in some truly bad weather. But he was in very bad shape, probably dying from a combination of his injuries, shock and, maybe, just maybe his having to try and figure out just what all those little plastic houses and people were doing standing around watching small plastic cars—the same ones every time!—pass by while a small replica of the trains he probably heard passing over the black bridge at the end of our street every day go zooming around and around this strange little village. In any case there didn't appear to be much left in the old guy. So, my father and his usually potted older brother took charge of the matter.

Since it was unlikely they would locate a veterinarian on this White Christmas day, they decided to take Toy outside and put him out of his misery. With the one weapon my mom allowed to stay in the house—a .22 caliber rifle—they planned to shoot Toy. I was horrified and, of course, saddened. Fortunately, I guess, Toy expired before a .22 caliber bullet could spread his small body over the newly fallen snow in our backyard. My last memory of Toy is lying in the snow, bloody and still, a sight I was not supposed to see. Merry Christmas.

The memory of Toy's lifeless body, I think, reminded me of the dead cat lying on top of the books in the Erie Art Museum. Or, I suppose, the image of the dead cat reminded me of Toy. In either case I was transfixed at this site and could not get it out of my mind as I slowly returned to a condition where I could at least attempt to control the ontology of time. And it was time for dinner, so I left the museum to join the ensemble. About 90 minutes later I returned with everyone to change into our "gig clothes" and prepare for the performance. Of course the first thing I saw upon re-entering the museum: the *Cat on the Books*.

As we engaged in the usual pre-concert ritual, the ensemble tuned up, made certain all the instruments were in place, checked the sound levels for those works using either tape playback or another type of sound manipulation and arranged music on the stands. During this time I noticed two young guys looking at the *Cat on the Books* and talking between themselves, apparently disagreeing over the premise or "worth" of the work. Hell, they could have been arguing or debating if indeed this piece constituted a "ready made" work of art. These two guys weren't very animated. They were just well, intense in their muted conversation. In the heat of preparations I forgot about them and the *Cat on the Books*, concluding our pre-concert ritual and getting ready for the real thing.

The concert went smoothly, was well attended with an overflow audience which was attracted to the museum not only for our performance but also for the opening of the exhibition, a well executed marketing stunt by the museum's director. After the performance there was a reception. I was eager to attend, to meet the artists and the rest of the audience and gauge their reactions to and interpretations of the *Cat on the Books*. But a strange thing happened: the cat was gone, leaving only some funky strands of gray-black hair scattered on the top book of the stack of books that continued to teeter precariously on the antique rug in the gallery space. The artist who was attributed as having created the *Cat on the Books* did not show up, causing much consternation among the attendees. John Vanco, upon learning of the cat's disappearance, was understandably enraged. He immediately called the police to report a theft.

Unfortunately, I did not overhear his initial conversation with the police.

John then announced to the crowd what had happened and asked that everyone leave the gallery area and meet under the museum's dome to wait for the police. During the confusion one of the Relâche musicians came over to me and whispered that he saw one of those guys who earlier had been heatedly discussing the *Cat on the Books*' merits remove the cat and take it out a back door; one of the doors that did not have an alarm attached to it. I then informed John and, together, we went looking for these two guys.

Before the cops arrived we located one of the guys, sitting outside shivering in the frigid Erie night. Little did we know that during this brief period when everyone was leaving the gallery area the *Cat on the Books* re-appeared in its assigned place. The guy was sitting on one of the large steps leading into the museum from the street, his head down, appearing either confused or embarrassed and cold. I approached him and asked, directly, if he and his friend had taken the dead cat. He looked up at us sheepishly, his teeth chattering from the cold air and said, "Yeah, we took it. But I put it back," his tone brightening a bit.

"You put it back?" "When?"

"Just a few minutes ago, when everybody left the gallery."

"Why did you take it?

"I dunno, man, my friend was, well, upset by the thing."

"Then why did you put it back?"

"Hey, I just like art."

I looked at John, then at this poor guy and suggested we cancel the cop-call, telling them we made a mistake. John agreed and called the police then invited everyone back into the gallery to continue the reception. I returned to the gallery not knowing if I should be laughing or crying. I mean how can one argue with this guy's logic? The guy who likes art? He didn't join us at the reception.

Needless to say, on our subsequent trips to Erie over the next several years none of us could ever get the image of the *Cat on the Books* out of our minds. It is forever engraved, no, enshrined in our memories of Erie along with those of the long sinuous drive there from Philadelphia, eating *pasta fagiole* at Dominic's Restaurant in Little Italy (the Erie version), rejecting a Perch dinner—an Erie delicacy drawn from the muck of Lake Erie— and hanging out with local folks who, hopefully, we enriched by our performances.

Personally I cannot separate the image of the *Cat on the Books* from the image of Toy's bloody body lying in the snow on that White Christmas so long ago.

Hey, I guess I just like art.

In 1975 just after I left graduate school I was working as a freelance writer-journalist for *The Drummer*, an alternative weekly newspaper writing "Earshots," a column on music events, personalities, ideas, etc. The column was loosely based on writer, composer and *Village Voice* critic Tom Johnson's, who, for 10 years, chronicled new and world music events and allied developments in New York City. I had been a fan of Tom's writing and approached the editor of *The Drummer* with an idea to create a similar column for New Music that seldom if ever was featured in the Philadelphia media.

The editor, a savvy, hip guy named Bruce Buschel, thought it was a good idea and gave me free rein. "Earshots" ran for two-and-a-half years, ending shortly after I co-founded Relâche in 1977. During that time I interviewed and profiled local and touring musicians including then-emerging artists Phillip Glass and Steve Reich when they appeared in Philadelphia with their ensembles. I also reviewed New Music concerts anywhere in the Philadelphia area regardless of the venue. And one venue in particular proved memorable: Holmesburg Prison.

To some Philadelphians, it's an image seared in their memories: an ugly gray-brown twenty foot high brick wall with guard towers perched atop each end of the wall visible from Interstate 95, the wall one of four similar ones configured in the shape of a box. Holmesburg Prison, one of the oldest and notorious prisons in America.

It's also an image most people view out of the corner of their eyes, a blur as they speed past driving north or south on I-95 or riding on AMTRAK heading north to New York or south returning to Philadelphia. It's a place we all acknowledge as sort of being there but few of us want to talk about it. As a kid I got to know Holmesburg Prison because some relatives lived not too far from it in a section of Philadelphia known as Torresdale, an aging working class neighborhood with small duplex homes not much larger than the ubiquitous row homes characteristic of neighborhoods closer to downtown Philadelphia. Many of the prison guards and other professionals who staffed the place lived in Torresdale. I often visited my aunts and uncles and cousins who lived there or accompanied my father when he visited one of several trucking companies located throughout the area.

Every time I went near the place I thought of the notorious bank robber, Willie Sutton, one of the few (if not the only) prisoner to escape from it. Willie was kind of a folk hero to some Philadelphians, especially the dead-end kids who grew up in my neighborhood. During my youth Holmesburg Prison was a place I observed warily sometimes from a location a little too close for comfort. That changed about ten years later.

After returning from military service and between times spent in school, studying, and working, I played basketball once a week with a group of guys at a high school gymnasium in Torresdale. One of the guys was a prison guard and asked if a group of us would be interested in playing ball with some of the prisoners. With early images of dreaded Holmesburg Prison hovering in the background I reluctantly agreed to do it. We met the following week at the entry gate for our first encounter inside "the joint."

Once we were admitted inside the main entrance we entered a guard station located in the center of the complex with five long corridors leading out from the center in a spoke-like configuration. After we signed in with the guard he opened a large steel gate made of thick gray bars. Passing through the gate, I heard a dull "clank," a sound I will never forget, its echo reverberating down the narrow corridor...the door locking behind us. We continued down the corridor to a gymnasium and played several ball games with selected prisoners. There were no incidents and we continued our weekly visits for about three months or so until I simply did not have the time to do it any longer. Each time we visited the prison, the sound of the gate closing appeared to settle in my jaw and I instinctively bit down on my back teeth. "Clank." No escape, I thought. Be careful." When I left the prison for what I thought would be the final time the sound of the gate closing behind stayed with me, although over time it gradually receded until one day in 1975 Joel Thome, the conductor-director of the Philadelphia Composers Forum called me.

He invited me to accompany him and his ensemble to a presentation-performance inside Holmesburg Prison. If I remember correctly, Joel had been awarded funds from the Pennsylvania Council on the Arts to conduct outreach activities at "unusual venues." You could not find a more unusual venue for New Music than a prison! I further learned that he planned to conduct these events at prisons around Pennsylvania. I thought this was a less-than-brilliant idea but was not in the position to tell him how I felt, unless I was asked, which I wasn't. He figured I would write about the event and promote his efforts to "expand the audience for New Music." I certainly agreed with his intention to build audiences and spent many years later on pursuing similar ideas, but a prison? New Music in a prison? Holmesburg? I didn't like the sound of it but agreed to go.

Among the works he selected to perform at Holmesburg Prison was George Crumb's *Makrokosmos I* or *II* for solo piano. Now I could not for the life of me figure out why he wanted to play a work by George Crumb in a prison! Crumb's music is, well, so precious, suited only for the hallowed confines of a recital or concert hall. To perform Crumb's music successfully with its air of cerebral melancholy, varying degrees of dynamic shadings, and quasi-theatrical gestures is difficult enough for performers and listeners alike. It requires a trained ear or at least an inquisitive ear to make sense of his work. But to play his music for a group of prisoners who have few "classical music" references is really sort of odd. As I entered Holmesburg Prison I heard once again that sound: "Clank," as the gate slammed shut behind us, our entourage slowly ambled down one of the long corridors striding along with the echo of the metal meeting metal, the sound I remembered so well from my previous visits. I was the only one in our group who had been inside this place before, but it's safe to say I was not the only one who was a bit nervous, not knowing what the prisoners would think or how they would react.

I soon found out.

The ensemble set up in a large auditorium which seated around 300. After tweaking the sound a bit and rehearsing a few passages from each work, we saw the guards bringing the prisoners into the auditorium, filling it almost to capacity. From a position in the rear of the space I could observe the behavior of the mostly black population and observe some of their faces as, inevitably, they smirked or sneered at this fairly unusual sight: a concert grand piano surrounded by a battery of percussion instruments and about four chairs for the string and woodwind players. And in the front of this stash of expensive instruments was the conductor, smiling like the proverbial Cheshire Cat as he prepared to explain to these guys what was going to happen. I held my breath.

I remember the first piece on the program featured a lot of percussion sounds, loud explosions interspersed with jagged dissonant bursts from the winds and strings, the conductor conducting away with those strange gestures they seem to relish. Nobody in the audience was tapping their feet and nobody was finding a groove to settle into. *There was no groove!* This was one of those jagged determinedly modernist pieces of music composed in a *serial* or *quasi-serial* musical language. The prisoners just sat there looking around trying to figure out what these weird white guys were up to. At the conclusion of the piece there was an eerie silence then mumbling from throughout the room, heads shaking up and down and from side-to-side. I couldn't figure out if some of the guys liked it or if they were conspiring to leave the auditorium for the perceived sanity of their jail cells. A tension seemed to build as Joel began his running commentary on the next work, George Crumb's *Makrokosmos I* or *II*.

As the piece unfolded, sort of, with those tiny pianissimo gestures so characteristic of Crumb's music, the pianist stood up and reached into the inside of the piano and started plucking the strings, gradually playing louder. Then he began hammering on the strings with a mallet increasing the dynamic until all you could really see was this guy wailing—or was it whaling—away at the piano with what looked like a hammer, his longish hair flailing this way and that way. Then from the left side of the auditorium a guy stood up and yelled, "Hey! Motherfucker get your fucking hands off that piano! Stop pounding on it, man!" The outraged prisoner remained standing, defiantly staring at the piano player who, needless to say was scared shitless. Thus encouraged, others chimed in, loudly remonstrating the pianist to stop beating on the piano. By this time he had stopped playing and was slowly and tentatively settling back onto the piano bench, looking worriedly at Joel, the prisoners and the guards. The guards moved in and quieted the agitated crowd of guys down, eventually restoring order. Needless to say *Makrokosmos I* or *II* was through for the day.

The remainder of the concert's program consisted of more traditional ensemble works. Short ones, fortunately. As the prisoners left the auditorium they were joking with one another, mimicking the players' gestures. I don't think New Music gained any converts that day.

I got to thinking about this incident. Here was this guy incarcerated for perhaps the next twenty years, maybe longer, possibly coming from a background where the piano was a revered instrument of family life, of celebration, and community. Maybe he grew up hearing his family or neighbors singing traditional songs accompanied by the piano or maybe he grew up listening to jazz or rhythm-and-blues, the piano a comforting presence. Maybe the guy always wanted to learn to play the piano but, for a variety of reasons, wasn't able to. And here is this guy pounding the hell out of the piano, an instrument he cannot own or perhaps did not have access to, whacking it to hell. I understood perfectly well why he was upset.

And so I realized that day if I were to continue creating and eventually presenting "new" music, then I would make certain it is presented in the proper venue with respect to the audiences' perceived knowledge of the music and the cultural contexts in which it has been created.

As we left the prison everyone was pretty quiet, the echoed "clank" of the gate closing behind us put closure to misguided attempts like this one to force music into spaces and places it has no right being in. For me I was exiting Holmesburg Prison for the last time.

A musician is trained to listen to music structurally. We focus our attention on some ethereal point-in-time, fixing our ears on the harmonic contours of a musical line to determine the tendencies of the pitch order or the resultant chord structure. When I listen at this level, I imagine a psychic caldron whereby those tonal elements combine with rhythmic patterns to produce a musical stew that swirls around in my mind until the internal logic of the piece reveals itself. Throughout this disciplined listening activity I attempt to leave a little to the imagination in order to reveal the "majesty and mystery of performance." It stands to reason that one requires time after the sounds end, a period of internal silence to allow this processed information to settle. One evening, in this uneasy spiritual state of discovery—and recovery—I discovered a concept that has guided me through my life. I discovered the Wing Nut Theory.

A makeshift auditorium in the African-American Museum in mid-1980s Philadelphia was not a particularly conducive venue to experience the deep dark secrets churning in the soul of an American original: Cecil Taylor. Contrary to the uneven acoustical properties of the room an in spite of its rather clinical ambiance, the room allowed the listener to revel in two vague yet powerful notions: the majesty and mystery in the ritual of performance and why white guys, alas, seem to rule the Western world.

Essentially, the auditorium was then a large multi-purpose room with rows of chairs deployed in a stadium seating configuration, ensuring that no matter where one sat there was sure to be an obstruction of some kind, usually someone's head with a large hat sitting atop it. In those days there were few organizations in Philadelphia with the guts to present artists even remotely controversial, and the African-American Museum was willing to present controversial black artists, so they certainly had my patronage. On this particular night the "controversial" artists they presented were Cecil Taylor and his quartet.

A pianist and composer renowned in New Music and "avant-garde" jazz circles, Cecil Taylor is an uncompromising artist who defies the constructs of most straight-ahead jazz musicians, and equally straight-ahead listeners with his fierce virtuoso playing. His dynamic improvisations and distinctive compositions yield a complex tapestry of sounds with the bobbing and weaving of pitch material and rhythmic cells seemingly in conflict with one another as they seek their eventual points of logical rest and resolve.

His keyboard technique is awesome: a unique amalgam of "avant-garde" Euro-American articulations interspersed with harsh percussive attacks and tone clusters formulated within rapid multi-note passages, often embracing formal designs from Western "Classical Music" (i.e., the "Sonata-Allegro Form," A-B-A) or traditional "Blues." When employing these identifiable forms, he invariably subjects them to a non-linear deconstruction; all the more reason to listen intently to the message imbedded in the maelstrom of sound which leaps from his piano. And leap it did. On this particular night in this odd space the Cecil Taylor Quartet was on fire!

They began their performance from off stage, the musicians chanting a slow undulating song sung in unison. A few odd uneven and un-tempered sounds from shells or beads being shaken by one or more of the musicians jangled underneath the voices. Gradually each of the players emerged from stage left, their chant and beads-song becoming more audible as they moved toward their instruments: bassist beginning with a fundamental tone or drone, saxophonist sounding a melodic line, an outline built on the bass' fundamental, Cecil at the piano lightly fingering in the upper register a flurry of concordant notes, finally the drummer slowly enters with soft brush strokes that eventually explode into furious pan-rhythmic patterns erupting from the full drum kit.

The vocal chant now merges into a sinuous instrumental line defiantly stated in the piano then extended by the saxophone, the bassist sounding a steady pulsing richly harmonic accompaniment, weaving in and around the piano and saxophone lines—pushing, pulling and coaxing each player into what at times appears to be a supernatural state. One composition lasted for over 90 minutes, guiding the listener through a maze of emotions and experiences, ending with the same vocal chant as each player left the stage in the same order as they entered, their voices gradually trailing off . It was truly transcendent.

I sat in my chair for a good 10 minutes trying to decipher what I had just heard; the intensity of the performance had rattled my bones. I was trying to get them back into place, not certain if they wanted to go back in place. I was elated and a bit shaken and somewhat confused. At that point in my life I had been around the "new music" scene for a considerable time and had heard some fairly intense performances but nothing, absolutely nothing compared to this extraordinary event. Cecil Taylor and his ensemble had taken me to a new place and it would be quite a while before I recovered, if indeed I ever would. Now, some 17 years later I can still hear that performance ringing throughout the odd symmetry of the African American Museum and resonating deeply within my now experienced—and somewhat jaded—middle-age psyche.

I had attended the concert with five friends who were perhaps not in the same psychic state after the concert as I was. After a suitable recovery time we agreed to meet for drinks. I think I was the last to arrive at our agreed upon location: one of the watering holes we frequented in Old City Philadelphia. When I arrived I sat down and said, simply, "this was one of the most impressive performances I've heard in a long time. Cecil simply amazes me." Everyone appeared to agree although they did not appear to be as moved or shaken as I was. Everyone that is except for one, a percussionist, a drummer of skill and precision whose knowledge of the hardware of the drummer's catalogue far exceeds his understanding of the mystery of the drummer's reckless inner soul.

He looked at me in some disbelief, trying to understand why I was so taken by the performance, and asked querulously, "Why didn't the drummer tighten his wing nut? His wing nut was loose the whole concert. It really bugged me. I couldn't listen because the wing nut was rattling around the head of the ride cymbal. Very sloppy playing," he griped, while shaking his head from side-to-side and lowering his eyes from my stare. I gazed at him not knowing what to say, just sitting there with my mouth open looking around at my other friends in total disbelief. The bleeping wing nut was loose. Damn!

For those of you unaware of these fine discernments, the wing nut is, well, a standard wing nut but burnished and polished to a fine brass finish in order to better fit into the trap set's elegant plastic, metal and brass hardware. The wing nut is screwed into place atop each cymbal on a tubular column, part of most drum sets or kits so that the cymbal doesn't fly across the room after an especially elegant smash delivered by an inspired drummer. There's the "ride" cymbal, "sizzle" cymbal and "high-hat" cymbal, each calibrated to exact specifications by a variety of percussion instrument makers adhering to ancient formulas derived from the Turks. The torque of the wing nut's placement over the cymbal controls its eventual sound: if loosely tightened, the cymbal will resonate longer and with a more vibrant character; if tightly wound, it will inhibit the cymbals resonance and restrict its decay. Usually a drummer will fix the wing nut in a uniform way that delivers the overall sound quality he/she desires. In the heat of performance the last thing on the drummer's mind is the wing nut. Or so I thought.

"But," I said to my friend, the drummer, "weren't you able to listen through the wing nut's position to what the drummer was doing, what he was saying, how he supported each of the other musicians, how he used the cymbals to change directions and color the players' collective and interactive ideas?"

"No," he replied, shaking his head slightly.

"You mean you were not able to just give in to the passion of the moment and join this transcendent and spiritual flight of virtuosity and exploration?"

"Nope," he said. "You can't play with the wing nut loose like that."

Now it was my turn to shake my head in disbelief. "How sad you're forced to listen to music in this way," I said. "Imagine how much you miss." I continued, "how much of the message is missed by listening to the music through the prism of a schematic which for all intents and purposes is not the *ur-text* in instrument set-up and placement, but rather something you have affirmed as a means to establish your credentials as a practicing musician."

He shrugged as if to say, well, yeah, you're right. How sad.

That night, at that precise instant, in a crowded bar in Olde City Philadelphia I developed the Wing Nut Theory: white guys who simply don't get it!

Since then, through numerous experiences in various levels of the music business I have unfortunately been able to apply the Wing Nut Theory to way too many situations. I remain amazed at how some truly talented musicians—and some not so talented—continue to miss the action by focusing their attention on the minutiae of placement or carriage of equipment at the expense of the spirit of the playing, of the moment, of the journey.

Tighten that wing nut!

The drummer in Cecil Taylor's quartet that night was Rashied Ali, one of many driving spirits in John Coltrane's later ensembles. Then as now I don't think Rashied Ali concerns himself with wing nuts.

Located in a box canyon at an elevation of 10,000 feet with mountains on either side rising to 12,500 feet, Telluride can be an unsettling experience as one wanders around fighting for breath in the rarified atmosphere while browsing restored buildings that formerly housed feed stores, blacksmith shops, brothels and other equally important businesses. Many of these weathered storefronts have long ago been transformed into boutiques or trendy restaurants and bars.

Once a thriving Colorado boomtown, like so many other boomtowns in the old West, Telluride fell into disrepair only to be revived by wealthy individuals or state agencies in the mid-to-late 20th century, and transformed into a tourist Mecca for those seeking solace from urban America. Over the years Telluride has become well known for its downhill ski trails and yearly film and folk music festivals. Between 1988 and 1993 New Music composer, performer and producer Charles Amirkhanian, with assistance from a group of philanthropists, hosted a different kind of festival, one that attracted a different breed of musical enthusiast to this jeweled town along the southern front of the Rocky Mountains. That event was the Composer-To-Composer Festival and, for five successive years, the Composer-To-Composer Festival transformed Telluride, Colorado.

Renowned and emerging composers and performers were invited to share ideas with a public audience and perform or hear their works performed in the Telluride Opera House. Recently renovated and listed on the National Historic Register, the Opera House is an intimate theatre similar to others built in Western cities throughout the 19th Century, ostensibly to provide "cultural experiences" for the rough-and-tumble characters that searched for gold and other minerals in the mountains and streams populating the American West. Sometimes one felt that a few of the attendees at the Composer-To-Composer Festival seemed to mistakenly wander in, attracted perhaps to the folk or "hippie" lifestyle so closely identified with Telluride's legacy. One thing is certain: the venerable Telluride Opera House had not experienced the likes of contemporary "new" music artists prior to the festival.

I attended all five of the Composer-To-Composer Festivals. Laurel and I planned our summer vacations to coincide with the festivals. After visiting parents in Arizona and New Mexico we leisurely drove around the Four Corners region in a borrowed van or pick-up truck, stopping at various points to camp, hike and take in the solitude and majesty of the high desert. As we wound our way either due north from New Mexico or northeast from Utah or Arizona we would arrive in Telluride to meet new friends and hang out with old ones and listen to some new works.

For the most part our roles on the Composer-To-Composer festivals were limited to our being part of the paying audience, although Laurel did premiere a new work for flute and piano by John Cage on the 1990 festival.

For the final festival in 1993, Relâche was a resident ensemble, collaborating with, among others, composers Louis Andriessen, Fred Ho, Paul Dresher and Larry Polanski and performers Zakhir Hussain and The Piano Duo from Amsterdam. Although memorable, it was overshadowed by an incident three years earlier on the 1990 festival featuring, once again like an encounter in Miami in 1988, a virtual meeting between John Cage and James Tenney.

John Cage and Conlon Nancarrow were two featured composers on the festival that year. Their joint appearance thrilled everyone as two icons of American experimental music were brought together to reminisce and comment on their works and other experiences from their long productive lives. A feature of the festival each day was a panel discussion with Charles Amirkhanian serving as moderator. Charles' role was to entice each panel member to discuss their work or comment on other composers' music and tell stories from their lives, providing insight into an artistic time and place. There were, at times, dissonant moments when one or more personalities on the stage clashed, but overall each of the panel sessions was cordial and sometimes extremely revealing.

The image of these two revered men, Cage and Nancarrow, on stage together was memorable. Both were quiet and dignified, not prone to talk openly about their work or criticize others. With Charles moderating the discussion and each of them answering his questions quietly the session was, to my mind, somewhat uneventful. And, especially for those of us with a deep understanding of the development of their music, and their respective roles in 20th century music history, the session was a bit understated. And then Charles posed a simple question to each of them, "If you were thirty years younger whom would you study with?"

I distinctly remember the look on each man's face. Cage was a bit startled, his eyes fixed on Charles' staring, then looking away and smiling to himself. Nancarrow stared at Charles with a blank look on his face. "Conlon," Charles asked, "who would you study with?" After a long pause Nancarrow replied, "I really don't know. I have no idea." Cage immediately replied, "James Tenney." He then told the story—in considerable detail—of having heard Relâche perform *Critical Band* at the Miami New Music America Festival and the subsequent correspondence with Jim, ending with a comment that "changed my mind about the role of harmony in music." From the audience I beamed, knowing that I was part of this quite extraordinary development. That was the last time I saw either John Cage or Conlon Nancarrow alive.

Like everyone who worked with New Music in the late 20th century John Cage was a singular presence. Sitting in the same theatre with him, consulting on a new work or simply being in the same room with John Cage gave each of us a sense of purpose. He was perhaps the most influential person in our professional lives.

During my life with Relâche I had the privilege to be around John on numerous occasions, to hear him talk on a variety of subjects and comment on Relâche's interpretation of a given work. Following are two of many stories about John Cage.

In 1985, the Relâche Ensemble was part of a consortium to commission a new work from John Cage. Funded by the then National Endowment for the Arts' commissioning program, the piece—titled *Hymnkus*—was a commission for three ensembles, each sharing the costs for the creation and initial performances of the work.

Each of the ensembles had a different complement of instruments so Cage wanted to create a score that could be easily adapted by each group. All agreed to use a vocalist. As he prepared to write the piece John called the Relâche office to ask some questions about the players, and especially about vocalist Barbara Noska.

At that time there was a new guy working for Relâche as administrative assistant named Jon Mire. He had just arrived in Philadelphia from Thibodeaux, Louisiana, his clipped Cajun accent providing a nice contrast to most of the other Relâche folks' who had a refined sort of "Philly-speak." Despite having been a proud member of his high school drum-and-bugle corps, he did not have much of a grasp of music and especially music history. I hired him precisely because he possessed the very administrative skills that were needed by a growing organization. Among his duties was answering the phone. One day the phone rang while I was in the office, actually I was in an adjoining room looking over some new scores that had just arrived. "Hey, Joseph," he called across the room, "there's some guy on the phone wants to talk with you. He says his name is John Cage. Do you want to talk to him? Who is he anyway?"

I grabbed the phone from our guy and before I could apologize to John I heard him say very quietly and not the least bit disturbed, "Hello, Joseph. I wonder if you can tell me Barbara Noska's vocal range?" "Of course," I replied, and did so. When I finished talking with John I sat our new guy down to give him a brief course in late 20th century music, and a lesson in answering the phone.

Sometime in the late 1980s the Relâche Ensemble was performing John Cage's piece, *Ryoanji*. Scored for voice, flute and percussion, it's a work of extreme beauty with glissandi performed by the voice and flute overlaying a mat of delicate percussion sounds played on non-tuned instruments, each articulation punctuated by dramatic silences. The piece is intended to invoke the meditative quality of one of the famous stone gardens in Kyoto, Japan, named appropriately Ryoanji.

Needless to say a successful realization of this work requires that the musical sounds emerge from silence then recede back, audibly appearing and disappearing, ebbing and flowing, over 15-minute duration. For this performance Relâche was in a small recital hall in downtown Philadelphia, The Ethical Society, a place where many Relâche concerts took place during its long history.

As vocalist Barbara Noska, flutist Laurel Wyckoff and percussionist Helen Carnevale gently played and sang their parts, a noise could be heard from somewhere in the rear of the hall, a slight suckling sound. It was a baby nursing, her mother staring intently at the performers. Everyone nearby who heard the baby smiled when they learned just what it was, and the sound essentially became one with *Ryoanji*. And then from a location not too far from the nursing baby and her mother I heard someone whispering. It was John Jonik, a friend of Relâche.

As I focused my attention on the delicate sonic contours of *Ryoanji*, I heard Jonik whisper to his then-girlfriend, Michaela Majoun, a local radio personality and friend of Relâche, "From now on this is going to be our song." It became hard to hear the delicate sounds sung by Barbara and played by Laurel and Helen amidst the muffled laughter coming from those who overheard Jonik's endearing paean. While the baby continued to nurse and the players continued to play I could observe groups of people shaking as they tried to contain their laughter. A few weeks later I sent John Cage a letter telling him of the incident with the baby. Cage's response later on was, "how nice." I did not mention Jonik's comment. Maybe I should have.

John Jonik, activist, artist and social commentator, with a face like the late cowboy actor-sidekick, Gabby Hayes (sans beard) is one of the more colorful characters from my Philadelphia days. His wry observations on daily life were infused with an alert, acerbic and active sense of humor and if he didn't make you laugh with one of his weird comments then he would show you his collection of "junque." A true pack-rat, he amassed hundreds of collectibles, untold items made of metal, rubber, wood, plastic, anything that might be used in a work of art or in some Rube Goldberg-esque device whose significance resided solely within John Jonik's expansive imagination. His Upper-Kensington row house was packed—basement to roof—with stuff. Like a fully loaded Philadelphia Hoagie squishing out of the role, his junque seemed to overflow its appointed space, threatening to slosh out the windows and onto the crowded street of that working-class neighborhood. When things got relatively boring, John collected cars. Sort of. He collected Volkswagen Squarebacks.

Remnants of the late 1960s and early 1970s, these rickety beasts were part station wagon and part Bug. Other than their being fuel-friendly, they were dismal attempts at car-making. John owned five of them, parked in several different cities between Philadelphia and Portland, Maine he registered each of them at an address in Latvia so when one of them was ticketed it would take years for the ticket to find its way back to Philadelphia, if, indeed, it ever did. In addition to his never-ending searches for treasured urban detritus, making odd surreal snow globes and collecting Volkswagen Squarebacks, he drew cartoons.

Appearing in the pages of *Playboy*, the *New Yorker*, *Esquire* and other respected magazines, John's cartoons were often brilliant. One of my particular favorites has two men walking down a street while miniature people are raining down on them. One guy says to the other one, "See, I told you no two of them look alike." In response to a request for a cartoon to hang in the Relâche office John gave me one with a guy walking past what appears to be a hardware store with gadgets and tools of numerous shapes and sizes hanging on the wall. On the window the sign says, "Dave's Hardware and Avant-Garde Music Supply Co." If only it had said, "Joe's..."

In addition to these and other passions and talents, John was known to those of us in the Relâche family as an early fan of Philip Glass' music. I'm not exactly sure what drew John to Philip's music. I like to think it was the sheer "revolutionary" audacity of Phil's early music that appealed to artists and audiences eager to identify with a sound and a process of making music that wove the disparate threads of cultural disintegration left over from the 1960s into some sort of composite whole. In any case, John was totally won over by Phil's music; as was I. So I guess it's an odd twist of memory that I often think of John Jonik when I listen to or think of Philip Glass.

A cartoon by John Jonik

My first exposure to Philip's music was from a recording made on Chatham Square Records, a label owned by Philip and dedicated to his works from the early 1970s. This was radical stuff, especially for a guy like me who was then just entering graduate studies at Temple University and who had been fairly well disenfranchised by the Euro-American music of the Modernist composers of the post-WWII generation whose maniacal devotion to Serialism was lethal. After an intense study of this music I concluded that it was not the music I wanted to write, let alone listen to. How could I? I didn't hear it. At that time, Philip's music was as refreshing as anything on the scene. And I heard it!

I heard in the loud repetitions the songs of the neighborhood I grew up in: predictable—yet oh-so-subtle variations—in the sound of the El as it hurtled over the mad streets of North Philadelphia or in the sounds of the relentless machines that gushed from the factories down the street and around the corner. I heard in the defiant arpeggios of Phil's *Music In Fifths* how that seemingly pure harmonic interval could sparkle and put to rest the absurdity of its role as a despoiler of music from the "common practice period." I responded enthusiastically when the root tones of those four-note patterns thumped its authoritative stamp on my chest, the part of the body that seems to collect deep bass tones before channeling them to other receptive neural points of passion. No doubt about it: I was hooked and wanted to hear this music live, to place my body squarely in the path of this audacious sound. I found the opportunity one summer night in New York City.

I remember the moment vividly: a hot summer night in New York's SoHo, walking down Mercer Street to attend a performance by the Philip Glass Ensemble at the original Kitchen, the lingering tastes of spinach linguini and a fine Barolo from Alfredo's Trattoria at Hudson and Bank Streets settling on my tongue. As we approached the Kitchen—we were early for the performance—we heard the final section of *Music In Similar Motion* spilling out of the wide-open second floor windows of the Kitchen. I was with Annson Kenney, Maralyn Polak and Barbara Noska; three of my Philly new music conspirators. I looked over at Annson whose eyes sparkled in anticipation as he sort of nodded to where the sound was coming from. His body language seemed to say, "This is the place. C'mon in." We did, just as the rehearsal was ending, the sound of Phil's amplified ensemble slamming off of the walls of the buildings along Mercer Street.

Over the years I attended a number of performances by Phil's ensemble, including the astounding premiere of *Einstein on the Beach* at the Metropolitan Opera. Once in Philadelphia after a blistering performance of several of his works from the late 1960s such as *Music in Similar Motion* and *Music In Contrary Motion* at the University Museum I found myself invited to a party with Phil and the ensemble by a well-known art collector whose penthouse apartment atop the old Drake Hotel was not prepared for this collection of ultra-hip writers, painters, musicians and hangers-on that happily made the trek up into the clouds that misty night. She—the well-known art collector—knew that it was trendy to like Philip Glass's music. So I guess having a party for him would give her instant celebrity in Philly's "hip" arts underground. Maybe, but what I remember most is how out-of-touch many of these party-goers were when they actually had to come to terms with the music, then try to have a conversation with the musicians while they frolicked in-and-out of her rooftop swimming pool. It was comical, yet sad. But, alas, it was a pretty good party!

As the Relâche Organization grew in size and quality, adding tune after tune to its rapidly expanding repertoire, I searched for ways to commission a work from Philip. It wasn't easy. Many of the granting organizations that Relâche had access to and who provided full or partial funding to commission new works by American composers were not eager to aid organizations who wanted a work by Philip. They viewed his success as beyond their mission to help underserved and under-performed composers find a voice in the American new music wilderness. On several occasions I presented the idea to sympathetic funding agencies, only to have them dissuade me, preferring that I concentrate on relatively lesser-known artists. While much of these "lesser-known" composers' music was being performed regularly (in some cases gaining reasonably large followings) they simply could not compete with composers like Philip Glass, Steve Reich and John Adams, among others, for the listeners' attention. The new music marketplace could absorb just so much, with other quality composers residing in the margins. After having had success in developing a long-range commissioning program in the early-to-mid 1990s I decided to focus my fundraising attention on generating money to commission not only Philip Glass but other composers whose music had gained commercial success through film scores and collaborative performances and recordings with world music and popular music artists. But my main target remained Philip Glass.

Although I knew Philip from having spent time talking with him at concerts, festivals and private parties, I felt I should approach him more formally to learn of his interest in writing a piece for the Relâche Ensemble. In times past he had expressed a respect for what we had accomplished in Philadelphia, commenting to a mutual friend once that, "Joseph has established an outpost of sorts in Philadelphia." This I took as a supreme compliment. I knew Philip's then manager, Jed Wheeler, Executive Director of International Production Associates (IPA) through meetings at various booking conferences such as the Association of Performing Arts Presenters (APAP) and the Western Arts Alliance (WAA). At those events I found Jed to be friendly, knowledgeable and respectful of my efforts to promote new music. So I called Jed and asked for a meeting in his New York office. We met in the spring of 1994.

My idea was quite simple: Philip would compose a new piece for Relâche lasting approximately 20 minutes. For the premier performances in Philadelphia, Philip would play keyboard as a guest performer with the ensemble. Following the premieres Relâche would have exclusive rights to perform the work for a period of two years. Jed thought it a reasonable request. He approached Philip who agreed to the deal, with the understanding that he would write a second keyboard part that could be removed after the initial performances. The fee for a commission and two appearances as a guest performer was $35,000, a figure that heretofore was well beyond Relâche's means, having offered a high commission fee of $15,000 a few years prior to composer-arranger George Russell. Jed and I agreed to the fee while he and Philip agreed to all parts of my proposal except that Relâche would have the exclusive performance rights for one year, not two. I then set about raising the necessary money.

Having established a reputation for developing large projects, Relâche's credibility with certain funding agencies and foundations was pretty solid so I naturally approached those funding officers with whom we had developed a relationship. My plan was to include the large commission to Philip in the context of a broader commissioning program that would, essentially, allow the Relâche Ensemble to present an (almost) entire season of premieres. I also targeted Meet the Composer, Chamber Music America and the American Music Center, all of whom had initiated various projects to help performers and ensembles create new works. Drew Keegan, Director of Marketing for Relâche, who had been instrumental in finding marketing and promotional funds from large and small corporations over the preceding couple of years worked with me to develop a fundraising strategy and set about finding the money to make this entire project happen.

Despite the good relations we had developed with enlightened businesses they were simply not of a mind to donate or invest money for the creation of new works. Philanthropic agencies, service organizations and state and city governments were a much better bet. As was often the case in those days, the Arts and Culture Division of the Pew Charitable Trusts immediately saw the wisdom in helping Relâche develop new musical works. And as knowledgeable arts funders, they clearly saw the wisdom in helping a local performing ensemble commission a new work by Philip Glass. As part of a larger general operating grant to Relâche they agreed to sponsor six commissions, one of them being to Philip Glass. That gave me approximately one-third of the fee. I then turned to Meet the Composer in New York.

Meet the Composer (MTC) was then under the visionary leadership of John Duffy, a composer and tireless advocate for American music and musicians. Under his guidance MTC raised substantial funds to make grants to composers and composer-ensemble-presenting organization alliances. Many of their programs provided essential operating funds to any number of individuals and organizations. When one approached John to talk about an idea or make a proposal, you knew he and his staff would give a good listen and try their best to offer assistance. I knew John mainly from having created an identity with MTC and meeting him at various concerts and functions in New York so I felt quite confident in asking for a meeting to talk about my commissioning projects. We met in his small unadorned office on Broadway and 96th Street one rainy afternoon.

As I sat down across from him I observed a black-and-white photo of a young boxer. Shoulders rounded and hunched up so that the neck seems to recede into the upper torso, a stance taken in anticipation of sticking a quick jab then sliding off the counter punch, it's the kind of promotional photo that adorns every boxing gym's office. That young boxer was John Duffy. Needless to say we launched into a long conversation about our shared boxing exploits then spent a good deal of time discussing the state of "the game," and how it had lost its luster and appeal for the average sports fan. Each of us had read the great writers on boxing and loved the poetry of the sport as much as the physical challenge it offered. I remember clearly how he related the content of a documentary on Mike Tyson that he had just seen, sadly remarking how Cus D'Amato's and Jim Jacobs' protégé had been fed to the dogs after their deaths. One could say John and I sort of bonded that day. When I finally got around to explaining why I wanted to talk with him, I learned that he was a big fan of Philip Glass' music. How appropriate!

I think John was as impressed with Philip's organizational skills as he was with his music. The fact that Phil had created a well designed and managed operation to include an artist management service (IPA), a publishing company (Dunvagen Press) a recording studio (Looking Glass Studio) and a record label (Point Music) all intended as a means of controlling the creation, production and distribution of Phil's music (as well as those composers whose music he liked) was appealing to both John and me. After explaining my commissioning plan to John and asking him if MTC would consider an application from Relâche to help with the commissioning fee to Philip, he encouraged me to apply. I did. After several months of waiting for the peer panel review process to make their recommendation to John I learned that they did not approve a commission fee for Philip. The usual reason was offered: he doesn't need it. "Yeah," I countered when I learned of their decision, "but Relâche does!" I shared my frustration with John over this decision, inferring that as long as peer panels are comprised of primarily composers then there is a good chance that well-known "established" artists would be left out of the mix. Accordingly, those organizations—like Relâche—who were adept at designing projects that celebrated popular artists as a means to enhance opportunities for those artists who are not as well known would suffer. John agreed and decided to make an executive decision to award Relâche $15,000 to be applied directly to Philip's commissioning fee. I now had $25,000 toward my goal. Figuring I could raise the remaining $10,000 from local sources we finalized the deal with the premiere performances scheduled for April, 1995. As part of the overall arrangement Philip and Jed agreed that Philip would conduct master classes at the Curtis Institute of Music and the University of the Arts and he would appear as special guest at a fundraising event for Relâche. Not a bad deal at all. We at Relâche set about organizing the premiere performance as part of the 1994-1995 Season.

In anticipation of attracting larger-than-usual audiences for the two premiere performances I approached Steve Goff, Managing Director of the Annenberg Center at the University of Pennsylvania. I and Relâche were involved with Steve in a successful partnership to present a world/new music series in addition to the Relâche Ensemble's concerts. I asked if we could perform Philip's new piece in the 1,000 seat Annenberg Theater rather than the

400 seat Prince Theater, Relâche's usual home. He agreed and as a co-presenter generously waived the rental fee. Nancy Weiss, then the chair of the board of directors at the Annenberg Center and a fan of Relâche offered to organize and host a reception in Philip's honor to benefit Relâche at her home in Bryn Mawr. To our surprise the Curtis Institute of Music agreed to pay Relâche for Philip's master class that would be offered to their composition students. The University of the Arts' Music Department followed suite. The package appeared to be complete. Philip and I met at his home in New York City to discuss the piece, agreeing easily on the overall concept of the work, a date to receive the score and parts, a rehearsal scheme and the two performances. We were off and running with one of the most anticipated events in Relâche's history.

Everything went according to plan, until early December in 1994 when Jed Wheeler called me and asked if I could meet with him in his office. Something had developed regarding the new piece. My first thought, of course, was that Philip wanted to move back the premiere dates or, worse yet, that he had to put it aside in favor of another work. But that wasn't the case at all. Jed informed me that the piece Philip was writing was just about complete, that he had titled it *TSE* and an Italian presenter had come forward requesting that the new piece become the instrumental component in a site-specific theatrical performance piece to be directed and staged by long-time Glass collaborator, Robert Wilson, at an ancient volcanic ruin somewhere in Sicily. Would, they asked, the Relâche Ensemble consider being the performing entity for this piece if, they—the Italian presenters—could take credit for the world premiere performance.? If Relâche agreed to this offer the ensemble would be paid well in addition to all travel expenses and a two-week residency in Sicily. The residency-performances were to take place in March, 1995, one month before the scheduled performances of *TSE* in Philadelphia. After consulting with the members of Relâche to see if this were feasible, I agreed to the initial offer. Jed began working on finalizing the deal.

I would like to report that everything went smoothly and that the Relâche Ensemble enjoyed an especially enjoyable trip to Sicily to work with two of the major American artists of the late 20th century, then return home to present this new work to its Philadelphia audiences. Of course, I can't but I can report that Relâche came away from this experience in very good shape. The Italian presenters, you see, decided that it would be way too expensive to pay the Relâche Ensemble's fee and travel expenses for this project. So they offered to subsidize our recording of *TSE* if we agreed to their using the recording in the new theater piece. Further, the recording would be made at Looking Glass Studios under the supervision of Kurt Munkasi, the highly respected recording engineer and producer who has been Philip Glass' long-time collaborator. I eagerly agreed and after two weeks' rehearsal with Philip the Relâche Ensemble spent two days in the recording studio laying down the tracks that would become the recorded version of *TSE*. The recording fee allowed Relâche to handsomely pay each ensemble member and recoup a portion of the original commissioning fee to Philip. As they say in the world of the suits, "it was a win-win situation."

In preparation for the Philadelphia performances we could now use the cachet of both Robert Wilson's and Philip Glass' names to promote *TSE*. And we did, tapping into as much of the Philadelphia theater audience as was possible. Not to mention the dance and visual arts audiences as well. Overall, everything went almost according to plan. The Relâche Ensemble now knew *TSE* quite well and were comfortable with the keyboard part that Phil had written for himself as well as when that part was extracted from the mix. It turned out to be a beautiful work that the ensemble enjoyed playing and, by most accounts, the audiences enjoyed listening to. Despite the general sense of *esprit de corps* that informed the whole project, there were the usual odd and disappointing elements.

With a world-renowned composer preparing to make several appearances in Philadelphia as part of a one-of-a-kind performance by the home-grown new music ensemble, Relâche, that had just been part of a collaborative project with the esteemed theater director, Robert Wilson, one would think that the Philadelphia media would leap at the chance to interview the principals and, essentially, help promote the event. No such luck. Other than with the entertainment editor of the *Philadelphia Weekly*, Relâche's promotions people couldn't stir up much excitement.

During the following year the Relâche Ensemble performed *TSE* throughout the U.S. and on tours to Europe, usually to enthusiastic responses from the audiences. I don't know if the Robert Wilson-directed theater work of which *TSE* was a part was ever performed again. I don't think it was. I had hoped that Philip and his production-recording team would consider recording *TSE* with Relâche but was told that due to Phil's exclusive recording deal with Nonesuch that it would be difficult to make it happen. I kept pushing the idea but to no avail. And what did John Jonik think of the piece? "It was nice," he said politely after the Philadelphia premiere and, after being

Poster for TSE premiere

introduced to Philip at a post-concert reception said, "I really like those fast pieces of yours."

No two of them are alike, I guess.

He was the quintessential Irish-Catholic artist. A gregarious and outgoing Leo with a mischievous grin and outrageous sense of humor who was still living with his widowed mother in the same North Philadelphia row house where he was raised. As much at home in the small neighborhood gym lifting weights as he was on the stage performing one of his many musical works or in one of the art galleries that exhibited his pieces, Annson Kenney was unique and important in the context of late 20th century Philadelphia art history and integral to the early years of Relâche and beyond. Throughout the 1980s and into the 1990s, Relâche experienced tremendous growth, which would never have happened without having spent a good deal of my life with and around Annson.

The scene: Circa 1980, Sassafras, a bar in Philadelphia's Olde City section where my friends and I often gathered after a concert or gallery opening or when we sought refuge from one of the ubiquitous in-your-face hangouts that were far more prevalent throughout the city in those days. At times Sassafras was the kind of place where you might feel that you had stepped out of dreary Philadelphia and into romantic Paris, into a small dark mysterious bistro populated by just the right mix of hipsters and wannabes dressed in the uniform of those in the know: black-on-black. The drinks and food were quite good, served by a knowledgeable and friendly corps of bartenders and waitresses who could just as easily have slipped out of their server's uniforms and joined the clientele in conversation. On this particular night the place was packed.

We were standing at the bar...me, Annson, Arthur, Merilyn and Maralyn and a few others and it was fairly noisy. A large guy dressed in a suit was sitting at the bar a few stools down from us, his tie loosened at his puffy red neck while he swiveled back-and-forth trying to find someone to latch on to. He was friendly but from what little conversation we heard him having with some others nearby he probably was not the kind of guy we had much in common with. Rather than being rude, or appearing to be rude, I remember avoiding him, as I engaged in one of my normal conversations with Arthur—him talking at me, me listening, nodding my head in recognition of one of Arthur's many astute articulate deconstructions of whatever was on his mind that particular night.

Annson was leaning, his back to the bar just to my left, with a familiar bottle of beer clenched in his meaty hand. Holding court as usual, this time he was describing in detail a wrestling match he had seen the night before, carefully explaining a similarity he observed between the scissors-lock the Iron Sheik had applied to the large muscular torso of The Assassin and a new performance piece he was working on that deconstructed the phrase "I am not a liberal." To his left was the guy in the suit who, trying to find a way into this highly conceptual moment blurted out, "Hey how about if I buy you all a drink? On me." Annson stopped in mid-sentence, looked at Arthur and me then said to the guy, "Sure, but does that mean we have to talk to you?"

Paradoxically, Annson Kenney was well known throughout subterranean Philadelphia more for his street antics and late-night escapades than his insightful yet playful art works. He employed linguistic constructs as a basis for written works, performance works, video and film works and, finally, a large body of neon art that confounded gallery visitors by creating, in essence, written pages on gallery walls containing statements and phrases scripted in elegant neon colors, complete with footnotes placed, of course, near one's feet

It was inevitable Annson and I would become friends.

We were born on the same day: July 26th. In the same year: 1944. Almost at the same time - two hours apart - in hospitals located close to one another in North Philadelphia. We first met as teenagers in the early 1960's at one of the many weekend dances held in church basements throughout the city as a means to control teenage angst. Controlling teenage angst was a service that even the church couldn't manage but they did provide opportunities to socialize and learn the hustles that would either propel us beyond the neighborhoods or teach us to survive within them. And they provided plenty of opportunities to dance away the fears that a soon-to-be-delivered draft notice was beginning to instill in us.

As we remembered, our first meeting was at "The Mott," a church on Orthodox Street in the Frankford section of the city, not very far from each of our respective neighborhoods. Or maybe it was at Saint Martin of Tours Church only blocks away on the Oxford Circle. Neither of us remembered the details, only that we met at one of these church dances then forgot about it as our lives took very different paths.

Annson had escaped the draft while settling in as an undergraduate at

Temple University, first as an English major then in Music Performance; he played the contrabass. I had returned from a tour in the Navy and was running on a fast track to make up for the time lost in service. By then Annson had left Temple University and was developing a reputation around town for his outlandish bass playing, within the context of a "free jazz" movement that was altering the sound of jazz. It was inevitable we'd meet again.

Sometime in the early 1970's I received a call from a saxophonist I was playing with. By then I was completely immersed in a musical culture, taking courses by day, studying and playing by night with whoever might be interested in my ideas and style. The guy who called was more conservative than I was, an excellent performer was but rather reluctant to dance along the edges of improvisational constructs that didn't fit into the usual theme-and-variation format. "Hey," he said, "I just left this session at Temple (University) where I tried to play with this crazy bass player. The guy has some serious chops but he's really crazy, out of control, doesn't want to work with anyone unless they're ready to step outside. I thought you might be interested in meeting him. Here's his number." Of course this crazy bass player was Annson Kenney. I called, got together, found that we had similar goals and agreed to keep in touch.

This time, we did.

Unlike many of Annson's other friends, associates, and hangers-on, I wasn't easily seduced by his outlandish and sometimes reckless behavior. Sure, it was fun being around him, especially late at night in some after-hours club in South Philadelphia where he would be engaged in conversation with a guy named Johnny Auto Body about Cha-Cha Muldowney's latest dragster speed record or dancing with Center City prostitutes who were gratefully off-duty after a night entertaining some screen door salesmen from Dubuque. I had experienced much stranger, and more dangerous, encounters in bars from Manila to Hong Kong during my Navy days, so rubbing shoulders with small-time Mafiosi and other assorted lost souls in Philadelphia did not particularly intimidate me. What could intimidate me however were Annson's quick brilliant powers of observation and analysis. I learned more from him about the demystification of the "art" experience or "art object" than from anyone else. Our long conversations on the phone, at boxing matches, at a bar, anywhere anytime was the equivalent of earning several graduate degrees. And they were a lot more fun.

Annson Kenney

In 1977 when I first had the idea to organize a performing ensemble that evolved into Relâche, Annson encouraged me and agreed to become a part of it. By this time he had pretty much moved away from music performance after years of developing solo works for the contrabass, sometimes in combination with varieties of electronic circuitry and computer generated sound realized either in real-time or recorded on tape. His creative energies during those days were devoted to writing and developing performance works which used his body as a vessel to disperse or display information.

In one piece from this period, *Interference Artifacts No. 5*, he attached electro-magnetic sensors to his bare skin at various points on his body to record the level of physical activity. The sensors were then connected to a transducer to convert the electrical impulses from his body into an audio signal that resulted in "white noise." He then articulated a series of long bow strokes across the strings of the contrabass without lifting the bow off of the strings and leaning forcibly into the strings thereby creating great tension at points where the bow hair excited the strings. The resultant sound was amplified and mixed with the white noise that accumulated from his intense bowing motions. Essentially, Annson worked up a sweat that was recorded by the sensors and transformed into audio sound that "interfered" with the sound of the contrabass. The interference overcame the musical sounds that became of secondary importance to the force of the body's movements. Another work in a similar vein is titled, *I'll Huff and I'll Puff and I'll Blow Your Impedance Match Down (Interference Artifacts No. 2).*

A large blackboard sets stage right with Annson standing in front of it with his back to the audience. A singer, usually Relâche's featured vocalist Barbara Noska, sits on a stool facing the audience, stage left with a microphone placed directly in front of her. In his right hand Annson holds sticks of hard white chalk, in his left hand a microphone. Each microphone is patched into an amplifier and mixer. Barbara begins singing unaccompanied a sacred or liturgical text, most often The Kaddish or at times Amazing Grace, repeating the song over and over while her voice is streamed back through the house speakers.

After Barbara completes the first round of song Annson begins writing on the blackboard the phrase, "If God had wanted us to listen he would have given us ears." He writes furiously with the chalk while pressing hard against the blackboard creating a screeching sound you no doubt remember from innumerable visits to the chalkboard as a kid in school. He holds the microphone close to the chalk so the screeching sounds can be picked up and routed through the amplifier and mixer then back into the house. As he covers the blackboard from top-to-bottom with this phrase, and in order to continue writing on the blackboard rather than erasing each phrase he writes over them repeatedly eventually covering the blackboard in white, a chalk curtain rendering each phrase indecipherable; in essence, erasing them. Over the duration of the piece —usually about 15 minutes—the screeching of the chalk combined with the attacks of each articulation builds into a loud blur which covers over the voice. Or, as Heidegger wrote,"Script overcomes scream..." The voice is interfered with and rendered inchoate.

Annson Kenney and Barbara Noska performing** I'll Huff and I'll Puff and I'll Blow Your Impedence Match Down **(Interference Artifacts No. 2)

Performance works like these, as well as many others by a variety of composers, gave each early Relâche concert a distinctive character. As the ensemble matured during its first years, Annson's presence was notable, attracting not only the curious music listener but also those from the visual arts community in Philadelphia who normally were not attracted to "New Music" concerts. In essence, Relâche wrapped its early image around the conceptual art world in much the same way that Philip Glass and Steve Reich did in the early 1970's within the downtown New York City gallery and loft world. Annson helped make this happen. He also helped Relâche develop its distinctive logo.

Adapted from the original script that appeared on promotional items announcing the premiere performance of Relâche, the logo for Relâche, The Ensemble strived to capture a fluid motion that was articulated so beautifully in the original. Like the original, our version appeared to unfold across the page from left to right, beginning with the capital "R" leaning just slightly to the right while the concluding lower-case "e" ended with a tail swooping slightly downward, giving the impression that the "R" would be whipped back and continue scrolling "R-e-l-â-c-h-e" forever across the page.

One day in 1979 while looking at a poster created for one of our concerts, I was standing with Annson, his hands in his baggy cargo pants, and Joe Showalter, his arms crossed in front of his chest in a pose that many people mistook for nervous displacement; all of us staring at the poster in critical repose. Joe said, "Hey Annson why don't you make a neon logo for us." Annson looked at me, then at Joe, took his hands out of his pockets and twirled his signature handlebar mustache and smiled, "That's just tacky enough to work." He set about designing it using a slightly eerie yet elegant magenta color. The Relâche logo was hung over every stage the ensemble performed on for years helping to define its unique image.

At first glance one might view the logo as a cute decorative component to the performances; indeed it was. But with its creation and emblematic placement, suspended above the action of the Relâche Ensemble, its diffuse magenta glow emerging from a black background, it appeared to be actually moving back-and-forth, front-to-back-to-front luring the observer away from the visual presentation on the stage and to it. And that is what was so magical: it signified "action," the act of writing R-e-l-â-c-h-e, the act of musical performance: translating symbols on pages—notation—into active sounds, the action of the gas moving through the glass tubes, the glow of the gas that, unlike musical sounds that disappear into the air, are trapped until the glass is fractured...and then, nothing. The piece ends?

Annson had an extraordinary facility with language. Many of his works were language- based. Over the years I assisted him in performances and installations, becoming, in the process, more fluent in my interpretation of language, granting me access to a meta-language that informed so much of Annson's world, including his playful teasing and twisting of metaphors that often served as critical barbs to the gullible gaijin who desperately wanted to be invited inside "our" world. I remember the night (or morning) when it all came together for me, at a time not long after when the Relâche logo was born.

At that time in Philadelphia one of the hipper bar-restaurants was named "London." Owned and managed by Warren and Dolores Browne and located in the Fairmount section of the city only a short distance from the Philadelphia Museum of Art and in close proximity to center-city, London was, as they said then, "a happenin' place." It was a nice bar populated by smart, irreverent stylistically alert smart-ass Philadelphians, many of them successful painters, graphic designers, architects, writers and savvy business-men and women. The second floor of the bar-restaurant was designated "The London Gallery" and featured a variety of artists' works, both local and international in scope. The space was small but accommodating. Local musicians, on the other hand, didn't necessarily frequent London, preferring instead a scruffy tavern on 15th Street around the corner from the Philadelphia Academy of Music named McGlinchey's, where the bartenders kept loaded weapons strapped to the underside of the bar.

The London's Warren Browne loved Annson's neon pieces so he offered him a one-man show. Annson recruited me and another long-time cohort, Nicholas Boonin, to help him hang about 15 neon pieces. In order to more effectively hang the works we decided to do it all in one day and night: Monday when the restaurant is closed. We started working early that afternoon and worked through the next morning. About 2 or 3 AM it happened.

I was installing a piece I later owned titled "Orgaspm!" trying to determine just how far above the floor it should be placed so that its piercing Day-Glo red color delivered with an on-and-off irritating regularity would have the optimum effect on a viewer, when I turned from facing the wall to ask Annson's opinion. I saw him standing perfectly still staring at a piece he had just finished securing to the wall. He just stared at it, his eyes maybe three inches from the glass. I walked over, standing next to him for a minute or so not knowing if I should interrupt him when he said quietly, "look at that, look at that gas, Joseph...see it moving along the inner edge of the tube, see how fast it moves." I moved closer to the glass and observed the speed at which the gas particles burst through the vacuumed space. I glanced at Annson and saw the sky blue color of the gas reflected in his eyes now beginning to reveal that playful gleam I was so used to seeing. And it hit me: he was metaphorically a gas particle streaming and screaming through an endless tube with curves and angles that had a clear logic yet was utterly out of control.

Finally, it all began to make sense to me. I understood completely his wild aggressive behavior and intense gestures so characteristic of his performances and writings, often one and the same. I understood why he was attracted to fast-paced games—he loved to attend drag races, often arranging for a press pass so he could watch and listen amid the deafening roar of the engines at the starting line. And I think I understood his need for physical pain, his penchant for getting punched out, seldom going after anyone who couldn't deliver a solid knockout punch or kick. From that moment on, in the early hours of another Philadelphia morning, until his death, he no longer had to step back and say, in John Cassavettes' elegant phrase, "Show me the logic." Though sometimes his logic was open to question, it was there. I got it.

Just months before he died in 1981, Annson received a fellowship from the Pennsylvania Council on the Arts, the first awarded to him after several previous attempts at submitting work that, to put in bluntly, left most peer panels scratching their heads. Finally, he was recognized by a regional arts agency. The cash award was something like $7,000. What did he do with it? He bought a sports car. Not just any sports car but a Lotus! I saw him the day he picked it up.

Scrunched down in its driver's seat, Annson commanded the bright yellow car into a parking spot near where I was waiting for him. He pulled up riding its brakes, the car vibrating up-and-down, its engine crying out to be stretched out on the open highway. Looking up, over the drone of the engine, he mouthed the words, "What do you think?" "Great, looks great," I said. "Where are you gonna run it?" I asked. "I can't drive it on the road yet, no insurance," he responded. "No insurance? What do you mean?" I asked. "I can't afford the blasted insurance," he grinned ruefully. "Too expensive." The car sat in a borrowed garage, never to run on the road while he lived.

Two days before he died, Annson called me to ask if I were going to be downtown that evening. I was writing an article about a pending strike by members of the Philadelphia Orchestra and had scheduled an interview with several of the players who wished to discuss certain grievances they had with the current administration and artistic direction of the orchestra. I offered Annson a ride. We hadn't seen each other or spoken for a week. I asked what he was up to. He was pretty upset over having lost a new jacket the previous night and was convinced it had been stolen from the back of a chair in a long-gone after-hours club appropriately named Purgatory. I offered to help in the search after my interview, but he said he could take care of it by himself. I then told him I would stop by Sassafras around 10:30 and see if he found the jacket and have a few drinks before heading home. He got out of my car and nodded his head okay.

That was the last time I saw him alive.

The jacket he was searching for had been custom-made for him by a designer friend. It was smooth, creamy leather, tan with red piping down the arms and along the shoulders with his name—in his distinctive handwriting, his autograph, really—stitched on the right-hand side front just below the shoulder. Sewn on the back of the jacket was a patch featuring the image of an eight ball, its perfectly contoured numeral rendered in red against the black of the ball. It was gorgeous and Annson was justifiably proud of it. Like every costume he wore, this jacket was distinctive. The thief had stolen more than a jacket; this jacket was Annson's identity.

He had been out drinking the night before and was absolutely convinced someone had lifted it while he was in the bathroom. He had his suspicions. When I left him off, Annson had some serious vengeance in his eyes. What happened after that is anyone's guess, but he wound up at a funky dive of a late-night bar-disco on Locust Street directly across from the Academy of Music. Maybe he had gone there at the same time I was interviewing the Philadelphia Orchestra musicians around the corner, I'll never know. There he apparently confronted a couple of guys who I assume he suspected in the theft. They promptly beat him up—which took some doing considering all the bodybuilding he did—inflicting some serious damage to his face. After the beating, he showed up at dawn on the downtown doorstep of one of his second-string squeezes, dripping blood all over his white-fringed buckskin as the shocked woman blanched. He did not recover the lost jacket that night, or ever.

Brilliant, provocative, engaging, feisty, loyal and dead at 37, Annson Kenney flamed out on a wet cold early day preceding New Year's Eve in 1981 on Germantown Avenue, as the car he was riding in—a Honda Civic—slammed into the rear of an electric trolley car, pinning him beneath for three grisly hours. The car's impact was judged to be in excess of 100 MPH, over steel tracks set in a cobblestone street. When the "Jaws of Death" finally pried him loose, one of the most dynamic voices to emerge in late 20th century Philadelphia was silenced. He died two hours later, never regaining consciousness.

After Annson's awful death, the tight circle of friends who revolved around his singular presence began to disperse. Arthur Sabatini, Nicholas Boonin and I raised money from the Pennsylvania Council on the Arts, local foundations and individuals and assisted by numerous friends created an alliance with Moore College of Art to organize a retrospective gallery show of his artworks. It opened February 1983, a little more than a year after he died and was, by all reckoning, quite successful, selling a number of his works posthumously, mainly neon. While many of his works had already been purchased for display in homes and commercial establishments throughout Philadelphia during his lifetime, later on, after he was gone, many of his neon sculptures were damaged beyond repair, like he was, the result of well-meaning friends mishandling the fragile glass and storing them in places less than secure.

For months, I would see in my daydreams the image of Annson peering out from behind that eight ball with an edgy grin on his face that seemed to say, "...hang in there, Joseph, remember it's tough being us."

And yet, there was something vaguely theatrical about Annson's passing, as if it were his final artwork. Even the photographs of his corpse seemed staged, his reconstructed face frozen into a mask-like apparition. But no, he was really dead, the first of our set to die, really. His funeral was held in the Catholic Church of his mother, three days after a subdued and truncated New Year's celebration. It was attended by a melange of Philly nightfolk: bar/media/arts types, disenfranchised hipsters who identified with Annson's brilliant, irreverent behavior, frayed entrepreneurs who somehow found in Annson a hope their failed lives could muster sufficient frissons to last at least until their next big deal, and stunned women certain he would father their future unborn children. The presiding priest, Father Suppé, was so impressed by the collective caring of Annson's friends; he performed the funeral service for free, refusing to accept payment. "There's just too much love here," he nodded solemnly.

I was in charge of the music . . .kind of "the last concert."

Assisted by my good friend Werner Strobel, I organized music I knew Annson liked. Werner and I carefully recorded selections or complete works to be played at various points throughout the service. I can't really call it a "Mass" even though it was held in Old Saint Joseph's Church, one of the oldest Catholic Churches in Philadelphia. From Ernst Bloch to the Bill Evans Trio featuring Scott LaFaro, from Rimsky Korsakov to the Rolling Stones, the music celebrated Annson's eclectic informed tastes and highlighted the testimonials given by his friends, typified more by the perverse humor of the stories we told rather than the descriptions of the unique works of art he created.

At the conclusion of the service, as we eight pallbearers lined up and prepared to lift Annson's body for the ceremonial trip to the cemetery, we heard from the speakers located throughout the church, "That's all right Momma, that's all right with you. That's all right my Momma anyway you do..." One of Annson's favorite songs: "That's All Right" by Arthur "Big Boy" Crudup, recorded by Elvis Presley at the original Sun Sessions Recordings. Annson often played it for his mother when she was mad at him. It usually caused her to become un-mad. Elvis's youthful plaintive voice stopped everyone cold in their tracks, allowing Annson's mother's pained cry to lift serenely upwards and settle in the Church's elegant domed ceiling.

As Elvis' voice trailed away we carried Annson's body out of the church and into a teeming rainstorm, convinced he had ordered "special effects" for the occasion. Heads down, balancing a body that never found balance in this world, we – his closest friends and fellow provocateurs – were about to step onto Walnut Street when suddenly from around the corner a truck screeched to a stop just a few feet from us. Startled, we looked up into the truck's cab and through the rain-streaked windshield into the equally startled face of the driver. "I'm sorry," he whispered, horrified at the prospect of running over a casket carried by eight wet guys in the middle of historic Philadelphia. We looked at him, then at the side of the truck. "Origlios's Beer Distributor," the lettering read. We looked at one another and started laughing; nearly dropping Annson into a street he had danced across on many occasions. Then we stopped for a moment and listened: from inside the casket we thought we heard that familiar cackle.

By the time the funeral procession wound its way up Fifth Street—the street where he had lived until he died—past the urban ghosts who danced along with him on his late-night escapades, through gritty drug-infested North Philadelphia neighborhoods, slipping alongside the hospital he was born in, Annson's body arrived at a cemetery located next to Lighthouse Field, where we knocked heads in sandlot football games, and where he and I sometimes found work and, always, adventure along the Midway at the yearly visit of the Ringling Brothers Barnum & Bailey Circus in the late 1950's. The rain had stopped leaving a soggy ground into which he was placed, ending a monumental era for many of us whose lives were transformed forever by our association with "Buzz" Kenney.

The collective consciousness of a people and their culture is often colored by the musical memories which inform their lives. As oral histories provide a background study, aural histories add an element of play. In many instances the musics of a people tell their life stories in more direct and personal ways through song and poetry with songs handed down from generation to generation. Unfortunately in today's world many songs are lost in the din of a commercial music industry that is as removed from the heart of a people as it is embracing of their hard-earned dollars. Song for many people is less about the celebration of their lives and experiences and more about false hopes embodied in the spin of the superficial "heroes" and "heroines" of popular culture. But, in the end, the song does not die. People do and we are left only with the memories, or, if we are fortunate, a melody. Among the more meaningful and resonant memories of my life with Relâche are those associated with composer and arranger Romulus Franceschini.

Born to Italian immigrant parents in 1929, Romulus lived a full life until his death in 1996 after a long battle with lung cancer. A native of South Philadelphia's vibrant Italian-American community, Romulus had just the right combination of street smarts and second-generation European sophistication. Music was a part of his life from the early years beginning with his study of the horn, or French Horn, and progressing through the Philadelphia School System's music programs. Like so many of us born into Philadelphia's working class families, his appreciation of music was nurtured by a love of jazz and other popular musics. After serving with the U.S. Army Occupation Forces in Japan following WWII, Romulus returned to study music—composition and theory—at the Philadelphia Conservatory of Music. Following graduation, he traveled to New York City to take lessons with Morton Feldman and became friendly with a group of "experimental" composers who had formed around Feldman and John Cage.

These years instilled in Romulus a passion for the "new," both in the classical music and jazz "avant-garde" worlds. He began writing and arranging works for a variety of ensembles including the Ro-Mas orchestra, an organization he formed with trombonist-composer Cal Massey in Philadelphia that included many of the leading "new" jazz players of the time. To earn a living Romulus became an editor at the Fleisher Collection of Music at the Free Library of Philadelphia, a job he held until two years before his death in 1994.

Despite his passion for the music of his time, Rom never lost sight of the contributions made by musicians of previous times. Never one to lock onto a specific "style," he was an eclectic composer, arranger, editor

Romulus Franceschini

and historian. He didn't talk very much about his work at the Fleisher Collection, preferring instead to discuss his experiences away from the job with the many musicians he was friendly with. As I was getting to know Rom, I came across an article on the American composer Charles Ives which mentioned Rom's name in conjunction with the Fleisher Collection, something to do with Rom having had a role in the restoration or re-interpretation of Ives' Fourth Symphony. I wanted to know more, but, initially, Rom was reticent.

After much questioning he finally filled me in on his participation, emphasizing, in his typically unassuming, modest way, he was not at all pleased with what had happened or the subsequent score which was published.

Charles Ives' Fourth Symphony was composed between 1909-1916, although parts of it were actually re-workings of material composed much earlier in his career. Essentially the work existed in manuscript form except for the second movement which had been published in 1929. Upon his death in 1954, Ives left the work in a confused and, to some, unplayable condition. Leopold Stokowski, conductor of the American Symphony Orchestra in New York, programmed the work twice but each time had to cancel the performance because a complete score and parts were not then available. With Stokowski's backing, a group of influential music publishers donated funds to the Fleisher Collection in order to prepare a workable score and parts.

As a valued member of Fleisher's staff, Romulus worked diligently with the existing Ives material to decipher the sketch and alone prepared the entire first movement. He also checked the previously published second movement against Ives' manuscript and discovered many errors. While assisting the chief curator at Fleisher, Ted Seder, Romulus pieced together the fiendishly difficult and virtually undecipherable fourth movement, using his advanced knowledge of 20th century musical language and notation to focus Ives' initial intentions and creating a score and parts that were now ready for performance. Finally, after many extra rehearsals, Stokowski gave the world premiere performance of Ives's Fourth Symphony with the American Symphony Orchestra in Carnegie Hall in 1965. In the published facsimile edition of the score there is a dedication to Romulus Franceshini.

Stokowski knew what others did not: Romulus was responsible for much of the work that others, perhaps, received credit for. In the end, Romulus remained unhappy with many decisions that were made by his senior staff colleagues but, as was often his nature, he kept his feelings private.

As was manifest by the Ives' Fourth Symphony reconstruction, Romulus' knowledge of music was encyclopedic. Despite his passion for the music of his time, Romulus never lost sight of the contributions made by musicians of previous times. Over the years he contributed essays and program notes to our publications and arranged a number of works for the idiosyncratic complement of performers who have been a part of the Relâche Ensemble. Among the composers who Romulus held in the highest esteem was John Cage.

I remember watching Rom throw the I-Ching to determine through "chance" procedures the overall structure of John Cage's *Fontana Mix* (1959), performed throughout the world by the Relâche Ensemble, often in conjunction with *Aria* sung by dramatic soprano Barbara Noska. Rom really used the coin toss as a means of determining events. One day I walked in to his office at the Fleisher Collection to discover him alternately flipping coins and writing notations on manuscript paper. This went on in silence for about 15 minutes while I sat and watched. Finally he realized I was in the room and then with a slight shrug of his shoulders said shyly, "...Just doin' Cage." Indeed, Rom did Cage well. John Cage knew Rom and remarked several times how much he enjoyed our/his version of *Fontana Mix* and *Fontana Mix with Aria.*

Sometimes, Rom could surprise you with a sudden upsurge of his aesthetic and cultural passions. Take the time Relâche had scheduled a work by composer Charles Dodge titled *Any Resemblance is Purely Coincidental.* Charles Dodge is known for his pioneering work with computer-generated music. This particular piece is scored for piano solo and pre-recorded tape, the material on the tape consisting of an old recording of Enrico Caruso singing the aria "Vesti la Giubba" from Leoncavallo's opera *I Pagliacci.* Dodge imported Caruso's voice into the computer and altered it, subjected it to a variety of changes: pitch displacement, rhythmic augmentation and diminution, timbral colorings, etc. The pianist "accompanies" the altered voice, reading from the score. The overall effect is hilarious, especially if one is familiar with Leoncavallo's well-know opera and equally well-known and popular aria. Over the duration of 10 minutes Caruso is resurrected, remixed, and then re-interred, depending on your state of mind and sense of humor.

As with musical works for tape and instrument or instruments a critical component in a successful realization is how the tape part is directed into the performance space with respect to the "live" sound of the other instrument(s), or in this instance the piano. The piano and tape parts are sent through a mixing board then processed accordingly so that the overall sound is clear and even, both in the auditorium and stage monitor mix. During technical and dress rehearsals I worked closely with our sound engineer Werner Strobel to ensure that the sound in the house was the best we could make it. I then asked Romulus and one of the other members of the Relâche Ensemble who wasn't playing to give their opinion so there was a consensus among a group of us who knew the specific sound quality we strived for at each concert.

At a Relâche Ensemble technical rehearsal, Joe Kasinskas, Romulus and I were working together balancing the sound. Joe and I moved about the auditorium between the rows of seats, from left to right, down and up the aisles, suggesting adjustments in sound to Werner. Romulus was positioned on the stage, downstage left adjusting the sound quality on stage and in the front of house, turning left then right, stooping down, turning back around. At a point where Caruso's eerie taped voice begins a dramatic crescendo, that glorious Italian tenor about to reach for a "high C," Romulus spun around, snapped his fingers and said loudly, "Damn, those old Wops really had it!" Man, what timing. Pianist John Dulik broke up laughing, as did we all. Irreverent or not, it was a perfect comment, from one aging Italian to another whom in some people's minds will never die.

Romulus was a rather prolific composer for orchestra, chamber ensembles, choral groups and soloists. He created music both with and without electronic and tape interplay. When discussing Rom's music, I often observed he was a fine composer but a superb arranger. His arrangements were always "clean," allowing the original musical elements to emerge even as his personal stamp was placed securely on the work. Of the many pieces he arranged I especially love his *White Spirituals*, re-workings of early American songs, supported by simple yet beautiful harmonies and orchestrations. A performance of the White Spirituals always brought a tear to someone in the audience, or to someone at the mixing board.

The memories of Romulus and Relâche swirl around me as I relive my remembrances of those days, now viewed from a point far from Philadelphia in the early years of the 21st century. Romulus' vision in 1977 was strong when he saw in two younger guys—me and Joe Showalter—a hope to rekindle the spirit of adventurousness in musical performance that was sadly missing at that time in the city.

Romulus was a gentle, honest man, yet fierce in his commitment to social change and intellectual sincerity. He hated musical charlatans and reveled in the power of song, in the elegance of an honest musical line emerging from the natural rhythms of the body, and through the body the song emerges, challenging the mind and soul of anyone willing to listen. The song tells us Romulus listened carefully.

While developing a performance career as a flutist in Philadelphia, Laurel Wyckoff also worked part time at the Fleisher Collection of Orchestral

Music on Logan Circle. There—in a rich, resonant "fated" coincidence—she encountered Romulus Franceschini and copyist Frank Deodata, the "South Philly Contingent" at Fleisher: two Italian-American guys with very different musical backgrounds and perspectives on the world who spoke the same South Philly *patois*, a combination of Northern Italian, Sicilian and urban English. The guys also shared a passion for pork sandwiches that were the house specialty at Willie's sandwich shop on South 8th Street. Romulus and Frank often took Laurel with them on their luncheon journeys to Willie's, or some other greasy spoon, like Pat's Steaks, located in the Italian Market. Delighted to be asked along, she became their *confidante*, someone they could share concerns about family and other assorted cronies they rubbed shoulders with in the deep recesses of Italian-American South Philly.

Laurel once remarked how exotic it was to hang with these two characters. "Where I grew up, in suburban Atlanta, I never knew an Italian," she marveled. "I never even knew a Catholic!"

One day over lunch Romulus asked Laurel if she had a piccolo. "Of course," she answered. Rom then asked her if she would loan it to the flute player who was playing with the Relâche Ensemble on an upcoming concert. Not knowing a thing about Relâche but sensing something was in the works and trusting Rom completely, she agreed to loan it for a couple of weeks. "You can borrow the piccolo," she declared, "but the next time you need it I'm coming along with it." When Rom reported this exchange to me I was intrigued. I had just met Laurel at a party. Although we only spoke briefly I mentioned I had recently formed a performing group to play New Music. She appeared to be interested in learning more. After Rom informed me of her interest to play with the group it was only natural that she be invited to play on the following Relâche concert. She did and stayed on to play at every Relâche Ensemble concert for the next 18 years.

When Laurel first appeared on the scene I sensed something special, I knew she'd have an impact on my life but did not realize how profound it would actually be. I should have known though by the way she presented herself in our first encounter: confidently and forcefully, yet seasoned with a touch of naiveté.

Laurel has been a part of my life since we first met in 1978. What began as a professional alliance developed into a life-long partnership, a marriage of contrasting personalities in pursuit of similar goals. Together we worked to achieve a level of artistic excellence and personal achievement as we have each, respectively, evolved through careers in music to executive management of the arts and humanities.

Laurel arrived in Philadelphia after a year's study in England and a short sojourn in suburban Atlanta, Georgia where she was raised. After graduating from high school she moved to London for flute studies at the Trinity College of Music, a good school if one were interested only in European classical music. Laurel had other ideas and wished to have a more complete academic education with an emphasis on contemporary literature and the humanities. She returned to Georgia, enrolled in a community college music program and prepared to audition for the Juilliard School of Music in New York and the Curtis Institute of Music in Philadelphia.

While auditioning for Curtis she met the late Murray Panitz, then the principal flutist for the Philadelphia Orchestra. After interviewing and hearing her play Panitz discerned an intellectual curiosity not only about music performance but also about literature, history and related subjects. Accordingly he suggested she enroll at a school that offered other academic courses to enhance music studies rather than a school focused entirely on music performance. And he offered to give her private flute lessons. She accepted his invitation and moved to Philadelphia in 1974, supporting herself and paying for expensive lessons as, briefly, an exotic dancer in New Jersey. Eventually she enrolled at the Philadelphia College of Performing Arts, formerly Philadelphia Musical Academy, now affiliated with the University of the Arts. After initial studies with Panitz she became a pupil of John Krell—Panitz's successor with the Philadelphia Orchestra—graduating with honors in 1978.

Along with other members of the Relâche Ensemble, Laurel experienced a period of real growth during the early years. Her innate musicianship and responsible behavior mixed well with the other instrumentalists in the group. People in the audience often remarked that she personified the Relâche player: steady, cooperative, focused; her stage presence epitomized the esprit that I sought to create in the core ensemble. Then in 1985 we became romantically involved, and our affair changed both of us. Our shared passion for Relâche's success along with personal interests in travel, food and wine and a general intellectual curiosity affirmed that together as a couple we would arrive at a heightened level of awareness and professional accomplishment. As we entered into this new period in our lives, Laurel perceived greater ways she could contribute to the organization, not only as a performing member of the group but also as a member of Relâche's staff.

She proposed to work part-time in the Relâche office, relieving me of some duties I had little time for; mainly logistical matters like scheduling rehearsals, creating a music library and archive, scheduling travel for the ensemble, communicating with our new production coordinator, David Michael Kenney; doing just about anything in the office to help the staff through an intense transitional period as we began to build for New Music America '87, and expand the Relâche Ensemble's presence in Philadelphia. And did she ever! Laurel's organizational and administrative skills were as strong as her musicianship; she became not only an invaluable member of the performing ensemble but also an equally invaluable member of the staff. By the time she left in 1996 to become director of the Suburban Music School in Media, Pennsylvania, she was Relâche Ensemble's manager and educational outreach facilitator, positions extremely hard to replace.

As our personal relationship deepened, Laurel moved into the small house I had been renting on Wharton Street in South Philadelphia. Two years later we bought a house on South 2nd Street just below Federal Street. In 1993 we married on Christmas Eve in her parents' house in Corrales, New Mexico, a place that had become a sanctuary for us since we first visited there together in 1988. She and I shared in all aspects of the "Relâche Experience" until 1998 when we moved to Montana. It was apparent to both of us that our lives with Relâche had run their natural course. Despite the intensity, the ups-and-downs, joys and difficulties of the previous 13 years, the decision to leave Philadelphia was significant. In an odd and curious way that was not clear to either of us, we felt that our lives together had really just begun. And the journey continues.

Life is a sound check. And then you eat.
—Singer-Songwriter Jimmie Dale Gilmore

ON THE ROAD

For some folks, "new" music is a revelation, for others, a violation of common decency. Not everyone "gets it." Alas, some of these folks happen to be music critics. One, with the local paper in Richmond, Virginia, barely concealed his loathing for the Relâche Ensemble when we were in residency at an art museum down there. In his review he contrasted our performances with those of a classically inclined string quartet which, just weeks prior to our concerts, had demonstrated their "commitment" to new and unusual works by performing a premiere by "P.D.Q Bach," nee Peter Shickele. "Now, *that* is New Music," the critic declared triumphantly, offering this caveat to his readers: "Don't even bother to attend their (Relâche's) concerts, stay home and watch the World Series instead." So, I figured as a guest in the genteel city of Richmond, Virginia I would behave like a Southern Gentleman and attempt to reason with him, perhaps over a drink. He declined to meet with me, but did talk over the phone. During our conversation I carefully explained the intention of each piece on our programs, their role within a clearly defined historical context, and chided him for having questioned the artistic integrity of several musicians in Relâche. For my conciliatory efforts, he dubbed me "The Che Guevera of New Music!" Now, that's a legacy to embrace, which of course I did. No question this guy thinks he won our ever so genteel skirmish. Little did he realize he had actually complimented me.

This would be his unwitting gift to the Relâche Ensemble, as we toured the Mid-Atlantic region several times during the 1980s, through subsidies from the Mid-Atlantic Arts Consortium and Pennsylvania Council on the Arts. And I will always remember how two trips in particular to Virginia gave us a perspective on the culture of the Old South, or more precisely, the cultural differences which still divide the Old North and the Old South.

Relâche had been scheduled for a weeklong residency at The Richmond Museum of Contemporary Art. The diligent museum director, Margo Crutchfield, presented a varied series of New Music and performance art to accompany the extensive permanent collection and visiting exhibitions of contemporary paintings and sculptures on display, including several by American painters from the Abstract Expressionist period of the 1950s. For the residency, I programmed concerts and outreach activities with musical works mirroring the artistic activities, inclinations and personalities of prominent artists whose works were in the collection. Accordingly, our concerts featured works by John Cage and Earle Brown, both influential collaborators and friends of artists in New York City during the 1950s.

The works by Cage and Brown each used graphic notation allowing the ensemble to demonstrate how these scores might be similar to some of the paintings in the museum. We found that museum audiences were often intrigued to learn how musicians "played" zigzagging lines and splotches of heavy inked patterns drawn on fields marked by references to time and space and not to specific pitch or scale. Of the many works from that period to gain some degree of notoriety—or popularity—was John Cage's *Fontana Mix with Aria*, one of his most enduring and often-presented works for small ensemble, and one the Relâche Ensemble performed exceptionally well.

Romulus Franceschini had created an instrumental realization of *Fontana Mix* based on Cage's chance procedures. For this realization Romulus used a coin flip to determine all aspects of performance: pitch variables, duration of each gesture, timbre, dynamics, etc. He then created a score with parts for each player. Singer Barbara Noska performed *Aria*—for solo voice—simultaneously with *Fontana Mix*.

Aria was composed for the late singer-actress Cathy Berberian, a pioneering New Music performer who developed a vocabulary of extended vocal techniques to enhance her sometimes outrageous performance personality. She was among the most sought after singers of New Music by composers from Europe and America during the mid-twentieth century, many of them wrote works specifically for her. The score for *Aria* is one of these. In it Cage provides the singer with a good deal of interpretive latitude. The score is comprised of drawings and implied vocal gestures taken from then popular comic strip characters from the newspapers. Depending upon the singer's style and interpretation *Aria* might result in a hilarious performance characterized by contrasting moments of "formal" and "non-formal" or folk-like singing.

Aria was essentially a picture-perfect role for Barbara Noska. She often dressed in clothes a young girl might wear, with likenesses of easily recognized comic book characters sewn or pressed on to her jeans and sweatshirt. I remember an image of Lucy from "Peanuts" pasted on one of Barbara's thighs pointing accusingly across a chasm at Little Orphan Annie who was affixed to the other thigh. Annie stared back with a characteristic round-eye vacant stare. Barbara's performances were coy, sometimes cute, with her voice swooping high-to-low sometimes imitating a child's voice. Concurrent with her the Relâche Ensemble revealed the quirky personalities of each member yet somehow these diverse folks melded into a cohesive whole, the essence of the evolving "Relâche sound." For some folks in Richmond, Virginia, *Fontana Mix with Aria* was a true "art experience." And, despite the unfortunate music critic, trapped as he was between flatulence and dyspepsia, we felt pretty good about the residency and were looking forward to the remainder of the tour, traveling further into the heart of Dixie.

After the final Richmond concert we arranged to have dinner with several museum functionaries at a venerable Southern manse converted into a restaurant featuring regional cuisine. We loaded our instruments and concert clothing into our van, and, armed with written directions to the restaurant, we drove off to have a relaxing dinner.

There were nine of us in various stages of post-concert recovery; varying ages, body styles and colors combined to fill the van's inner chamber with a decidedly non-Southern character. Within a few minutes I had no idea where we were heading, or which way to go, so I began a series of maneuvers to get back on track, resulting in multiple U-turns across dark highways and side streets. From behind the van a strobe light began pulsing, illuminating the area around us. Then a siren, its short staccato bursts in tandem with the blinking light, signaling we pull over. As I eased the van to the side of the road everyone grew silent, apprehensive over the possibility we were about to be hauled in by the local authorities. And all we really wanted to do is eat dinner! A big guy in a trooper's brown uniform and Smokey the Bear hat stepped up to the window of the van, his hand resting on his service revolver. He peered grimly into the van and after looking everyone over stared at me and, with an accent peeled from under a dry tree bark, demanded, "Just what the hell do you think you're doing weaving all over the road? You been drinkin'?"

"You see, officer," I began, "we just finished giving a performance at the Richmond Museum of Contemporary Art and..."

"What do you mean a performance? Are you some kind of a band or something?" he asked.

"Well, not exactly. You see we're a classical music group and we've been in residence at the museum of art all week and..."

"You been here all week and you still can't drive right?" he interrupted.

"Look," I sighed, "We're tired and hungry and lost. We're trying to get to this restaurant, here are the directions, and we just got lost. So I've been turning around trying to figure out if we're heading in the right direction, that's all. So, can you help us find our way?"

"You're classical musicians and can't find your way?" he taunted.

I suppose he saw a way to take advantage of our situation. I mean here we were, a bunch of "classical" musicians with funny accents who appear rather uneasy in the midst of the Po-lice, driving around in a van with Pennsylvania tags and a load of musical instruments. And the spokesman—me—with longish hair and trace of Philly attitude. Well the situation was getting a bit testy.

"Wait here," he ordered.

We waited for about 30 minutes while he checked us out, growing hungrier by the minute, sitting in a van at the side of the road with floodlights splashed on us inviting every motorist who passed by to stop and stare. It's now raining and the temperature has dropped, and we're famished. Finally, he walks over to us and gruffly warns, "Okay, get on your way but if I see you weaving on the road again I'll run you in." Southern hospitality at its finest.

We eventually found the restaurant. It was only a few blocks away. The museum staff had arranged for a late serving; the restaurant personnel treated us like celebrities. We needed a good send-off as the next stop proved much less unpleasant than our encounter with the Po-lice but equally strange, affirming just how different some of us Yankees really are from some of those old Rebels.

The College of Washington and Lee is situated midway between Richmond and Norfolk, near Colonial Williamsburg, best known for their historical re-enactment of tedious tasks, like cleaning the cobblestone streets with quaint straw brooms while wearing period clothing. We were scheduled to spend two days at the college giving master classes, workshops and a concert.

We arrived at the college after a relatively short drive from Richmond—in a pouring rain. After being met by two cautious clean-cut students we were directed to the campus chapel that set atop a fairly steep grass incline. My task was to back the van up the incline to the rear door of the chapel, a fairly easy maneuver under normal circumstances. But the circumstances on this October day were not normal: it was raining hard and the ground was soaked. While easing up the steeply graded incline the van's wheels could not grip the muddy turf causing it to slide sideways slamming into a tree resulting in minor damage to the front fender. Rather than continue this impossible climb we unloaded the instruments and equipment and sloshed into the chapel to dry off and supervise the placement of instruments and chairs in preparation for our dress-technical rehearsal, open to all students and faculty. While rehearsing and setting audio balances I noticed two young guys peering at us through slats in a wall at the rear of the sanctuary which served as the stage area.

All I could see were their eyes, shifting back-and-forth from the players to me trying to determine perhaps what their next move should be in the face of "the enemy." It was a bit eerie having these mysterious eyes overlooking us so I said with genuine earnestness, "Excuse me, guys, would you like to join the others out front and observe the rehearsal?" No comment, they just kept staring at me through the slats in the wall. I looked around at the other students and faculty in attendance and noticed they appeared embarrassed, looking down at the floor or glancing around at one another. To ease the tension I called for a break. As the ensemble wandered off I stepped through a door leading to an area behind the stage area. In doing so, I looked directly into the two pairs of eyes I had seen through the slats in the wall. It was a sight I will never forget.

They were both short slight guys, maybe 19 or 20 years old and dressed oddly—an assortment of clothes fashioned like gray uniforms of the old Confederacy; they didn't fit very well. Images of smooth and smartly pleated wool dress blues that adorned my young body as a prim-and-proper U.S. Navy sailor appeared before me in stark contrast to the "uniforms" worn by these wannabes. Each of them had a Confederate cap scrunched tightly on their small heads with the distinctive emblem of two crossed sabers fixed above the little visor shielding their eyes. "You're welcome to join us out front," I suggested, explaining we were conducting an open rehearsal in preparation for a concert that night. They just stood there, stooped over, peering up at me from under their caps. Finally one of them said, "Uh, sir, do you mind if we pay our respects?" I was confused.

"Pay your respects?

To who?" I responded.

"To Robert E. Lee," one of them said.

"Isn't he dead?" I said, trying to lighten the load a bit.

They both stared at me in disbelief, horror actually at the suggestion that the patron saint of the Confederate cause was no longer leading the charge. And they were probably pissed at me for making light of such a serious issue.

"Well, sir, he's buried down there," one of them said while nodding to the floor then pointing straight down.

His body is there along with all of his family," the other guy said solemnly.

We just want to pay our respects today, on his birthday," the first guy said.

"Jeez, guys, I'm sorry. I didn't know today was a holiday," I responded not having the heart to inform them that Robert E. Lee's birthday is not something we tend to celebrate up North.

Go ahead, please. Pay your respects. But if you don't mind we're going to continue our rehearsal."

They nodded in unison then proceeded down a stairway leading below the sanctuary to a crypt containing the remains of Robert E. Lee and his entire family, their names elegantly inscribed in stone markers fixed to the wall. We continued with our dress rehearsal but I was haunted by the image of those two weird little guys with the funny hats wandering amidst the ghosts of Robert E. Lee et al. Imagine, "New Music" swirling above the remains of the South's most revered statesman. If we had known it was his birthday I might have programmed an arrangement of "Dixie" in a strict "Minimalist" style, arranged, or adapted, by any one of a dozen irreverent New Music composers who inhabited our marginalized world.

Eventually I became caught up once again in the business at hand, the image of our long-lost Rebel soldiers giving way to the challenges of explaining to a group of students and their teachers just what it is we're trying to do by playing this strange music. They were, I remember, a respectful group but completely at a loss to understand the music's history and place in the late 20th century. That is, I thought I had double-timed away from our boys in gray, when, out of the corner of my eye, I saw them standing just off the stage area, gesturing to me. I excused myself from the discussion and strolled over to them once more.

"Uh, sir, is that your van outside?" one of them asked me.

"Yeah, it slipped in the mud and banged into that tree while I was trying to back it up the hill there," I responded, a bit confused, wondering why these guys would care about our van.

"Could you move it?" one of them asked.

"Sure, but why? I'm sort of busy right now," I said showing some irritation.

"It's on the grave," one of them said.

"Excuse me? What grave? It's sitting on a patch of grass," I said now showing more than a little irritation.

"The horse's grave," one of them countered.

"What horse?" I demanded to know.

"Robert E. Lee's horse. He's buried there right where your van is parked," the other said.

"Oh," I said in disbelief. "I'll move it in just a few minutes," I assured them and walked back to the discussion not knowing if I should be laughing or pulling their hats down over their little eyes. If I remember correctly I reentered the discussion just when a student asked, "Why is the singer screaming?" It was to be a long couple of days.

Although it continued to rain heavily throughout our two-day visit to the College of Washington and Lee, the rain did not keep people from attending the workshops and concert. I can't say everyone in attendance was thrilled with all of the music but they were respectful, if a bit skeptical.

After the concert while the ensemble was talking with the audience and packing up, a man came up to us and complimented the musicians, expressing satisfaction with several of the pieces that had been played. During our talk he mentioned that he is a musician, a folk musician, that his mother had been a composer and was wondering if we knew of her. Laurel asked her name and he replied, "Ruth Crawford Seeger." I looked at Laurel then at the man and said, "you must be Mike Seeger." He was. We sat down with him for a half our or so and talked about his mother's music. He was impressed we knew so much about her life and work. Now, fortunately, many more people know her work.

We were destined to return to the South again in the future but next time we would be better prepared for the "cultural differences" that awaited us. The next morning we left for home in our battered van while the weather slowly improved, skimming up I-95 while whistling a dozen different variations on "Dixie."

During the 1980s arts councils in many states throughout America allocated funds to support presenting organizations in their efforts to broaden audiences' understanding of and awareness for new trends in music, dance and theatre. Essentially, arts councils provided partial or full subsidy to presenters when they programmed new works performed by established companies or ensembles that despite their high professional caliber, do not generate large audiences or revenues. During this period the Relâche Ensemble fit the profile by having created a unique repertoire of works by living composers performed with a distinctive sound and style. Arts councils throughout the Mid-Atlantic region listed Relâche on their touring rosters, ensuring a reasonably healthy number of out-of-state performances for the group. Among the states which generously supported Relâche was the New York State Council on the Arts.

Traveling by van throughout the East Coast, Relâche normally spent two or three days in each location conducting outreach activities and workshops in addition to a concert performance. Often a good deal of time gets spent working with secondary or music school students explaining our repertoire and how certain pieces are performed using newly developed or unusual instrumental and vocal "extended techniques" that were part of every New Music ensemble's arsenal. These experiences usually proved productive and ensured that we had a good if not excellent audience for the concert performance. There were times, however, when a particular presenter did not schedule outreach activities as a means to promote the performance nor did they conduct a meaningful marketing campaign. The result was usually a small audience turnout that did little to lift the spirits of the musicians or enlighten the local citizenry. Relâche was engaged to perform a number of concerts in upstate New York over a two-week period. One such event, scheduled for Schenectady, threatened to become one of the most dismal experiences Relâche had during those years, but we turned it around.

Like many mid-to-large cities in New York, Pennsylvania and Ohio, Schenectady in the 1980s was in transition. The manufacturing plants which had sustained these economies were in decline or gone completely, forcing the population to develop new methods of production and services. In the downtown areas of these cities there was usually a large Art-Deco theatre catering to the local citizens' interest in commercial Hollywood-generated movies and large touring shows like "South Pacific" or "The Music Man." Seldom does the program director at theatres like this one present performances deemed out-of-the-ordinary. Relâche was scheduled to perform in such a space, The Proctor Theater. Well, presenting the Relâche Ensemble in a place like this is indeed out-of-the-ordinary.

We arrived in the middle of the afternoon after spending several days in Ithaca and Utica. With nearly a week on the road, we were beginning to weary of the travel and rather dismal late winter weather: gray leaden skies and consistently cold temperatures. I was driving the van and, after a four-hour interstate cruise, couldn't wait to get to the hotel located just across from the theatre. So, I pulled into the theatre parking lot to first check in with the presenter and make preparations for the sound checks.

The equally weary musicians staggered out of the van to stretch, inadvertently leaving the van unlocked without anyone to oversee the luggage and, most importantly, an array of instruments. No sooner had we entered the stage door before two guys sauntered over to check out the van. Like a couple of low-level street thugs, they appeared to be peeking through the windows trying, I guess, to determine if this was going to be a good take. Observing this I bolted out the stage door and, in my best badass Philly *patois*, asked them "*whatdafucyadoin*?" Maybe it was the tone of my voice, or maybe it was the weary "don't mess with me" look on my face but they looked over, startled, then split, bounding down the street and disappearing into an alley. Damn, I felt right at home.

Making certain the van was locked and luggage and instruments were stashed under the seats, I returned to the theatre and met the program director. He led us up the stairs onto the upstage area. As we got closer to the stage I began to have this feeling that the stage and auditorium were part of a very large complex as I heard the approaching sound resounding off of the dark wood panels lining the stairwell. I was correct. The stage was huge, big enough to accommodate all of the New Music groups then active in America at the time! The auditorium had 2,500 seats, enough to accommodate *all* of the audiences for a year's worth of performances by all these New Music groups. I thought, what are we doing here?

After recovering from the initial shock and meeting the overly-excited sound engineer who was eagerly anticipating working with "real musicians for a change," I wandered out to the lobby to see what sort of signage they had put up and learn from their marketing department what sort of marketing and promotions they had done in preparation for our concert. Well, there were no signs other than the marquee announcing "Free Concert Tonight!" And the marketing people had apparently done nothing to announce our appearance other than a photo in their subscription brochure. No radio or TV promos, no interviews with college or NPR station and only one print advertisement, which appeared in the previous Sunday newspaper. I carefully explained the meaning of the name "Relâche," how when it's placed on the marquee of a theatre it means in French "no performance," that it's a play on words in the spirit of the Dada artists, Satie, Picabia, Cocteau, from whom we borrowed the term. How clever it would have been if they had placed—in bold letters—RELÂCHE! onto the marquee and invited a TV crew to shoot it while we stood looking up at it. Anything to pique people's curiosity, to get them interested in hearing music that they had little reference for. Nothing, absolutely nothing was done to promote the concert.

Disgusted, I asked the program director just why he had booked us into such a large theatre and why his staff did not do a thing to promote the event, explaining that nobody called our office in advance to learn more about Relâche and the subsequent concert. His answer, as you might imagine, was lame: "Well, you know New Music is a tough sell," he said, continuing with the usual line, "No matter what we do people just don't like contemporary music. I booked you guys because it was something different and because the arts council paid for it."

I really wanted to let Leo loose and give it to him, but refrained, responding, "Why bother, you're not doing anybody any good. There isn't going to be anybody in the seats tonight, it's going to be an embarrassment for everyone, especially the musicians." Then I asked him how many tickets were sold. He scurried over to the box office, returning to report, "Thirteen." My inner Leo was really rattled at this point so I walked away, down the long aisle of seats that I knew would remain empty, up the stage stairs and to the green room backstage to cool off. After a half hour or so I went back to him and suggested he place about 50 chairs on the stage, configured close to and around the musicians. Rather than give a "formal" concert in that huge, sepulchral, empty space, we would conduct a workshop including full performances of each work on the program. He agreed, relieved, I'm sure.

Well, true to form, that evening's turnout was just about what I predicted: perhaps 25 people showed up, all senior citizens. These were folks who probably attend every event at The Proctor either out of boredom or perhaps genuine curiosity. Just as everyone was seated in the chairs placed on the stage I noticed an elderly gentleman coming down the aisle, sort of swaggering. I waited until he reached the stage, stopped, looked up at us and asked, "What's everybody doing on the stage?" I explained the situation to him noticing that he was wearing various garment items of military uniforms, pants from the Air Force, a shirt from the Army, decorated with a WWII vintage Airborne insignia, and an overcoat from the Marines draped over one shoulder with a patch signifying the rate of Gunnery Sergeant. I invited him to join everyone else. He did, but not without reservations.

My job in these situations is to serve as master-of-ceremonies, introducing each piece by explaining the overall structure of the work to be performed, a brief history of the work and its place within a certain timeframe, introducing each player and asking them to elaborate on their role in the piece. Anything and everything that can be done to better illuminate the work for an audience about to hear music they've never heard before. Throughout the presentation this guy with the multi-military uniform costume kept looking at me, sneering at times, challenging me at other times. He sat cross-legged with his hands folded or clenched in a fist, squirming in and out of this position, often interrupting me with snide comments or dumb questions. Of course he was ticking off not only me but also many of the others who were listening quite attentively. I announced a brief intermission and without calling attention to myself walked over to this guy to see if I could reason with him, or at least shut him up.

The guy was probably homeless, I surmised, and came into the theatre to get out of the cold night. And he was pretty big, probably a veteran of WWII and years of working in the Schenectady steel mills, or some other rust-belt town. No problem, I figured, he's just like the old guys I grew up with in North Philadelphia. So, observing his Gunnery Sergeant insignia I mentioned that I too was a veteran, although certainly not of WWII, and I knew more than one ornery Gunnery Sergeant in my time. He looked at me with a bit more respect while I diplomatically asked him to cool it and give the musicians more respect as they attempted to explain and then play the music. It worked. For the remainder of the presentation he was quiet and attentive.

Afterward we held a question-and-answer session and, surprisingly, this guy had some pretty good questions. Somehow, someway we connected, not only with him but also with the rest of the folks in the audience that night. The experience turned out much better than I thought it would have and I like to think that we turned on some senior citizens to music that they would never have otherwise encountered. The music critic from the local paper attended as well and wrote a glowing review of Relâche which remained in our press kit for years after. As for the program and marketing directors at the theatre, they didn't even show up for the performance. Oh, well. But Leo was grinning. The box office manager delivered the check to me after sitting raptly through the entire performance.

Wesley Hall, clarinetist with Relâche during the 1980s, stands about 5'5" tall, straight blond hair framing his boyish face. An excellent musician with a superb ear for ensemble work, Wes was a good team player even when the overall concept of a particular work eluded him. His hobby was astronomy and sometimes on tours he entertained everyone by describing in vivid detail the alignment of the stars and their movement through the galaxy. On this particular night the stars were aligned in his favor.

We arrived in Troy late in the evening, a snowstorm severely hampering our short trip from Schenectady. By the time we found the hotel it was near midnight and everyone was tired and a bit on edge. Again, I had driven the van and was determined to get us to the hotel for a good night's sleep before beginning work in the morning at Rensselaer Polytechnic Institute, our host for this stop. I pulled the van into the hotel lot, unloaded it and got everyone checked in, everyone that is except Wes Hall. I couldn't find him anywhere.

After everyone was settled in their rooms I scoured the lobby for Wes. From somewhere near the bar I heard yelling that was definitely not of a friendly nature. It fact, somebody was mighty angry, and quickly cleared the area. Everyone in the vicinity backed away, some stumbling into lounge chairs that were scattered around the bar. I looked over toward the door and saw a large guy with his back to me gesticulating at someone outside, his huge arms moving in an exaggerated but aimless jab. He was about 6'7" tall and weighed in the area of 275 pounds, his bulk bursting out of a tight-fitting black suit with a large bald head sticking out from his massive shoulders. The guy filled the doorframe quite easily. What I didn't see was Wes Hall who was standing about five feet from him inside the doorway—obliterated completely by the man's huge silhouette. Wesley was looking up, way up at his face, Wes' own face frozen in a look caused either by severe fright or disbelief at the guy's size and fierceness. As the big guy moved outside to deal with whatever demons were disturbing him, I went over to Wes, still frozen in a silent stare. He looked at me and sort of pointed with his right hand, still not saying a word. Then, quietly and softly he murmured "The Sheik."

Who?" I asked.

The Iron Sheik," he repeated, and then he bolted towards the check-in desk. I followed him to the desk and authorized his check-in. He didn't say a word as he took his key and went to his room.

I stood there for a few seconds before asking the desk clerk what had just happened. He told me a bunch of professional wrestlers had arrived for a match the next night and the Iron Sheik was unhappy about something. "Oh," I said nodding. I went to my room resisting a side trip to the bar for bourbon or maybe two.

In C, Terry Riley's seminal "minimalist" work, consists of 53 short musical fragments or phrases played consecutively by each member of the ensemble repeating each as many times as they wish. Relâche had been performing *In C* for years, including a 20th Anniversary performance at the 1984 New Music America Festival in Hartford, CT with an "all-star" ensemble led by Terry Riley. Around that time, Rensselaer Polytechnic Institute's music department, headed by Neil Rolnick—a composer in the vanguard of innovative interactive electronic and computer technologies in creation and performance who has collaborated with the Relâche Ensemble on a number of occasions, including our recording a work of his for CRI Records in 1984—arranged for us to appear at Rensselaer, and included the work we had recorded with him, as well as Terry Riley's *In C*.

It's a dauntingly precise piece, which provides ample rewards for those in proximity. Values of all the notes in the phrases are divisible by two: whole, half, quarter, eighth and sixteenth notes, with appropriate rests. The idea of course is to listen carefully and decide when to continue repeating a phrase and when to move from one to the next in a manner that will match or contrast those being played by others in the ensemble, stringing together a tonally pleasing and prismatic tapestry of sounds that, when carefully realized, creates a meditative atmosphere for player and listener alike. Holding everyone together or keeping everyone in time is a "pulse" played in eighth-note values on the upper two C-naturals of the keyboard at a constant rate. If the pulse slows down or speeds up everyone can be thrown off tempo and the piece will not have the aural sheen that one has grown accustomed to hearing. To maintain a consistent tempo the player executing the pulse must work himself into a trance-like state as he's likely to sustain the pulse for as long as one hour, or more. It requires terrific concentration. On this night I needed it.

For this tour I was designated as the pulse player, a role I had assumed after years of playing the piece either on the marimba or vibraphone. Seated to the right of our pianist, John Dulik, who interprets the 53 phrases with the other ensemble members, I prepared to play the pulse by clearing my mind of extraneous "stuff." Usually this is a fairly easy task since the minute details of concert preparation and rehearsal have long since passed. Seated or standing to my right facing the audience in a semi-circle is the ensemble, my back—like John Dulik's—somewhat to the audience. The reason for this configuration is to allow the players to see John and me in case there are problems and all of us can visually cue one another with a shift of the shoulder or nod of the head. Over the course of many performances this set-up worked very well.

In C was scheduled to conclude the first half of the concert, just before intermission requiring a slight adjustment of the chairs and instruments. As this was being done I entered from stage right and took my seat next to John to wait for the other players to settle in. Normally during this brief interlude I use the time to enter into some kind of a trance or meditative condition by fixing my stare on an object at the rear of the stage, a piece of stage hardware or maybe the fold of a curtain. When the players are set there is usually a thirty-second silence before I begin playing the pulse. Just as I was about to begin John whispered to me, "can you lift the piano lid to full stick?" For this piece he wanted the full resonance of the piano to fill in with the ensemble. Needless to say this broke my concentration. I stood up, moved a few steps to my right to make the adjustment from half to full stick when I heard a very quiet voice say, "Hey, buddy, while your there how about checking the oil?" It was Guy Klucevsek peering out from behind his accordion, with a smirk which accompanied his pithy comments, or well-timed wisecracks. Everybody fell out laughing, me especially. Now I had to try to pull myself back together, to settle into a trance-like state once again. It was not easy.

I went through the ritual once again but could not concentrate. For a moment as I began playing the pulse I was fixed, steady, and then I began to chuckle, quietly, John Dulik trying not to laugh shushed me, the other players having the same difficulty as I was. Finally I eased into it and found a steady groove, everyone staying with the pulse to give a fine performance of *In C*. And it lasted exactly 30 minutes, the goal we had set for ourselves. After the intermission and another round of laughter the ensemble went back on stage and nailed the rest of the concert. This was the final performance of the two-week tour. The long drive home was punctuated with spasms of laughter as we recalled Guy's remark. It would be one of many such incidents that broke the boredom of long days and nights on the road.

JAPAN

I was about seven years old when I had my first nightmare, at least the first one I remember. I was about to have my tonsils removed and my mother was doing her best to assure me that the procedure would not hurt and I would only have a sore throat for a few days before returning to school. But I was not convinced and spent the days leading up to the tonsillectomy stirring in my sleep, worrying that with the tonsils out there went my voice. Years later I recalled this fear after reading Lorca: "*...the little boy has lost his voice, the King of the gypsies has it!*" On one of those long nights after hours of lying awake I fell asleep and entered for the first time the mysterious world of Asia.

Images from that dream are vague but I distinctly remember being with Asian women, their faces powdered white with elegant makeup which exaggerated their almond shaped eyes. Those beautiful eyes peered seductively into my young psyche. They wore colored robes that flowed with their movements and some had multiple arms moving at different angles, all enticing me to come closer. But I did not have to: their images floated in and out of view, some of their faces merged with my gaze, others swooped in and around me while still others pushed me away and pulled me towards them. I awoke frightened with a final image seared in memory: a chorus of women wearing gold pointed hats dancing behind a veil—*a scrim*?—enticing me to come with them, beckoning.

Were these women Japanese? Chinese? Thai? Vietnamese? Or were they Indian? I don't know. Nor did I know what this dream had to do with having my tonsils taken out. But somehow this dream opened up a pathway to Asia, one that I have followed over the years and one that has shaped my life in dramatic fashion. And for the first time in memory this dream introduced me to the "outside person," the me who looks through me looking at the world around me. The Japanese term for foreigner, *Gaijin*, translates into English as "outside person." I would eventually become well acquainted with this word. One question though: I wonder where the sound was during this dance of discovery? The women in my dream moved in silence.

Over the years I have tried to analyze this dream, to figure out what impact its meaning, if any, has had on my life. I was born in 1944 during some of the most vicious fighting between American and Japanese combatants throughout the Pacific Theatre. Exactly one year after my birth the atomic bomb incinerated Hiroshima and Nagasaki. In my early years the hatred of the Japanese among my neighbors, many of whom had fought against them, was evident. And of course television and Hollywood portrayed the Japanese people in the vilest way imaginable. Yet I found myself attracted to the Japanese, perhaps in defiance of the behavior of those around me. Their perceived dignity, reserved yet respectful, appealed to me, although I learned later on this reserved dignity could often conceal a steely arrogance and veiled racism. To gain a better understanding of these people and their recovering society I scoured magazines for photographs and articles; most often they focused on the "MacArthurization" of Japanese society, images of the general standing amidst the thankful people as he managed the reconstruction of their proud culture. Later in life I would stand beneath the statue of MacArthur located in a riverside park in Yokohama, burning and scheming for a rendezvous with mysterious women who seemed to be everywhere and eminently available.

Gradually the pervasive hatred and mistrust of the Japanese people began to diminish, replaced by a hatred, mistrust—and fear—of the Russians and then the Chinese. This led of course to another conflict, the Korean War, and yet another Asian foe: North Koreans. Now the images appearing in magazines and newspapers vilified the North Korean people who looked very much like their Japanese cousins who were being supported by the Chinese who had launched their communist society with visions of world dominance. Then in my teens during the early years of Camelot on the Mall the Vietnamese appeared, another Asian menace to be dealt with and kept from the imagined shores of an increasingly isolated America. Was my dream a foreshadowing of how Asian people would dominate life in America as I grew up? How Asian people would dominate my consciousness as I grew into manhood?

Was it also an early indication that Asian cultures would shape my aesthetic values, that exposure to what at first were alien exotic images would become signs, part of a value system and language to govern my life and career? I suppose the answer to all these questions is yes. But to what degree and how directly have these influences shaped me?

They began when I arrived in Japan in the mid-1960s, a young sailor with the U.S. Navy recently assigned to the Seventh Fleet, initially to an outpost outside a small village in Kamiseya located 20 miles equidistant from Tokyo and Yokohama. The Naval facility had been an ammunitions depot for the Japanese Army during the war. Just miles down the main road linking Kamiseya and Yokohama there was a Pepsi-Cola bottling plant which, 20 years earlier, had been a prisoner of war camp; barbed wire still encircled the unkempt grounds around the factory. Rice paddies dominated much of the landscape, tended by peasant-like workers who drove small three-wheeled Mitsubishi pick-up trucks when they weren't hauling goods attached to wooden braces settled on ageless shoulders. These images just miles from one of the world's modern cities—Tokyo—were startling for a young guy who had just been indoctrinated into the technological world of electronic intercept, learning to handle state-of-the-art equipment that could eavesdrop on conversations at sea thousands of miles away. The village of Kamiseya could have been lifted from the 19th century and dropped down in the middle of the 20th. What a shock!

During liberty and leave away from military duties I explored Japan, venturing into Tokyo and Yokohama, visiting the ancient cities of Kyoto, and Nara in the south and the mountains of Hakone just an hour or so from Tokyo. I developed short-term friendships with people I met at coffee shops and concerts in Tokyo or in bars in the Chinatown section of Yokohama. And like most young guys in my situation I developed even shorter relationships with the bargirls who lived off the largesse of U.S. military paychecks. I made failed attempts to learn the language while discovering which Japanese foods would find resonance with me. Few did. Despite my adventurous ways I never really developed a keen appreciation for Japanese food, especially sushi, although I like yakitori, skewered chicken meat grilled over charcoal served with soy sauce that brightened the taste of sticky white rice. But I did develop an appreciation for traditional Japanese design, especially the homes, apartments and ryokans (small inns), temples and gardens that define traditional Japan. Yet it was perhaps my exposure to Tokyo that shaped not only my perception of the Japanese but also my perceptions of a modern world on the verge of a radical transformation into the next century.

Tokyo then and now is an immense city, virtually rebuilt after the Pacific War, unyielding; its seductive colorful exotic rhythms coruscate along concrete corridors filled with sounds of industry, technology and play. A network of commuter and subway trains—always on time—glides overhead and below streets teeming with motor vehicles and pedestrians who somehow—amidst the seeming confusion—appear to be moving like a well conditioned army. The major sections of the city, Shinjuku, Shibuya, Ginza, Roppongi, etc., each have a unique character and sense of place with distinctive shops and restaurants, parks and museums, corporate headquarters and government offices that define their role in the megalopolis that is Tokyo.

I had been in Japan for maybe one month when I finally had the opportunity to visit Tokyo. That first month I spent learning my job and adjusting to military life overseas. Most of the guys stationed at Kamiseya were content to spend their liberty in Yokohama. It was only a half-hour bus ride to the main commissary—the Navy ran a shuttle bus to accommodate enlisted men—and from there you could walk or take a city bus to one of the main neighborhoods: Iseysaki-cho or the more popular Chinatown, neither particularly attractive to me, although I certainly spent more time and money there than I should have. When traveling to Tokyo I caught a train at Yokohama Station for the 30-minute ride to Tokyo Station. On my first visits there I rode the subways and walked the streets, losing myself, finding my way back; acclimating myself to the city.

After several months I knew my way around fairly well, having become familiar with the subway system and the streets which meandered out from the main subway stations. I distinctly remember my first image of bustling Tokyo: a huge electric sign advertising Sapporo Beer outside the subway station in Shinjuku. Thousands of light bulbs came on in sequence to depict the beer mug filling with beer, then overflowing down the sides of the mug. Spectacular!

The sounds of the city were deafening: a constant mechanical drone seemed to permeate the streets and buildings, at least in proximity to the trains and subways. This sound was unlike those I grew up with in Philadelphia, where the screech of the elevated train was distinctive but singular. In Tokyo, there were so many different trains all meeting and passing one another, their cacophony merged with, and modulated, the sounds of bumper-to-bumper cars, busses and trucks coursing up and down the streets.

Walking down narrow streets I heard recordings of Japanese singers singing popular songs, some I recognized others completely new to my ears. Clashing with these voices were the "ching-ching-chings" from Pachinko parlors that seemed to occupy every other building I passed, each packed with salarymen and housewives pouring coins into the pinball-like machines in hopes of a big payoff. And the smells: charcoal from outside street vendors' carts with fish and corn cooking on the small hibachi grill collided with the distinctive odor of fish cooking in gallons of vegetable oil wafting out from small kitchens behind equally small restaurants. Another smell not particularly appealing but memorable was of kerosene heaters warming numerous small bars in cold weather. I often walked these streets alone, trying to mask my appearance by dressing in a style setting me apart from other GIs. I could afford expensive shirts and tailor-made trousers, suits and jackets, even on an enlisted man's salary. During those years the U.S. dollar was worth 360 yen! I took advantage of the powerful dollar to buy clothing and shoes styled in Europe, worn with a sense of purpose and freedom apart from the conformity of most GIs who usually wore jeans or khakis and Banlon shirts, often without a jacket even in freezing cold weather. Although I sometimes passed for English my short hair probably doomed me in the eyes of most Japanese on the streets. I sometimes imagined them saying to one another, "another American GI, but at least he's well dressed and quiet." And I was unusually quiet when visiting cultural events, often being the only *gaijin* there.

I often learned about events by visiting the USO office in the Ginza section of Tokyo. There I could find schedules of events and purchase tickets at a greatly reduced price. I became acquainted with a young guy in charge of this desk. We often met at a jazz coffee shop to listen and talk about music. I was probably one of the few GIs he met with an interest in jazz and more "avant-garde" fare so he took a special interest in helping me out. I saw and heard so many different—and new—things during these years, from Noh Theatre to Kabuki, from the Miles Davis Quintet to recitals by master Shakuhachi flute players, from Indonesian to Japanese Bunraku puppets, from experimental films by Maya Deren and John Cassavettes to the mythical films of Akira Kurosawa, they were all available in bustling Tokyo. In this milieu I first saw and heard a new form of dance-theatre named Butoh which completely altered my perception of both dance and theatre, as well as music.

This memory is still vivid. I entered a small gallery someplace in the

Shinjuku section of the city; people were sitting on chairs and the floor in the darkened space. After a few minutes a light bulb clicked on to reveal a young Japanese guy wearing an oversized sports jacket and jeans. He then began to slowly remove his jacket without moving his head, his eyes staring straight-ahead boring into a gallery wall. The only sound in the space was made by people shifting in their seats and re-positioning themselves on the floor, and of course the sounds of the city seeping into the gallery. For well over an hour this young guy went through the motions of removing his jacket, first one sleeve then the other, then folding the fabric before draping it over a chair located next to him. When he completed the task he slowly reached up and clicked off the light bulb. The performance was over. I was astonished at the control he had over his body and how effortlessly he seemed to executive these movements perfectly in tune with the internal rhythms of his body, his breathing patterns in sync with the force of gravity that seemed to plant him securely into, or onto, the floor. I left quietly, not knowing how to behave, although I desperately wanted to ask someone what had just happened.

A week or so later I returned to my friend at the USO who directed me to this event. He explained Butoh to me in simple terms and suggested I find out more by researching it at the American Cultural Center's library. I learned that Butoh was then a very new form of dance and theatre that uses very simple movements to explore feelings and beliefs deeply imbedded in the psyche. These works are performed in silence and require enormous physical and mental strength since they often are designed to literally defy gravity. The dance form evolved through the work of dancers and theatre artists who matured during the dark difficult days following WWII, gaining a certain amount of popularity among new dance enthusiasts in Europe and the United States. I never saw another performance of Butoh until years later in New York, but the image of this man slowly taking off a jacket is memorable.

I had begun the process of self-discovery by experiencing new and challenging performances in all media. I had yet to begin to fully understand these experiences and place them in the proper relevant contexts, but I knew I was eventually going to become a part of something I could not yet articulate. With six months or so left on my duty assignment I was now faced with the prospect of trying to explain my discoveries to shipmates, most of them content to bury themselves in mediocre rock-and-roll and popular country and Western musics while, in the parlance of the military, "getting short."

When I returned to the states to begin my life anew I attempted to keep myself informed of developments in Japan with the intention of returning one day to experience life there as a civilian. It finally happened in 1989.

After numerous failed attempts trying to organize a tour of Japan for the Relâche Ensemble I received a letter from the American Consulate in Tokyo asking if Relâche were interested in performing at the 1990 Interlink Festival. Of course I responded immediately, informing them of our interest and inquiring what expenses we were expected to cover, knowing full well that the U.S government would not cover all of the considerable expenses for Relâche to travel there for a lengthy visit. The cultural attaché at that time was a man named Christopher Rochester who did everything imaginable to make our trip affordable including assistance with fundraising. Fortunately the Interlink Festival had a reasonably large budget so most of our expenses would be covered. To ensure that the Relâche musicians would be well paid, I raised money from the Fund for U.S. Artists Abroad to supplement the fee, travel and accommodations paid by the U.S. government and the Japanese co-producers of the Interlink Festival, an organization named Min-On Productions.

The Interlink Festival was a yearly event that happened between 1987 and 1994. Its mission was to create good will and share information through cultural exchanges between musicians in the United States and Japan. Each year a prominent Japanese composer was selected as artistic director for the festival, a good idea that ensured each festival would have a different artistic vision and profile. The artistic director worked closely with the U.S. Cultural attaché and Min-On Productions to select American and Japanese participants. It was unique because it focused solely on New Music. The artistic director for the 1989 Interlink Festival was Toshi Ichiyanagi.

Ichiyanagi was well known to New Music artists in America and Europe. He had been a close friend and sometime collaborator of John Cage's, having studied and worked with John on numerous projects early in his (Ichiyanagi's) career while living in New York City with his first wife, the artist Yoko Ono. It was probably through his association with Cage and Cage's interest in Zen Buddhism and other Asian spiritual studies that helped make Cage such a revered and honored figure in Japan throughout the late 20th century. In addition to overseeing all of the logistical matters for the tour I collaborated with Ichiyanagi to program each of the concerts and related

Festival of New American Music

INTERLINK 1989

Relâche

The Ensemble For Contemporary Music

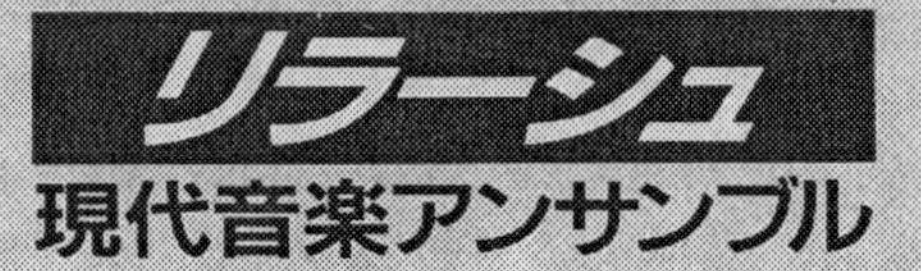

Interlink Festival poster

events Relâche would be giving. We agreed to include two works by contemporary Japanese composers on each of the concerts. As a courtesy I suggested we include one of Ichinayagi's, a work for solo piano titled "Piano Media" which Relâche pianist John Dulik had taken a liking to. Ichiyanagi was pleased. He also asked if Relâche might be interested in having a Japanese guest ensemble appear on one of the concerts. I immediately agreed, certain Relâche would benefit from a peer-to-peer association with Japanese New Music performers. Ichiyanagi then mentioned a group named "Kirik," a suggestion I thought was brilliant.

"Kirik" was a new ensemble founded by a quartet of young Japanese musicians who specialize in *Gagaku*, the music of the Imperial Japanese Court. Although trained in the rigors of Gagaku style and musical language, associated with the renowned National Theater of Tokyo, Kirik's mission was to both preserve the ancient form of *Gagaku* music and to create New Musical works in those traditional forms. Each of the musicians in Kirik was trained on Western instruments, from piano to oboe and flute and was therefore versed in reading and interpretation of Euro-American musics. As performers in Kirik however they performed on traditional Japanese instruments like the *Sho*, *Hichiriki* and *Ryuteki*, all wind instruments. After hearing a recording of their work I suggested to Ichiyanagi that Kirik not only perform on a concert with Relâche, but also join Relâche on two of the works we were planning to do that were composed for open instrumentation. I proposed a plan to Ichiyanagi whereby Kirik and Relâche would meet shortly after our arrival in Japan and rehearse Daniel Goode's "Wind Symphony" and Pauline Oliveros' "The Well," each group exchanging performance ideas and techniques. Ichiyanagi was especially pleased with this proposal. With artistic matters settled we prepared for the trip.

The Relâche Ensemble arrived in Tokyo in early October 1989 after a delayed departure from Detroit due to a mechanical problem with the plane. We were scheduled to begin a two-week residency in Japan with a performance and presentation at the American Cultural Center two days after arriving, resting and adjusting to the time difference. Our delayed arrival meant that the American Cultural Center event would occur less than a full day after settling in to the hotel, not a particularly good situation. Even though we all felt a bit tired we prepared for the festivities with little or no complications.

For this event we were to perform and discuss with an audience of Japanese musicians, artists, writers and scholars several compositions scheduled for performance at the formal concerts at Casals Hall in Tokyo. We decided to perform and talk about sections of Frederic Rzewski's *Coming Together*, John Cage's *Fontana Mix with Aria* and *Parterre* by Mary Ellen Childs, three distinctly different works. The presentation was scheduled for 5 PM After introductions by Christopher Rochester, Toshi Ichiyanagi and me, Relâche began to perform the sections we had selected. Somewhere into one of the final sections of *Coming Together*, when the ensemble and narrator have worked themselves into a controlled yet chaotic condition, as the music demands, I noticed Christopher Rochester was trying to get my attention from across the small performance space. Immediately at the end of the final section I walked over to Chris who then walked me into another room while the ensemble took questions from the audience. Without saying anything Chris pointed to a television screen containing an image of the damaged Oakland Bridge in California. A major earthquake had struck just minutes before and early reports arriving in Tokyo were alarming, reporting many thousands of dead and injured. Chris asked if we should cancel the remainder of the presentation after informing the ensemble and audience what had just happened. Of course I deferred to him.

We took a break and informed the ensemble while members of the audience began talking among themselves, having learned of the earthquake from the reports coming from television monitors located in the cultural center. Although shocked and not knowing precisely what the real facts were we agreed that there wasn't much to be done at the moment and decided to go on with the remainder of the presentation. After doing so, the questions from the audience became an odd combination of musical and cultural queries, some quite oblique, mixed with sobering recollections of having experienced many earthquakes as residents of Japan. After the presentation we were taken to a local Japanese restaurant and there began to learn more details in the aftermath of the earthquake which had struck the Bay Area in California—the death toll was fortunately low, although the material damage was severe.

As we began to prepare for the two major concerts in Tokyo—technical set-up, open rehearsals, interviews with the media—we found ourselves stretched pretty thin. Although there was time to explore the city, those intervals were at a premium since our hosts and producer, Min-On Concert Association, was shuttling us from point-to-point on a bus that appeared to be terminally stuck in some of the worst traffic jams any of us had ever experienced. Even though the men and women assigned to assist us by Min-On were extremely friendly, helpful and generous there was something not quite right in the way some of them acted. It took a few days for me to figure out just what that something was. It came as something of a surprise to me as I recalled a series of events occurring while I was stationed in Japan 20 years earlier.

During that time, a political party emerged in Japanese society whose mission included returning Japanese culture to a more militaristic or some might say "Imperialistic" society. "Soka Gakkai," as it was named, was then viewed as a splinter movement and too extreme in praxis to gain a popular following. Their organization grew in part by recruiting young poorly educated girls who worked as barmaids and prostitutes in clubs situated close to U.S. military bases located throughout the country. While I was stationed at Kamiseya, Japan, I learned some of the guys stationed with me were associating with these girls, clearly unaware of Soka Gakkai's cultish influence on them.

Most of us stationed at Kamiseya were involved in intelligence-gathering work so the command's officers were directed to steer their young enlistees away from any undue outside political influence for fear of their disclosing sensitive intelligence information to the locals. There was an apparent concern that these young girls, toughened as they were by their chosen profession, were unstable and impressionable, the result of having been raised in rural poor areas or being the daughters of low-life thugs from broken homes. Soka Gakkai offered some of these girls a family that they might never have had.

Some of them became attached to young American GIs and were eager to indoctrinate them to their cause, however vague it might have been. Although at the time I felt these concerns were a bit overly dramatic, and maybe even a little paranoid on the government's part, I also observed some strange behavior by a few guys, the result of their becoming a little too close to one or two of these young girls. Eventually and within a relatively short period of time the establishments where these girls worked were placed off-limits to U.S. servicemen. Over the years after I returned to civilian life I learned that Soka Gakkai's influence and impact on Japanese society grew considerably to become a serious political party. In the mid-1980s several prominent members of the Soka Gakkai Party were elected to the Japanese Diet, their mission to steer Japan away from U.S. influence had gained more credibility. My early and transient experiences with Soka Gakkai came back to me when I met employees of Min-On Concert Association.

As we were being shuttled around Tokyo, hustled in and out of restaurants and media offices our guides, or hosts, would ask questions about life in the U.S. Generally these questions were innocent ones centering on personal lives, families, feelings about current political conditions and personalities, how the Japanese—then per capita the wealthiest nation in the world—were perceived by average Americans. I cannot remember ever being asked a question about art—music, dance, literature by any of these folks. They usually asked questions in a manner coming across as *too* nice, *too* respectful. Underneath that nicety was something almost sinister; I felt they really were not listening to our responses but were forming—in their minds—answers they really wanted to hear from us. It was all somewhat strange, a bit disconcerting yet done with absolutely no disrespect whatsoever. In fact most of the ensemble members of Relâche did not detect whatever I was picking up. I resolved to put this feeling away and just enjoy the experience of being in Japan. And then I learned through the interpreter assisting us that the Min-On Concert Association was affiliated with Soka Gakkai, that Soka Gakkai subsidized either all of a part of their operations. Strangely, I was relieved to learn this, affirming whatever I was feeling, and absolving me of a perceived paranoia on my part. This knowledge now colored some of the professional experiences I had while working with Min-On Productions.

Our interpreter, an attractive young woman who spoke flawless English without a trace of an accent, was the daughter of an American GI and Japanese mother. Born in the mid-1950s during the American occupation of Japan, Keiko was educated in a bilingual program at an American school in Yokohama before attending a prominent university in Tokyo. I was especially intrigued with her since it was likely she was one of many young schoolgirls I used to observe during my military service walking around Yokohama in their blue plaid uniforms, giggling while trying to decide which of the girls was going to practice their English on the young *Gaijin*. Keiko would have had no such problem since her first language was English! She and I spent much time talking about our lives, she as an outcast in her society and me as not quite an outcast but someone who never quite felt at home in America. There was no contest in terms of our perceived roles: as a mixed race woman living in Japan she was definitely an outcast. And the behavior of some people we came in contact with proved this beyond a doubt.

The officials from Min-On Productions who accompanied us during our visit behaved oddly around her. It wasn't like they were rude to her, but almost. Keiko appeared to accept directions or commands from some of these people in a way that was both deferential and distasteful, at least to her. When interpreting for us she was a consummate professional with knowledge of American behavior and current trends and fashion, the result of having worked with many American scholars and businessmen. This knowledge produced nice easy-going exchanges between all of us. But I could not help noticing her demeanor was different during exchanges with some of the Min-On officers. I learned later in our trip that my observations were accurate and the Min-On people regarded her—as a mixed race person— as not their equal and treated her with less formality and friendliness than they would have treated a "full blood" Japanese. Keiko was not happy with this situation but clearly had become accustomed to it. When I asked her if she might be more comfortable living in the states she responded that her position as a free-lance interpreter was fairly lucrative, one she probably could not match in the U.S. And she—in her heart—viewed herself as a Japanese person since she had lived there all of her life. One situation in particular magnified this unfortunate condition, and it had to do with the president of Min-On Productions.

Kanami Yoshida was his name and despite his elegant posture and official position he revealed his true identity to me one evening at an otherwise extraordinary event.

He personally invited the entire Relâche Ensemble to dinner at one of the most luxurious traditional Japanese restaurants in Tokyo, located in the Roppongi district. The specialty of this restaurant was Shabu-Shabu, wafer-thin slices of Kobe Beef cooked at the table and served with numerous garnishes and flavored sauces by Kimono-clad women. The wine list was extensive with exquisite wines from Bordeaux and Burgundy among the higher priced items. Yoshida-san spared nothing, the waitresses kept coming and going with fresh food while the expensive wines were opened, tasted and approved by our host before filling everyone's glass. For those who preferred beer, Sapporo was the chosen one. As the director of Relâche I was seated at the center of the table directly across from Yoshida and was expected to communicate directly to him even when addressing other members of his staff. We hit it off quite well.

Unlike conversations with other member of Min-On's staff, Yoshida-san was interested in talking about music, visual art and especially film. Over the years I have acquired a reasonably good database for things Japanese, especially film and music. This served me well during my conversations with Yoshida. At one point he asked me if I were familiar with Akira Kurosawa's films. When I responded, yes I was and proceeded to discuss in some detail aspects of my favorite Kurosawa films—"Kagamusha," "Ran" and of course, "Rashoman"—Yoshida was surprised. He then inferred I must also be familiar with Toshiro Mifune, the actor who worked closely with Kurosowa during their long association. Yes, of course, I informed him. He then revealed Kurosowa and Mifune are among his closest friends and drinking buddies. I informed him that Kurosawa was immensely popular with filmmakers and film buffs in the United States, surprised that he found this surprising. When I referenced sections of some of the films with the accompanying musical scores, by Toru Takemitsu and others, well, he appeared to be deeply impressed. Good thing too, since our exchanges were becoming more fluid, the result of a never-ending supply of excellent wines. He began to make little remarks that would normally have been expressed in private, maybe in the men's room. This is when he expressed his disdain for Keiko, our interpreter.

He whispered to me that she was not a person of honor, forgetting, I suppose, that the part of her that ostensibly dishonored her was the American part. This comment stunned and angered me. The fact he said it with a little smirk on his face was especially troubling. Even though I was enjoying the hell out of the evening, ecstatic that the members of Relâche were being exposed to another level of Japanese society, this guy's nasty comment almost caused me to react. Fortunately I did not; I remember nodding my head and excusing myself to go the bathroom. When I returned Yoshida-san was in deep conversation with his second-in-command. Shortly afterwards he stood up, thanked everyone, accepted our gratitude, then left the restaurant. We lingered for another hour and continued to talk with Min-On's staff. I suppose Yoshida was "corrected" by his lieutenant and to save face, was the first official from Min-On to leave. At the subsequent concert performances we shook hands but never engaged in another conversation.

The Tokyo concerts at Casals Hall, a beautiful, recently opened 800-seat music recital facility, were successful in every aspect. Each concert was well attended, perhaps to 70% capacity. The overall response from the almost all Japanese audience was respectful but reserved, except for Frederick Rzewski's *Coming Together* when some in the audience responded with cheers and "yips," clearly caught up in the driving, rocking character of this piece. A number of Japanese dignitaries from the music world attended including composers Toru Takemitsu, whom I had a chance to meet, and Somei Satoh, with whom I and Relâche developed a professional relationship resulting in several superb works for the ensemble in the following years. Everyone associated with Relâche felt good: we had performed very well and had conducted ourselves with professional aplomb and personal good will. I'm happy to say that we received very high marks from the U.S. Ambassador to Japan and the president of Min-On Concert Productions.

I was home from Japan for a month before heading to Europe to work on details for our first European tour, scheduled for early 1992. While traveling by train from Amsterdam, to Berlin, Vienna, Warsaw, and other cities interested in presenting the Relâche Ensemble, I found myself mentally reliving the times I spent in Japan both during military service and the more recently completed trip. At this time the Japanese were riding high, their economy and luxurious lifestyle were the envy of many advanced countries in the West, especially some European countries who were experiencing social and economic trauma after the changes from communist control to free market economies. In comparing those experiences in Japan with my relatively newfound experiences in Europe—extremely meaningful and educational ones—I still felt the pull of Asia. I wanted to get back to Japan and tour other parts of the country as well as visit countries in Southeast Asia that were beginning to exert their independence after years of wars and genocide, their indigenous musics beginning to find resonance in the U.S. I wished to follow-up with the Japanese musicians I had recently met and hopefully develop exchange projects with them. I decided that I would return to Japan in a year or so. In which capacity and how I would afford the extraordinary expense was not at all clear. Eventually in 1994 I did.

Radio producer and on-air host for WNYC-FM in New York, John Schaefer, presented an excellent series of live concerts at Merkin Concert Hall for many years. One of these concerts was dedicated to New Music from Japan and featured, in addition to performances by the charismatic pianist from Singapore, Margaret Leng Tan and guest performers from Japan, a work featuring the American shakuhachi player Ralph Samuelson, who was also the executive director of The Asian Cultural Council. Having heard numerous Japanese master shakuhachi players over the years, I was curious how an American would sound, both in tone and style. Ralph was a student of Katsuyo Yokoyama, then one of the great shakuhachi masters, so I should not have been surprised at his (Ralph's) expertise on the instrument. I was impressed and decided to introduce myself to him at a reception following the concert. Turns out he knew much about the Relâche Ensemble, having heard the group perform in New York. As the executive director of the Asian Cultural Council he had received reports of our past appearance on the Interlink Festival. He suggested we meet sometime in his office to explore other exchange projects that might be of interest to Relâche and me.

When we met, Ralph explained one of the programs his office manages is a travel fellowship to send an American artist, arts administrator, writer or anyone interested in exploring current and future projects with Japanese artists to Japan for a lengthy visit. Given my background and interests in developing strong exchange projects between the countries, he encouraged me to apply for this fellowship. I developed a comprehensive proposal outlining the kinds of exchanges I envisioned, along with a potential itinerary which would place me in contact with artists throughout Japan, not just in Tokyo. Ralph liked my approach, remarking that too many applicants, and visitors, spend all of their time in Tokyo, forgetting Japan is an artistically, and culturally, diverse country, especially in other large cities such as Osaka and Kobe. I applied to the program and was awarded funds for travel, accommodations and a daily stipend to spend two months in Japan as a visiting artist. My goal was to travel around the country to meet with potential artists and performing arts presenters to develop an exchange program. Once again I headed back to Japan, only this time I was to discover a different country, one that allowed me to put closure of sorts on my Japanese life.

I prepared for the trip by initiating contacts with numerous Japanese artists and producer-presenters and arts administrators, many of them already known to staff at the Asian Cultural Council. On my previous European journeys I developed relationships with contemporaries through a network of contacts provided by musician friends. For this trip to Japan I would have official introductions made by staff in New York and Tokyo, these in addition to ones that I had already developed. Essentially I was given an itinerary by the Asian Cultural Council with the understanding that I should add meetings and visits to the ones they arranged. It took only a few months to organize the trip, scheduled for May and June of 1994.

The day before I was to depart from Philadelphia I met with Ralph

Samuelson in New York, the day when the U.S. dollar dipped below 100 Yen, to 98 Yen on the dollar, the lowest value the dollar had ever had against the Yen! To compensate, Ralph increased the fellowship award so that my visit would be almost manageable. It was, but barely.

I spent a total of six weeks in Japan and, as planned, traveled to other parts of the country in pursuit of new contacts and projects. Laurel joined me after the first three weeks, and together we discovered small community based arts and crafts festivals while exploring Kyoto, Kobe, Osaka, small villages in the mountain regions of central Japan and of course Tokyo. Once again Tokyo was the anchor. We had rented an apartment in the Nakano section of the city, convenient to rail and subway lines, just one stop from Shibuya, then the most densely populated section of the city, slightly ahead of Shinjuku with their newly constructed skyscrapers, monuments to the almighty Japanese Yen. These skyscrapers were also monuments to newly developed steel and design techniques allowing the Japanese to build skyscrapers over the roiling undulating inner terrain of the earth, a condition that produces daily earthquakes, most barely perceptible to the average citizen and some, utterly destructive. Despite the joy of discovering new regions of the country and meeting new people, the overall experience in Tokyo was not particularly memorable. How Tokyo had changed in just four short years! Or was it I who had changed?

Tokyo had become the quintessential late-20th century world power city with super highways forming complex geometric patterns as they weave around the city supported by huge concrete pillars, the roads packed with expensive cars which sometimes appeared to zoom in-and-out of the low lying clouds. Narrow distinctive streets I once walked along during my early journeys of discovery were now wide concourses to commerce, their distinct character gone; they all look the same. The train stations were still packed with people standing shoulder-to-shoulder waiting to buy tickets or enter one of the numerous passageways leading to the railroad tracks. Throughout the station a platoon of Middle-Eastern-looking men—young guys—stood in small groups eyeing tourists, purportedly stealing phone card numbers and selling them to other *Gaijin* who were now a ubiquitous presence throughout the city. The playful seductive neon signs which once gave Tokyo its unique character had been replaced by huge high-definition television screens that transmitted cute oversized images of men and women hawking products which could be purchased in any city anywhere throughout the "developed" world. And the sound of Tokyo was pervasive: a constant menacing low rumble looped in and around the calculus of a city that never sleeps. Despite being given a raise by my hosts, the Asian Cultural Council, it was virtually impossible to make ends meet during the six weeks of my visit. This was exacerbated by a visit I made to a small tearoom where I ordered a sandwich and cup of tea. The sandwich was essentially the size of those served at teatime in Britain, but without the ceremony. The bill for this small treat was $25.00!

I would virtually spend an entire day in Tokyo traveling to and returning from just one meeting. Sometimes I was able to schedule two meetings, managing the time it took me to walk and ride the subway or taxicab between meetings that, although in the same quadrant of the city, still took an inordinate amount of time to negotiate. People were still relatively nice but their manner had changed from that of earlier visits to Japan. At least I perceived a change due no doubt to all of the *Gaijin* who now lived in Tokyo; I was no longer an exotic but just another white guy on the prowl. As the trip wore on I began to look forward to our departure, first to Singapore, then home where I would dive into a new project I had created: "Music in Motion." The train ride from downtown Tokyo to Haneda Airport was a bittersweet one. I felt truly relieved to be leaving a country and a people that had helped to shape my aesthetic perspective as I came of age at different ages of my life. I have no desire to return to Tokyo. Do I wish to return to another part of Japan? Maybe sometime in the near future I'll get that old feeling once again.

EUROPE

If you build a retaining wall to keep a delimited portion of the earth from bursting through it, the wall should have a 5-degree pitch—leaning toward the retained patch of land. And the wall should be porous to allow water to flow through it so as not to build up moisture and ultimately decay the structure. This I'm told by my father-in-law, John Wyckoff, who erected a similar wall in rural New Mexico using large rocks placed carefully in interlocking patterns the way the Anasazi people, the "ancient ones," constructed their walls and dwellings throughout the region over one thousand years ago. Apparently it works. John's wall has withstood numerous onslaughts of rain, snow and high winds for 15 years, growing stronger with age. The Anasazi's engineering miracles have withstood even fiercer winds, snow and rain for 1,000 years as a visit to any number of restored ancient dwellings scattered throughout New Mexico and other southwestern U.S. states will prove.

During Christmas 2000 I visited John's retaining wall. Well, I visited him at his retreat in a desolate area in the mountains of southwest New Mexico. On Christmas Eve Day we sat on his wall at the foot of a steep rough-hewn mountain watching a flock of hawks circle overhead, observing, we thought, a mountain lion spotted in the area but out of our sight and sensibilities apparently at the top of the mountain. For some strange and totally unaccountable reason while talking about the durability of his wall and its pristine design characteristics, my mind flashed to an image of the Berlin Wall, that hideous structure erected by the Soviets during the darkest days of the Cold War. And I wondered why the Soviet engineers who designed and built the thing hadn't considered the elegant pitch of the wall we were sitting on in Hop Canyon, Magdalena, New Mexico at the end of the first year of a new century.

From 1960 to 1990 this monstrosity stood defiantly erect, running for miles along historical sections of north-central Europe, a decisive barrier dividing the people of East and West Germany. "The Wall," as it was usually called, was not constructed of porous material, and it was not pitched 5 degrees—leaning towards East Germany and the alleged comfort of a Communist controlled Soviet sponsored regime. No, it was ramrod straight, constructed of cinder blocks and concrete topped with barbed wire. Guard towers were placed strategically along its perimeter manned by armed East German soldiers, many barely out of their teens, who peered tentatively at their friends and families in East Berlin, when they weren't looking longingly at the free-spirited, affluent former friends and families in West Berlin. The Berlin Wall served as a stanchion, held in place by the polar spikes that divided the Communist and Capitalist worlds for much of the 20th century.

During this time West Berlin was alive with possibility, its streets, shops, restaurants and bars crowded with residents and tourists from throughout the world basking in the bright lights and freewheeling lifestyle. On the other side of "The Wall," East Berlin appeared to be in an eternal state of gloom, the city always seemed gray, its streets clogged with people who marched dutifully from job-to-home with the weight of Soviet military and ideological history placed squarely on their collective shoulders. The shops were often jammed but usually with people in need of necessities not luxuries. I remember walking into a bakery one time and, before placing my order, noticed a sign taped to the wall written in black crayon on brown wrapping paper: "Today's bread is not hard. Having no bread is hard." I ordered something sweet and left feeling foolish.

When "The Wall" finally came down in 1990 the frustrations of people on both sides seemingly blew the thing to smithereens; its remnants scattered throughout the now unified city of Berlin. The ghost of "The Wall" remained however for years after reminding everyone of its power to divide and oppress. But its memory also served as a symbol of a time past and a source of renewal for the new Europe. When, in 1990, the Relâche Ensemble visited Berlin everything appeared positive and eerily joyous.

This was the first European tour for Relâche after years of work in the trenches of postmodern America and following—a few months earlier—

a tour of Japan. After 15 years together with many of the players having served with the ensemble either from the very beginning or very nearly so, Relâche faced a crisis of sorts: the need to change some personnel. Several of the long-time members had begun to establish solo careers while others became disillusioned with the evolving repertoire, preferring works featuring their particular skills in solo, duo or "modular" contexts rather than a purer ensemble configuration we had slowly constructed. Through several unique collaborations the group had forged a distinct ensemble sound. Pauline Oliveros' *The Well*, described earlier in the chapter about The Yellow Springs Institute, is one such work.

"Listen...Merge...Match...Support...Soar." These are the keywords, the guiding words of the piece—the *urtext*—stated at the beginning in the "score" as a point-of-departure for the ensemble to develop the work: from an ethereal slowly evolving, soothing, meditative opening first section to a rhythmically steady second section propelled along by a staccato figure played ostinato by a percussionist on the claves, and then a return to a deliberate devolution of the opening character. *TheWell* assumes a dramatic participatory quality, with the players and audience merging with one another, each anticipating a gesture here resulting in a sound there...supporting, listening...soaring.

The opening section played by the full ensemble actually evolves from a brief two-three-minute prelude played by Pauline Oliveros on the accordion. When, on numerous occasions, she performed the work with Relâche, accordionist Guy Klucevsek, an original member of the first Relâche Ensemble, joined her. If the ensemble performed the piece without Pauline, Guy performed the opening solo, bringing to it his distinctive sound and personality, giving it a shape or context for the others to enter into. On this night in Berlin in a reconstructed ballroom amidst the ghosts of "Old Berlin" and in the shadow of the once infamous "Wall," the Relâche Ensemble with guest artist Guy Klucevsek gave one of the more exuberant and strange realizations of *The Well*.

Normally Guy, Pauline, or Guy and Pauline played the opening section seated along with the rest of the ensemble. For this performance Guy decided to enter from off-stage, slowly developing the opening figures and intending to wind up seated in his chair. The opening figures usually consisted of a series of long tones or sustained chords that build to a moderate climax then return to a point of silence or repose. Not this night!

Guy came blasting out from stage right, ripping off a series of loud dissonant chords shifting into even more dissonant chords. As he moved across the stage he turned from left to right, back to the audience then facing the audience; a dance not unlike the dance of the small man in David Lynch's fabled TV series "Twin Peaks" which haunted viewers in the early 1990s. As Guy moved past the seated members of Relâche, most of who were smiling in disbelief, he wound up in the audience who, in turn, were watching and laughing at the audacity of this stunt, loving every minute of it. Guy appeared to be in a trance, or some other state-of-mind; he was really rocking! But all of a sudden he fell from, I suppose, the unrestrained energy propelling him across the space. Wham! He fell flat on his back smacking his head against the floor. *And he kept on playing*! The Relâche players were in stitches as was the audience, then realizing that Guy was approaching that point where they—the players—were to join in, they hunched down in their chairs and began playing along slowly *merging...matching...supporting.* Guy then soared up and slowly—amidst cheers from the audience—took his seat along with the other members of the group. They proceeded to "The Well" with conviction. It was a truly fantastic performance.

After the concert we joined members of the audience for drinks. Everyone was talking about "The Well." It was the highlight of the concert and endeared Relâche to this hip European audience who, unlike some of their United States contemporaries, respect and celebrate the unpredictability of the American experimental spirit. As for Guy? Well he was ecstatic despite the rather large bump on the back of his head.

An invitation for Relâche to appear on the Prague Spring Festival was the result of having met several officials of the festival at previous New Music America festivals during their visits to the United States. We were asked if an invitation were tendered to Relâche, would we be able to raise funds sufficient to at least match a performance fee and expenses that the festival could cover. I informed them that yes, indeed, I felt confident that I could raise the money once an invitation was made. The formal invitation arrived at our office in early 1989 to appear at the festival in 1991. Shortly afterward it was changed to 1992,

And so, in the spring of 1992 The Relâche Ensemble left Philadelphia for a two-week tour to two former eastern-bloc countries: Czechoslovakia and Lithuania. Although the ensemble had driven through Czechoslovakia before on a previous European tour it had not performed there. This time

Relâche Ensemble in Warsaw following their Berlin performance

we were going to perform at the prestigious Prague Spring Festival prior to visiting Vilnius and Kaunus, Lithuania.

This was to be an extraordinary experience. For most of us Lithuania could just as easily have been a distant planet circling some moon in an unknown galaxy. We knew little of its history especially when compared to Czechoslovakia and its legacy within the historical contexts of WWII and the resultant Cold War which shaped our lives as teenagers growing up in the United States. And Prague! Here was an opportunity for us to experience first hand one of the world's great cities, one rich in Western music praxis and history, and a repository of European culture that was quickly fading away. And we were to discover in Lithuania a country that was emerging from behind the scrim of misery that so divided the east and west throughout much of the 20th century.

With a tour of Japan in 1989, a tour of Europe in 1990, including numerous visits to European cities to attend festivals and meet with producer-presenters, preparations just under way to develop a strategic Five Year Plan for the organization including an extensive commissioning effort, planning and presenting an expanded season in Philadelphia and now an invitation for another potential tour in 1992 placed the administrative division of Relâche on full alert. For an organization that had expanded precipitously between 1985 and 1987 in order to produce and present New Music America '87, and then carefully "downsizing" to a more manageable level we were, to put it mildly, in a precarious position. But to create the kind of international identity I envisioned for Relâche, it was essential to look far down the road and assume the challenging organizational responsibilities inherent to any aspiring world-class organization.

I began the fundraising effort almost immediately by meeting with representatives from Arts International's "The Fund for U.S. Artists Abroad" with money provided by the Rockefeller Foundation. The U.S. State Department—in a dramatic change of policy—lessened their support for programs of cultural exchanges and the National Endowment for the Arts—in the pre-"Culture War" days—did not subsidize tours abroad by American artists. The Fund for U.S. Artists Abroad was just about the only program of its kind during those years.

At the initial meeting I informed them of Relâche's plans, how we were making an effort to encourage exchanges of information and music among a variety of countries, and impressing on the Fund's officers how their assistance would aid the cause. Since Arts International could not commit to a multi-year grant, and also because grants to assist with tours abroad were awarded on a yearly basis at the recommendation of a "peer panel" review system, Relâche would have to submit detailed application proposals for each separate tour. As we were combining the trips to Prague and Lithuania into a single tour we were able to use the Prague Spring Festival invitation as an "anchor" to fund the entire package. The peer panel awarded Relâche monies sufficient to match the performance fees from Prague and Lithuania. We now finalized travel plans for the tour.

From Philadelphia we flew to Brussels on Swissair, then one of the world's finest airlines. After an overnight stop in Brussels where we could easily have purged our group per diems, but didn't, we flew to Prague. When the plane landed at the Prague airport the audio system played Smetana's

"The Moldau," a perfectly obvious welcoming tune and one that caused most of the musicians to smile, warmly recalling just how many times they had played it throughout their respective careers.

Our performance was scheduled for an old castle located downtown, across the street from a puppet store which seemed to personify Old Europe: small dark and musty smelling with wooden puppets hanging from the walls and ceiling of just about every square inch of the store. What character the place had! And what character the castle had as well.

Sparkling white walls decorated with ornate Baroque fixtures and figurines painted with gold leaf adorned the rectangular space, the acoustical character extraordinary. The Relâche Ensemble's sound fit nicely into the space, the natural acoustic properties embraced the ensemble's warm rounded tones and gave separation to the concertante sections. There was no need to electronically enhance the group, something we had to do in most venues. At least for this performance the ensemble would be viewed from the audience not through a network of cables and microphone stands but through a veil of historical events that transformed Relâche while Europe was transforming itself.

When Relâche arrived on the afternoon of the evening concert for a technical rehearsal we learned that the performance had been sold out for two months. Two months! Relâche had performed for full houses in the past but never had tickets been sold two months in advance of a performance. We were stunned. In addition there were television cameras and crews milling about the hall filming the rehearsal for a documentary about the festival. And a radio recording crew was marking audio levels for a live broadcast of the concert over a government-sponsored station. This was a very heady experience for the group and energized everyone to play with a bit more resolve.

It was a memorable moment for Relâche and a highlight of the organization's 15-year tenure. I felt redeemed. Relâche received little honor, or respect, in our hometown Philadelphia but here, in one of Europe's oldest and most treasured cities we were treated with dignity and respect, affirming stories I had heard for years from American artists who performed abroad. And although we had toured overseas before and been treated well, this appearance in Prague just seemed a little more dignified. Relâche played beautifully that night and was given a standing ovation from a clearly enlightened and enthusiastic audience.

We left Prague feeling pretty good about ourselves, not overly confident, just good with the assurance that we had represented American music of the late 20th. Century with dignity and honesty, imparting a balanced sense of playfulness and seriousness that characterizes much of the repertoire we champion. After the concert we celebrated with some of the festival officials and a few Czech musicians we had gotten to know. Among the places we went to was a bar featuring a Reggae band; the place was packed with Rastafarians! Jamaican men with elaborate dreadlocks dancing in the middle of downtown Prague was not something I expected to find and perhaps more than anything else that night prepared us for the two-hour flight to Lithuania scheduled for the next evening.

As the plane approached Vilnius strings of lights suddenly appeared illuminating the airport runway below, switched on by workers just as the aging Soviet-built jet began its descent. We later learned that those lights—as well as others throughout the airport terminal—were actually left off until just before a plane arrives to save much needed energy and money. After passing through a numbing series of check points at the small airport, the members of Relâche, with their entourage, continued a journey of discovery and illumination, when the simple act of turning on a light became a metaphor for lives lost in time and place and a realization of just how lucky some of we Americans had been during the final quarter of the 20th century.

Proud ancient Lithuania was awakening from a long sleep when the Relâche Ensemble arrived in June 1992. The oppressive Soviet occupation of the past fifty years had been deposed. Young weary Soviet soldiers who enforced stringent controls over a community of workers in Lithuania and throughout the Eastern-bloc countries were now slowly drifting back to an uncertain Russia. A long period of isolation, alienation and horror for the people of this barren land had ended.

This was the first time an American New Music ensemble was scheduled to perform in Lithuania since before the Soviet occupation, and musicians from throughout the country were looking forward to hearing music by American composers whose works they knew only from intermittent radio broadcasts or an occasional CD that found its way into the black market. Relâche's arrival coincided with a national folk song festival, the first held in Lithuania in many years. What timing! After settling in, the Relâche Ensemble—from another side of history—eased into town amidst the sounds of massed voices echoing off the sand-colored walls of buildings lining the narrow cobblestone streets of this beautiful old city. Dressed in colorful traditional clothing, choirs were on every street corner singing songs from the reliquary of their pre-Soviet past; the downtown areas of Vilnius resounded with an Ivesian cacophony of sounds celebrating the resolve of the people of this city within a country of song catchers. For this special visit Relâche brought a gift: *Lithuanian Dream Songs*.

Like so many other trips abroad, our journey to Lithuania was the result of months of planning and dreaming. The Relâche staff made dozens of phone calls and wrote numerous letters to convince various government "cultural" czars—on both sides of the diplomatic abyss—that our intentions were indeed honorable. Lithuania was one of several former Eastern-bloc countries targeted by Relâche to share musical information with. Our intention was to perform new American music while at the same time discover musical works by their composers whose styles and interests were compatible with the ensemble's.

Previously Relâche had developed exchange projects with Hungary, Czechoslovakia and Poland. The plan was quite simple: Relâche would perform in these countries, invited by various organizations through an alliance of personal and professional contacts with financial support from government agencies and private philanthropies. In exchange Relâche invited composers from these countries to visit the United States and hear their music performed by the ensemble. While visiting Philadelphia and New York City the composers gave lectures and workshops to a variety of audiences and conducted interviews with radio and print journalists. Overall these exchanges proved successful for all concerned, with Relâche gaining access to potential new audiences while enhancing their repertoire with works seeded in 20th century Eastern European histories. The link to Lithuania was more tenuous, the result of close personal relationships with members of the extended Relâche family, specifically Bridget and Joseph Kasinskas.

Joe Kasinskas is one of many composers who have had a long and rewarding relationship with the Relâche Ensemble. He has made a number of works for the group, several settling into the repertoire and performed numerous times. He is among those with whom I have worked throughout my career whose music always satisfies me. It is hauntingly beautiful music, honest, direct and void of any academic pretense. It is, simply and elegantly, the music he hears filtered through a variety of experiences drawn from a working class Connecticut background and re-discovery of his Lithuanian ancestry.

After military service Joe returned to school, eventually earning a DMA in Composition from the University of Colorado and launching a teaching career at Glassboro State College in New Jersey, now Rowan College. After enduring the insular politics of this institution he decided an academic life was not one he wanted to pursue and instead, bravely, took a job as a letter carrier with the U.S. Postal Service, a decision that has given him more time to compose and help raise a family while living in Cherry Hill, New Jersey just a 15-minute drive from downtown Philadelphia. Beginning sometime in the early 1980's Joe and his wife Bridget became interested in their shared Lithuanian heritage and with access to the Lithuanian communities of Philadelphia and surrounding areas Joe was able to dedicate a portion of his creative energies to study Lithuanian folk music. Bridget was an essential ally in this effort as she forged friendships and relationships with many in the Lithuanian-American communities through family ties and fluency with the language.

An accomplished violinist and fiddler, Bridget is as easily at home with the standard repertoire as she is with folk material. Born to Lithuanian parents—her father died in WWII having been conscripted into the German Army—she along with her mother and sister endured several German refugee camps until arriving in Philadelphia after the war. Like many of the early Relâche musicians she was raised in the neighborhoods of Philadelphia in close families which nurtured unwavering Catholic solidarity to the ethnic traditions of their particular country of birth or allegiance. And like so many of her generation she pulled away from these traditional bonds to create another life with less reliance on neighborhood connections and values only to be drawn once again back to those roots. And like so many others, the force of music lured her back.

After they were married in the early 1980s, Bridget introduced Joe to a Lithuanian immigrant named Bronius Krokys who survived the Stalinist purge at the end of WWII to arrive in the U.S. where he worked as an engineer for Kodak in upstate New York. After retiring he moved to Philadelphia to be closer to his daughter; he and Joe met at an informal gathering of Lithuanian-Americans residing in the area. During their initial conversation Joe mentioned to Bronius that he's a musician, a composer, and guitarist. Bronius then informed Joe that he sings; in fact he knows many Lithuanian folks songs having learned them by ear. When Joe asked how many he knew, Bronius replied, " Oh hundreds." Joe was intrigued and impressed by the man's sincerity. He was then in the early stages of studying the Lithuanian language, and although a novice, felt secure enough to ask Bronius to teach him a few of the songs he knows. Bronius, confident and eager, agreed. When they began meeting, Joe learned that Bronius did not read music—the fellow had learned by ear over 200 songs, an archive and living historical catalogue of Lithuanian folk music. Thus, Joe discovered a treasure trove of old and newer songs many unknown to other members of the local Lithuanian communities. He suggested that they continue meeting, with Bronius teaching the songs to him while Joe notated them by hand. After months of meetings and notating the melodic lines, Joe informed Bronius that he had enough and now it was time to begin harmonizing the melodies. Bronius, puzzled over this, asked Joe what he meant by "harmonizing" the melodies. After Joe explained how he would set them in a simple four-part harmony, Bronius replied, " Oh I can sing all those parts too." Startled by this revelation, Joe then began the process of notating all four parts. The result of their work was the creation of the "Lithuanian Folk Song Project."

In order to perform these songs they formed a quartet with Joe playing guitar, Bridget playing violin and Bronius and his daughter singing the leads. Joe and Bridget accompanied them and sang the back-up parts. They called themselves the "Lithuanian Folk Song Quartet" and began performing at festivals and events in Philadelphia, New York, Chicago, Toronto and other cities with Lithuanian populations. Joe was then awarded a grant from the Pennsylvania Council on the Arts to serve an apprenticeship with Bronius, something he had already been doing but now the relationship became "formal" and provided them with money to invest in the project to record and publish a number of the songs. Eventually the quartet performed a concert in Philadelphia at the Fleisher Art Memorial as part of the Pennsylvania Folklore Project, a program designed to celebrate the diversity of folk traditions in Philadelphia and the surrounding areas. At this concert I heard the folk songs performed in a context that Joe and Bridget had dreamed of for a long time. It was simply beautiful.

After the performance I suggested that Joe consider arranging a group of songs for the Relâche Ensemble and vocalist Barbara Noska who, by virtue of her Hungarian ancestry was especially adept at interpreting music derived from folk song traditions. I distinctly remember Joe's response to my suggestion: he looked at me and smiled, his bushy mustache spread across his face and said in his deliberate and slow manner, "Yeah, I think that will work out. I like the idea. Let's do it!" He did and titled the piece *Lithuanian Dream Songs*. Bridget coached Barbara in pronunciation and interpretation of Lithuanian folk styles and the piece premiered in Philadelphia in the spring of 1991.

Lithuanian Dream Songs is a haunting, gut-wrenching work of elegance and lyrical beauty. Comprised of seven separate songs that arc across a field laden with images of emotion and longing, the simple lyrics of a wedding song starkly contrast to a lament for those lost in the isolation of Siberia, the result of Joseph Stalin's wretched attempts at ethnic purity. Barbara Noska's voice rises and falls along the contours of the lines, coaxing the poetry from the text while the distinctive sound of the Relâche Ensemble provides strong instrumental support and commentary, the viola lines played with precision as Kathleen Carroll provides a fiddle-like playfulness to the songs. Overall *Lithuanian Dream Songs* was well received by the audience including a hard-to-impress contingent of Lithuanian-Americans who turned out for the performances.

At the reception following the initial performance I was standing with Joe and several Lithuanian-Americans who were discussing recent events in Lithuania. Each of these people—in addition to Joe and Bridget—had relatives still in Lithuania in need of certain items, like blankets, clothing and cooking utensils, among other things. I learned of monthly shipments of goods organized by the community and offered to spread the word among my friends in Philadelphia and contribute some items. In the course of the conversation I commented that it would be great if *Lithuanian Dream Songs* could someday be performed in Lithuania. To my surprise one of the people said, "Why not? Now might be the perfect time for Relâche to visit Lithuania."

I looked at Joe and asked, "What do you think? Want to try to make this work? Relâche is already scheduled to perform in Czechoslovakia at the Prague Spring Festival in June of 1992. Lithuania isn't too far from Prague. If we can get an invitation from an official agency in Lithuania and if they can provide hotel rooms plus a small performance fee and we can raise a little money from the local Lithuanian community then maybe we can develop a tour around our Prague Spring performance." Once again Joe looked back at me and with a sly smile said, "Yeah. You think we can do it?" "Why not?" I replied, "it's just a matter of finding someone in Lithuania to invite us. That shouldn't be too hard." In order to pull this off we set our sites on Vilnius and Kaunus, the two largest cities in Lithuania and residence of a number of friends and relatives of those living in the Philadelphia area. The process was underway.

After a year's worth of fundraising, letter writing and phone calls with Joe and Bridget heading the effort, Relâche secured an invitation from The Young Composers Society, a quasi-government agency in Lithuania to visit and give two performances. I was able to increase the amount of a grant that was initially awarded by Arts International for our appearance at the Prague Spring Festival to help defray some of the costs. The Young Composers Society offered a performance fee to be paid in rubles, a useless currency outside of Lithuania that provided certain luxuries: members of Relâche were able to eat quite well in the few restaurants open in Lithuania during that time. While in both Vilnius and Kaunus our entourage stayed in "official" hotels, large post-Soviet concrete bunkers that were dilapidated by our pampered privileged sensibilities but relatively safe and acceptable. The government picked up the tab for everyone.

Our first concert was scheduled for Vilnius in the theatre where the symphony orchestra performed. The theatre stage was small and acoustically dry which required that the ensemble have some type of sound enhancement system in order to balance the instrumental/vocal parts and sweeten them up a bit so as to project as even a sound as possible into the auditorium. The Relâche Ensemble, like most other New Music groups, is used to working with sound enhancement not only to project a more even sound into an auditorium but also to rely on a stage mix in order that each performer can better balance their parts against one another. Having been warned in advance that an adequate sound system was virtually impossible to locate in Lithuania we traveled with two small guitar amplifiers, microphones and a portable mixer, just for this type of situation.

The theatre, a medium-size proscenium hall with perhaps 1,000 seats did not have any audio enhancement system at all so Joe Kasinskas and I set up our equipment to provide a stage mix for the ensemble. The system proved to be adequate for the players to balance their parts within the group but did not enhance the sound delivered to the auditorium. And for this performance there was an additional problem: a new singer unfamiliar with the ensemble and its inherent composite personality.

Barbara Noska had declined to accompany the ensemble on this tour. Since most—if not all—of the vocal/instrumental works in the repertoire were created for Barbara's unique vocal style, having her not perform in these concerts would have normally been a serious problem. And since we planned on performing the *Lithuanian Dream Songs*, a work composed with her voice in mind, this posed more of a problem than usual. But Joe and Bridget Kasinskas had an idea: they asked a European singing star, Veronika Povilioniene, to perform with the group as guest vocalist.

Veronika Povilioniene was at that time among the most revered singers in Lithuania, or as someone described her, "the Joan Baez of Lithuania." She was a prominent researcher and interpreter of Lithuanian folk songs, having performed throughout Europe and the United States, including an appearance in Philadelphia with Joe and Bridget for the Lithuanian-Americans in the area. The decision to sing the *Lithuanian Dream Songs* was made just as the ensemble was leaving for Europe, so she didn't have much time to learn the piece. Fortunately Veronika knew many of the original songs that constituted the work, so it was a matter of her learning how Joe had set them with and against the instrumental accompaniment. To facilitate the learning process Joe and Bridget arrived in her hometown of Kaunus a few days before the Relâche Ensemble arrived in Vilnius to go over the material with her. This proved to be a valuable decision, one that not only gave Veronika more security in her interpretation of the songs but also avoided potential embarrassment for Relâche.

While rehearsing the piece with Veronika, Joe and Bridget discovered it contained several words which had taken on new meanings during the long Soviet occupation of Lithuania. For example in one of the songs the word "draugas" is used as a modifier for "swan" ("friend swan.") When Bronius Krokys grew up in Lithuania "draugas" meant "friend" and was a much-used colloquial term. During the Soviet occupation the word "draugas" was used to denote a much different person: it meant "comrade." When Veronika came upon "draugas" she became upset and was certain it would upset other Lithuanians in the audience. So they changed the word to "dear swan" instead of "friend/comrade swan."

In addition, they decided that Bridget would play along with Veronika, doubling her vocal line at the octave on violin.

Those decisions proved excellent ones with Bridget's violin lines adding a new timbral weight to the work's overall power. Veronika felt more at ease with the changes they agreed upon, her powerful voice—big gutsy tones—wrapped around each phrase, adding natural inflections and colorings the result of her familiarity with the songs and distinct regional accents in her native language.

Bridget Kasinsaks and Veronika Povilioniene in Kaunus, Lithuania

Back in Vilnius Joe, Bridget, Veronika and the Relâche Ensemble joined forces to give a moving performance of *Lithuanian Dream Songs*. Overall the concert was well attended and well received with Bob Ashley's *Outcome Inevitable*, Thomas Albert's *A Maze With Grace*, Lois V Vierk's *Timberline* and Eric Stokes' *Three American Folks Songs* performed for the first time in Lithuania. But it was the *Lithuanian Dream Songs* that stood out. To hear them performed in this context was powerful indeed.

We thanked our "hosts" and returned to the bus for the ride back to our hotel. A few new friends we had met joined us for a post-concert celebration at the hotel bar that was sufficiently stocked with black market spirits from Western Europe and the U.S. The next morning we headed out for Kaunus, a city even more out-of-touch with our 20th century American sensibilities than Vilnius had been. After a bumpy two-hour drive along roads cutting through an agricultural region of Lithuania that had not delivered much of a bounty in many years, we arrived in Kaunus, a city most of us had never even heard of.

Much smaller than Vilnius with a population right out of an old Hollywood studio's central casting department replete with elderly ladies in long skirts and frayed scarves on their heads and men in knickers, billowy shirts and tattered hats on their heads, Kaunus seemed to emerge from a mist, a medieval city of small winding dirt streets and pock-marked stucco buildings arranged in an Escher-like pattern. In the middle stood an old theatre and on its marquee was emblazoned a sign saying, "Relâche."

As we were leaving the bus to enter the theatre for a dress rehearsal, we heard someone say in English tinged with a distinct Polish accent, "Hey Joe, over here. I'm over here." I was as surprised as everyone else to hear a greeting in English and I assumed "Hey Joe" was meant for Joe Kasinskas, perhaps a distant relative or "postal pal" he had been communicating with trying to get his attention. So, I looked for Joe but he wasn't around having entered the theatre already. Again, "Hey Joe, over here. It's me, Litwinski." The rest of Relâche looked around at him then back at me and started laughing. "Damn," Douglas Mapp asked with a grin, "can't we go anywhere without someone knowing you?" I looked at him in total disbelief. He was smiling broadly as I went over to greet him.

Myszyslaw Litwinski, a composer-performer from Poland who creates magnificent vocal works set in an updated version of Byzantium Chant, singing while accompanying himself on harmonium, was living in Kaunus. He had moved there from New York City where for five or six years in the late 1980s and early 1990s he performed his music while shuttling back-and-forth to Warsaw. I was alerted to him by Guy Klucevsek and New Music radio-concert producer/host John Schaffer of station WNYC-FM in New York. I was immediately attracted to his eerie beautiful music and voice; a crystalline high tenor always impeccably tuned. His work was totally unique in the context of the then American New Music scene. After attending several of his performances primarily in churches around New York I was convinced he could make a compelling work for voice and the Relâche Ensemble. And I wanted to present him in Philadelphia as a guest performer on a future Relâche concert. After several meetings to design a plan to fund the work and schedule performances—a plan that sadly did not materialize—I lost touch with him. And now a year or so later here he is in Kaunus.

Apparently Kaunus is—or was—home to numerous mystical religious sects, which stood apart from the dominant Catholic faith observed by a majority of Lithuanians. These sects practiced an ancient form of worship that, if I remember correctly, may have deified, or was it danced with, the devil, I'm not certain which. In any case, many Lithuanians perceived them to be a bit odd or maybe even dangerous, and their presence cast a strange shadow on this sleepy old city. Litwinski was attracted to these sects, explaining in vague terms how he had always wanted to learn more about them while growing up in a rural region of Poland. Clearly Litwinski was compelled to shed his Polish-Catholic skin, to find solace in a mystical religion that, I suppose, fit more easily within his artistic vision. It was never clear to me just why he was living in Kaunus or just what his attraction was to these religious sects, but I was happy to see him and happier still that his connections to the artists living there would provide us with a valuable resource.

The theatre where we were to perform was not in particularly good condition. Although home to the local symphony orchestra, it was an uneven sound chamber and in disrepair with flaking walls, threadbare carpeting and uncompromising chairs. It was a barely usable almost derelict relic of a once elegant European culture. The dressing rooms and attached bathrooms were a mess, designed and outfitted for people more accustomed to living with detached outhouses on rural land or the perennial camper who prides himself on being able to thrive without modern sanitary conveniences. Inconveniently, the plumbing was spotty, sometimes not working at all or just barely. The toilets were similar to ones used in Japan: oval openings fitted with ceramic housing shells. Only these were very old and cracking, offering little in the way of creature comfort.

Having traveled extensively in Eastern Europe I had become somewhat accustomed to the abrasive quality of the toilet paper usually doled out by large unsmiling women stationed just outside the bathroom, a few scraps of paper in one hand while the other waited —palm-up—for a tip. With that in mind I prepared myself to use the facilities only to discover that there

Relâche Ensemble with Joe and Bridget Kasinskas kneeling in front of Kaunus theatre

were no large unsmiling women in waiting, in fact there was no one whatsoever to oversee the place. When I settled on the toilet I looked and saw in the toilet paper dispenser or shelf a few old brown pieces of paper. I reached up and took one only to learn that these scraps of paper were actually old program notes from some past symphony concert. Given my long-standing issues with the institution of the symphony orchestra I could have had a field day making certain less than obvious connections between that aging out-of-touch institution and this particular aging almost out-of-touch facility. But rather than state my case with references or jokes that might have been perceived as "insensitive," I finished the task at hand. As I was leaving the bathroom, Lloyd Shorter, the oboe player in the group and, like me, an irreverent ironic soul, looked at me with a disconcerting smile and said, "Did you see...?" "Yeah, I did," I said interrupting him. We left shaking heads that were full of wicked thoughts.

Like the theatre stage in Vilnius this one was also acoustically dry, necessitating once again that we employ our small sound system on stage. As Joe Kasinskas and I set up the equipment we discovered a problem: we needed six electrical outlets but only had five available on stage. Pianist John Dulik, who was traveling with his synthesizer and keyboard, had left his power strip in Vilnius, otherwise we would have had enough outlet sources. To remedy this situation we began making phone calls to find out which stores might carry an electrical strip. We discovered there were no stores in Kaunus who sold these strips. Stumped, we prepared to rehearse without electronic amplification, causing a little concern in one or two of the players, especially violist Kathleen Carroll who always felt she was being swamped by the winds and percussion. Then, from a seat in the auditorium that now familiar Polish-English accented voice floated up to the stage, "I think I know where we can find an outlet strip." It was Litwinski. "Come with me," he urged. Joe and I followed him out of the theatre while the ensemble took a break.

We left through the back door and walked down a narrow street into what appeared to be an old village. It was of course downtown Kaunus. Continuing we passed a large building with every one of its windows wide open, white curtains flapping in the breeze deflecting, I hoped, the dust that was being carried through the cool air. "A school?" I asked Litwinski. "The hospital," he answered. Occupied with this image of a hospital with its windows wide open I stumbled over something that turned out to be a someone. A guy was lying in the street just outside the hospital, his eyes closed and mouth hanging open, his face battered and bruised; he wasn't moving. Joe and I cast troubled looks at Litwinski and suggested we do something. Litwinski shook his head from side to side and said, "Come on, we're almost there, just around this corner." "But the guy could be dead," I said. Litwinski shook his head again and motioned that we continue on. We turned the corner and continued down an even narrower street with pedestrian overpasses connecting colorful buildings dusted with layers of soot. I felt as if we were entering the Underworld. Maybe we had.

We continued walking down this narrow street for another block or two when Litwinski suddenly stopped and pointed to a door. "This is what we're looking for," he said. I looked at Joe with some concern and tensing a bit I clenched my fists waiting for whatever action might develop. Of course I reverted back to my Philly upbringing—when faced with a situation I'm not comfortable with I prepare for battle. This turned out to be a foolish reaction as we soon learned.

Litwinski knocked on the door then responded to a voice behind the door that asked who was there. After identifying us a guy opened the door to reveal a site I will never forget: an attractive young woman in leopard-skin pants and halter top sat on a stool, her blond hair cut short so as to accentuate her small heavily made-up face, her legs curled around the legs of the stool. Behind her three guys were standing behind a synthesizer, guitar and drum set while a fourth stood holding a bunch of audio cables, interrupted I suppose as he was connecting the cables to input jacks on a large console rack-mounted against the wall. A rock band! In the middle of what to me was a dilapidated old town from some storybook past, these folks were recording in a studio that was well equipped with comparatively recent recording gear! And to blunt any concerns that were building in my Philly bones about perceived danger, these people were extremely friendly and gracious, eager to talk with us upon finding we're American musicians.

After the usual greetings, Litwinski explained our situation. The engineer reached down, unplugged some cables and handed me an electrical outlet strip with the request it be returned the next morning. I thanked him, reached into my pocket and pulled out a twenty dollar bill, U.S. currency and handed it to him. He was stunned. I'm not certain just how much $20 was worth when compared to the rubles these guys had stuffed in their pockets, but I wouldn't have been surprised if it just about covered the costs of their recording session.

On our return trip to the theatre we once again came across the guy lying in the street. He was still unconscious but now lying in a different position about ten yards or so from where we had first seen him. Again, we looked at Litwinski and asked him if we should help the guy out, take him into the hospital or something. Litwinski said it would be better if we didn't touch him. "See, he's okay. He reasoned. "He is in a different position now." Although Joe and I did not agree with him we figured he knew something we didn't and clearly did not want to get involved in something that could prove highly problematic. We continued on to the theatre, plugged in the equipment, ran through a rehearsal, took a break for dinner then returned to play for a small appreciative audience.

Following the concert there was a reception so the musicians from Relâche could meet and talk with members of the audience. During the reception Veronika confided to Joe and Bridget that she had to leave the reception to attend her husband's birthday party. As a courtesy she invited Relâche to attend the party after the reception and dinner. Little did she realize that the group would indeed show up.

Our Lithuanian hosts arranged for Relâche to have a bus and driver as well as an interpreter for those times when Bridget was off visiting relatives but at this particular time it wouldn't have mattered who was doing the interpreting since the misunderstanding, if indeed that is what it was, reflected more a "cultural difference" than a literal interpretation, or misinterpretation, of the language.

We all piled into the bus, Joe and Bridget among us, and asked the driver to take us to Veronika's house, she having given Bridget the address before leaving. I remember the driver not knowing where to go, confused with the location and not having any written directions. Eventually he found it just outside the city limits of Vilnius located in a compact neighborhood. Carefully navigating the large bus through narrow streets he pulled alongside a small house that appeared to be bursting at the seams with people having what sounded like a pretty good time. Bridget and Joe went inside the house, I guess to make certain it was the right one. It was. And it was full of people who were more than a little surprised that we actually showed up.

It seems that Veronika's invitation to attend the party really wasn't an invitation at all but a gesture that was intended to show respect for our new friendship or relationship, never expecting us to, well, accept.

The Relâche entourage filed out of the bus and into the small kitchen—already stuffed with friends and relatives of the family—and attempted to mingle, but there was literally no room to maneuver and the food and drink was pretty much gone since the party had been going on most of the day. In addition the revelers were doing what many Lithuanians do when they celebrate: they sing! Folk songs, popular songs, drinking songs, and everyone knew the songs, each verse flowing easily from the small groups or ensemble standing near—*what else*?—the kitchen sink. So the Relâche entourage listened until, at the request of Veronika's husband—the birthday boy—we were asked to sing. "Sing? Sing what? We thought to ourselves. "We don't sing, we *play*." The looks on our collective faces must have been pretty revealing to our hosts but they weren't very convincing.

I remember Bridget sort of taking the lead and, in desperation, suggesting that we sing an American folksong: "I've Been Working On The Railroad." Needless to say we all felt a little dumb. We had essentially crashed the party of a man who, in addition to being married to a much-admired singer and folklorist, was a high-ranking political official. Here we were standing in the middle of a bunch of strangers who were clearly enjoying themselves by singing songs redolent of their country's history and we Americans couldn't think of anything more resonant than an old ditty whose story was as far from our post-modern consciousness as is the act of settling a dispute by jousting!

I've been working on the railroad
All the livelong day
I've been working on the railroad
Just to pass the time of day.

Well, we were passing the time of day all right—actually it was nighttime—as well as passing the key of song around a bit as we struggled to agree on exactly which key "I've Been Working On The Railroad" should have been in until, thankfully, it ended after one verse since none of us knew the second or third versus. I remember each of us reluctantly out of the corner of our eyes looking at one another and waiting for what could only come next: applause and the next request to sing another song. Bridget again: "How about 'Old McDonald Had A Farm?" After my initial reaction to this suggestion—a look that said "You've got to be kidding," I smiled at the recollection of the late comedian Andy Kaufman who used to do an outrageous bit with this dumb song: he stood silently next to an old portable record player looking at the audience while playing an old vinyl recording of "Old McDonald." his eyes wide open until joining the chorus when they entered "with an oink oink here and an oink oink there." In that small house in Lithuania I felt about as dumb as Andy Kaufman looked. And I probably sounded just about as bad as he had.

Finally, our recital ended with each of us leaning backwards, bending as it were towards the door and the relief we would find in the cool dark night where there would be no more requests to sing songs that are unfortunately not part of our daily repertoire. *At least not without a rehearsal!*

The next day we drove back to Vilnius for two days of sightseeing and meetings before heading home, glad to be in a city that at least made us feel we were indeed in a city. And Litwinski? The last time I saw him was after the concert. We had a drink and vowed to stay in touch. I never heard from him again.. . .

During our final days in Vilnius we were to meet with students from the Lithuanian Composers League to discuss our role in the context of late-twentieth century Euro-American musical praxis. And we invited composers to submit their scores and tapes to us for our review in the hope that one or more might be performed by Relâche on a future concert in Philadelphia. In addition, they scheduled a concert of new works to be performed during our visit.

The concert was held in St. Casmir's Roman Catholic Church, a revered structure that was in the process of being restored to if not its earlier grandeur then at least a grander version of the one that has stood for years in defiance of numerous conquerors. Named in honor of Lithuania's archetypal hero, St. Casmir's served as a museum during the Soviet occupation, *a museum of atheism*! The original wood pews had just been reinstalled over bare concrete floors. The altar appeared to be new, as were the statues of saints placed on both sides of the sanctuary. Paintings depicting the Stations of the Cross were newly drawn on the walls, their somber images muted, the result of soft straw-tinged lighting that enveloped the space. Stepping from painting to painting one heard the movement of soles reverberating back and echoing ever so slightly throughout the bare chamber. This," I said to myself, is a great place to hear a choir sing. And it was.

Many of the works on the program were composed for a small choir, vocal soloist or a variety of instrumental-vocal combinations and all performed beautifully by students or recent graduates of the music academy. Each piece had clarity, a point-of-view or historical perspective that defied their youthful composers' lack of experiences in a broader musical world. One sensed solidarity of purpose among these folks and a total lack of academic pretension. Overall the performances were striking for their precision and mature presentations. The members of the Relâche Ensemble were all impressed and perhaps a bit humbled at the musicianship of these students. The next day we met a group of the composers in their office, located believe it or not, in the official home of the President of Lithuania!

The then-president of Lithuania, Vytautas Landsbergis, was a musicologist, his wife an accomplished pianist who hosted—in a first floor office—the Lithuanian Composers League. We learned much about their recent history. A few blocks away, for example, stood an old official looking red brick building that has housed the Vilnius School of Music for many years. During certain hours each day as the percussion students were practicing in the basement, a room was set aside for "inquiries" of local citizens by Soviet soldiers, their cries ostensibly muffled by loud snare drumming, tympani tremolos and upper-register pingings on the xylophone. No jokes about chamber music, please! One of the composers pointed to a location in front of the music school where a huge statue of Lenin once stood. Now there was nothing, just a pile of concrete barriers remaining as a memorial to those who gathered and brought down the despised statue with ropes and muscle. After two exhausting days our visit with the young composers concluded, our sightseeing ended and we prepared to return home, with a one-day stopover in Brussels.

I think it's fair to say as a group the Relâche Ensemble was shocked to learn how badly prepared we were to understand both the social and economic conditions informing the lives of the Lithuanian people, shocked to come face-to-face with many of our inherited inadequacies as representatives of a powerful culturally elite nation which essentially shaped the dreams of thousands of disenfranchised people in many parts of the world. For me the joy of discovery was muted by the realization of just how out-of-touch I had become in some areas of basic social interactions, like participating and sharing in the joy of song. I'm being candid here: I viewed myself as a savior of sorts, the guy who would lead an envoy of "culturally enlightened" artists into the "developing world," and, essentially, offer the natives the bounty of America's musical largesse. How wrong I was.

Then music must at times terrify,
It must shake men by the throats,
It must extol the virtues of full stomachs and fat laughing babies,
It must bring social as well as aesthetic order to our lives

—Archie Shepp, Musician

NEW MUSIC AMERICA

It was a time in the history of 20th century music when the lines separating musical forms, styles and languages were dissolving rapidly. In the summer of 1979 the Kitchen, a venturesome performance space in downtown Manhattan, sponsored what would eventually become "New Music America," yearly festivals of New Music, installation art, video and performance art produced in a different city by different people and organizations over an 11-year period.

"New Music New York" was a series of events, a "mini-festival," really, organized by an alliance of professionals led by Mimi Johnson, Director of Performing Arts Services, Mary Griffin (then Mary MacArthur), Executive Director and Rhys Chatham, Music Director for the Kitchen. Its intent was to showcase New Music and other hard-to-pigeonhole performance art works and broaden the audience base for these works. The festival's producers hoped to forge closer alliances among performers, presenters, producers and journalists interested in New Music by hosting discussion sessions to explore issues of programming, promotion, marketing and fundraising. This was the first time the term "New Music" was used to reference New Musical works that were emerging from the furtive artistic streams flowing away from American Modernism.

Rooted in the American experimental traditions of John Cage, Lou Harrison, Conlon Nancarrow and others, composer-performers like Phillip Glass, Steve Reich and Robert Ashley were developing musical forms which combined new tonalities with theatre and evolving audio technologies to create collaborative ensemble, solo and inter-media works. The European-derived concept of "the composer," someone who writes music for another person or group of performers using a musical language based on Euro-American theories ands styles, was changing in concept and practice.

Composer-performers residing mainly although not exclusively in downtown New York City were giving concerts in any "alternative space" that would host them, from art galleries and artist's lofts to retail stores and street corners. These artists were primarily performers with interests in non-traditional performance practices. Some were trained in conservatories and/or university music schools in the practice of Western "classical" music. Others developed their skills by playing in rock or "jazz" ensembles and bands. All sought to create new works they would then play either as soloists or with others in the context of small groups.

Many composer-performers integrated evolving computer and electronic technologies in their works, collaborating with engineers and designers to develop new performance techniques and, in some instances, new instruments to alter or manipulate real-time or recorded sounds. Others, like Glass and Reich, formed ensembles of highly skilled musicians to play only their music while serving as conductor-performers in their ensembles. Visual and conceptual artists—also skilled musicians—created site-specific interactive sound installations to explore the acoustic characteristics of a room or other similar locations. Improvisational musicians in a variety of styles from "jazz" to "world" musics became an integral part of this loosely defined, impossible to categorize period of burgeoning artistic activity.

"New Music New York" celebrated the music and artistic vision of these artists. I attended the festival with my friend, the late Annson Kenney. We were attracted to the festival not only to hear new works but also to hear others who had gained some degree of popularity (or notoriety) within the shadow world of New Music in America. Among the works we were most eager to hear and see was *The Wolfman* by Robert Ashley.

To our knowledge, only Robert Ashley had previously performed *The Wolfman*. It requires a performer to sing loudly—very loudly—into a microphone a tone that slides over the range of an octave (or more). The voice is "accompanied" by a separate taped composition. The performer is required to, (from Bob Ashley's instructions that appeared in the July 1968 edition of *Source – music of the avant garde*) "slide the top front surface of the tongue from extreme front (against the teeth) to extreme back along the roof of the mouth, thus producing a range of 'vowels'.") By manipulating the tone production technique, the vocal sound (in combination with the taped sounds) becomes increasingly louder and louder. Then the sounds are controlled in a manner that causes severe audio feedback at a level that is approximately comparable to ½ watt of available power for every seat in the performance space.. The resultant sound can be painful, causing members of the audience to flee the space with hands over their scorched ears. In its brief history *The Wolfman* caused controversy wherever it was performed and this night was no exception.

Almost everybody fled the Kitchen as Bob, bathed in an amber light, dark wrap-around sun glasses hiding his intense stare and sweating in tempo while leaning into the microphone, produced a very, very loud sound. It was loud, but strangely soothing. Annson and I stayed throughout the performance, among a handful to do so. There was no other work on the festival which profoundly elicited an immediate reaction from the audience as *The Wolfman* did. There were a number of other works that were successful, some entering the repertoire of performers and ensembles for years thereafter. Of course there were others that were honorable failures and still others that were downright awful, but that's the joy of events such as these.

The festival was memorable not only for having the opportunity to hear a continuous stream of New Music works but it provided for me an opportunity to meet artists I had been listening to via recordings and reading about in journals and publications. *Source* and *Soundings*, for example, were among the few publications available during the 1970s dedicated exclusively to interviews and analysis of pioneering works in New Music and performance. It was an event that brought the emerging East Coast New Music community together, giving me access to what was then a fairly small, insular group of people. To them I became known as "the guy in Philadelphia, the Relâche guy," becoming, I suppose, something of an insider myself.

"New Music New York" was a transforming experience for me. I felt an immediate kinship with other artists and producer-presenters there. I sensed movement—something was beginning to happen that would take this music out of the margins and place it before the public. Since there was not an audience sufficient to support the work it became essential to develop an awareness and appreciation of "new" music within the offices of foundations and corporate philanthropies; to encourage their contributions to present the music and develop long-range marketing, promotional and fundraising strategies to propel the music forward and hopefully build an audience to support future endeavors. Other participants felt the same enthusiasm. A group of producer-presenters and composer-performers met informally to discuss ways to keep the momentum going and urge someone somewhere outside of New York City to present another festival, hopefully within a year's time. The organization to step up and meet the challenge was the Walker Art Center in Minneapolis who organized and presented a festival the following year called "New Music America."

"The New Music America Festival" officially premiered at the Walker Art Center in the summer of 1980 under the artistic direction of Nigel Redden, Director of Programs at Walker with assistance from composer Libby Larsen, then director of the Minnesota Composers Forum, now renamed the American Composers Alliance. Many of those who attended "New Music New York" also attended and performed in the Walker's "New Music America" festival. Others were selected from a corps of artists living in the Midwest and West Coast.

The Walker Art Center promoted the festival well. Once word started getting around the New Music community, the festival began to attract audiences from the east and west coasts, Chicago and smaller cities throughout the Midwest, Southwest and Southeast as well as from Toronto and Vancouver, Canada. Each day during the festival public meetings were scheduled to continue the dialogue begun in New York the previous year. Since more people attended the festival at Walker more attended the public meetings. These resulted in our learning what was happening in New Music circles in other cities around the country. Others began to speculate on how a similar festival might energize their cities and communities. Essentially, we began to share information and determine the potential to present festivals in a different city each year. As a consequence of these meetings an organization named "The New Music Alliance" was formed.

Consisting of presenters, artists' agents and composer-performers, the New Music Alliance began as a loosely organized group which planned to hold meetings before and during future New Music America festivals and continue a dialogue for action among members. To provide leadership to the fledgling group a board of directors was elected by the members. The board drew up a set of by-laws and elected officials. It was determined that there would be no central office. Each year the producer-presenter of the festival would serve as president for the following year. And each year a new set of officers was elected. As you might imagine, the New Music Alliance was successful at some of their tasks and not so successful with others. But it was a start.

Eventually the New Music Alliance became a not-for-profit organization with the intention to raise funds to assist independent producers for future New Music America festivals. In reality the Alliance proved less than effective at fundraising but highly effective at giving a voice to New Music in America and assistance to producer-presenters of the festival. San Francisco was selected as the site of the third New Music America Festival in 1981. Under the leadership of the late Robin Kirck, a consortium of presenters from New Langton Arts to the Exploratorium presented the festival adding film and video to the mix of New Music and installation art.

Although eager to do so, I was not able to attend New Music America 1981 in San Francisco. I did however participate virtually since National Public Radio broadcast highlights of the festival each night. Fortunately for me and other radio listeners in Philadelphia WUHY-FM (now WHYY-FM) broadcast the programs nightly.

Since the programs were broadcast late at night in Philadelphia, I was able to hear live events in addition to others taped earlier in the day. Each performance had commentary by Charles Amirkhanian, the fine composer-performer of text-sound works and then pioneering music director for Pacifica Radio station KPFK in San Francisco. Listening to those broadcasts was a magical experience for anyone who loves the medium of radio.

Most of the performances featured on the programs were held at "non-traditional" venues or certainly in unique settings. For example, Ingram Marshall's beautiful piece titled *Fog Tropes* was performed along the waterfront of San Francisco Bay, a collage of recorded sounds from the maritime areas of San Francisco shimmered across the water and right into ones' living room. I began to envision performances in somewhat similar settings along the historic waterfront and Olde City sections of Philadelphia. I looked forward to 1982 when the festival would be held in Chicago.

"Mayor Byrne's New Music America Festival '82," named after the sitting mayor, Jane Byrne, and sponsored by the Mayor's Office of Special Events and the *Chicago Tribune* was slated to be larger and more diverse than the previous two festivals. The festival's producers, Peter Gena, Alene Valkanus and Kyle Gann programmed a variety of performances and events. For 10 days, from the Navy Pier's multi-faceted evening concerts to afternoon sessions at the public library to sound installations along the waterfront of Lake Michigan, the city was alive with New Music and related events. Many remain vivid in my mind: I especially remember a performance by Glenn Branca, who created music for a large choir of amplified just-intoned electric guitars, to be played loudly, very loudly, so loud in fact that many people streamed out of the performance. The next day at a public gathering in response to a question about the work, John Cage who customarily never said anything negative about another composer's work, remarked, perhaps jokingly, "Mr. Branca's music made my knees hurt." Later, after talking with Branca he was much more conciliatory.

I attended the entire festival, taking in as many events as I could, making new friends while expanding my personal network of performers, composers, producer-presenters and media artists. I also attended all of the public meetings of the New Music Alliance making it known to everyone that I was formulating plans to present the festival in Philadelphia. I made it clear that I welcomed their assistance and, essentially, made every effort to become a working member of the Alliance. At the final meeting I was elected to the board of directors, where, among other issues, the Alliance sanctioned festivals for 1983 in Washington, D.C. and 1984 in Hartford, Connecticut. I returned to Philadelphia with a sketch of a plan to present the festival in 1986.

Bill Warrell, Executive Director of District Curators, joined a coalition with the Washington Performing Arts Society and 9th Street Crossings Festival to present New Music America 1983 in Washington, D.C.. Although I could not attend that year's festival I did attend the New Music Alliance meetings Bill hosted in the months preceding the festival. During those meetings I continued to develop my plans, sharing ideas with other Alliance members and gauging if, indeed, 1986 would be the right year for Philadelphia. Although I calculated I'd need at least a three-year lead-time to draw up a final plan and fundraising strategy, events in Philadelphia and other cities interested in hosting the festival forced me to reconsider 1986.

Joseph Celli, then Executive Director of Real Art Ways in Hartford, Connecticut, and Vice President of the New Music Alliance, produced the festival in Hartford in 1984. Joseph and I had become friends and, among the issues we discussed over the phone and in meetings in New York City were plans for future festivals. Since composer-performers Carl Stone and Joan La Barbara were organizing a coalition in Los Angeles to present the festival in 1985 and Pauline Oliveros, along with a group of Houston artists working closely with the Houston Festival Foundation and Diverse Works—a leading performance venue—were doing the same thing in Houston it made perfect sense for me to concentrate on 1987. I prepared a first draft of a business and artistic plan and presented it to the New Music Alliance during New Music America '84 in Hartford, a festival that for many reasons was the most important one I attended.

The Relâche Ensemble was a performing group showcased at that year's festival. So, in addition to all of the business I had planned to explore with the New Music Alliance, I was responsible to coordinate the ensemble's performances which included two works commissioned by the festival, one by composer-filmmaker Phill Niblock and the second by composer-violinist Malcolm Goldstein.

Malcolm's work, written with the improvisational skills of the ensemble members in mind, featured him as a soloist. Like much of his music at that time, the piece had some truly beautiful moments but veered a bit off track when the cadenza-like sections took over. Overall, though, it was quite lovely and entered the repertoire over the next few years, Malcolm appearing with the group as guest performer. Phill Niblock at that time was working on a series of films about "work," containing long scenes focused on hands of workers from various cultures in close-up shots executing rituals of tying knots or pulling on ropes attached to fishing nets. The films are compelling, strengthened by the sound scores Phill composed for the ensemble that were performed live with the films. The combined effect of film and live performance was mesmerizing. But it was the performance of another work that I remember most about the festival.

The year 1984 was the twentieth anniversary of Terry Riley's seminal work *In C*. To honor Terry and celebrate the impact *In C* has had on contemporary music, the festival producers organized an "all-star" ensemble consisting of performers and composer-performers featured on the festival. In all there were 30 including singers Joan La Barbara and Barbara Noska. Terry Riley, rather than playing piano or saxophone – his usual instruments - joined Joan and Barbara in singing the 53 musical fragments which serve as the score or musical parts for the piece. To gain a better insight into this event, it's important to understand the personalities of this one-time only all-star band.

Almost all of the musicians recruited for this performance were soloists and composers, capable of delivering some truly remarkable performances on their instruments or voices using extended instrumental or vocal techniques, and employing electronic and computer systems to alter and/or expand the range and characteristics of their performances. Earlier in their careers, many of them had been members of orchestras and smaller chamber music ensembles while others were improvising musicians with roots in jazz or rock. Few of them—at that time—were currently part of an ensemble, most having established their current identities as soloists. Others were used to the give-and-take of improvisational groups where a different kind of ensemble precision was required.

In this context, a large group of highly individualized musicians with egos to match their reputations for artistic excellence strive to become a unified ensemble without the guidance of a conductor or other designated leader. It proved problematic at best. And to make matters more difficult, Terry Riley wanted to perform *In C* without the "pulse," the two upper high "C-natural" keys on the piano normally played in even eighth-note patterns by one of the players to keep everyone together. At the first performance of *In C* in 1964 Steve Reich, a member of the ensemble, suggested to Terry that they insert the "pulse" in order to keep everyone together. From then on whenever *In C* was performed the "pulse" was played on the piano. Into this mix of soloists and without the "pulse" to keep everyone together the Relâche ensemble's musicians served as a guidepost of sorts but not without creating some tension within the group.

By 1984 the eight core members of Relâche were on the verge of becoming a true ensemble, with certain alliances having been formed to serve as group or section leaders. A rehearsal and performance protocol had been established by the group which endowed each performance with a fluency and precision that would reach yet another level of excellence and maturity by the early 1990s. But at that point in its history Relâche was really playing well as a unit.

By the time of this all-star performance of *In C*, Relâche had been performing the work for about five years and had some clear ideas about ways to structure the piece, a tempo that worked well, and a reasonable length. All of this information was, essentially, conveyed to the Hartford group and, overall, each of the performers responded to, or sensibly questioned, Relâche's approach. Some others, by virtue of their well-earned reputations, took issue with Relâche assuming a role of "leadership," although that really wasn't their intention. In any case, because *In C* was performed without the pulse and because a true consensus was never reached in terms of certain performance details, the performance was shaky, and, I feel, possibly a bit too long. On the other hand, maybe it was just the right length and the shaky quality was viewed as a virtue: all of these individuals coming together to form a unified whole. Everyone, of course, hears a work like *In C* in dramatically different ways. The important thing was perhaps not the quality of the performance but the fact it was a celebration of Terry Riley's vision to create a work with such a dramatic, and enduring, effect on 20th century music. It was a very special night.

The *In C* concert concluded the Relâche Ensemble's performing duties on the festival, freeing me to concentrate all of my energies on presenting a business and artistic plan to the New Music Alliance for an East-coast festival in 1987. The presentation went well. I returned to Philadelphia with a clear direction and template in place for New Music America '87.

Although I attended both "New Music America '85" in Los Angeles and "New Music America 1986" in Houston and participated in all of the New Music Alliance meetings and activities accompanying those festivals, I was focused directly on my vision for Philadelphia. By actively participating in each of those festivals I discovered new works and emerging talent, several of whom were included on the Philadelphia festival. But my overarching intentions in attending these festivals was to observe the internal mechanisms of selection, production and presentation, to determine through consultation and observation how I might make the Philadelphia festival somewhat different from past ones and, essentially, elevate the event to a level of excellence which might attract a larger and more diverse audience.

Before describing how I developed a fundraising strategy and accompanying plan for New Music America '87, it is essential to first understand a little of that city's mechanism for supporting arts and culture ventures.

Like most large cities in America, Philadelphia's municipal services departments operated at various levels of efficiency through creative enterprise based on a system of graft. Part of this system required that money flow through various city accounts under the management, or mismanagement as the case may be, of officials placed in their positions of authority through an aligned system of patronage. In matters of arts and culture what little municipal support that existed for most of the late 20th century flowed through this creaky system of patronage and cronyism. Essentially, funds were dispensed to arts and culture groups through the offices of a city councilman.

In most instances, people elected to these offices were not exactly folks drawn to arts and culture. The funds emanating from their offices were usually distributed by someone on the administrative staff, who just might have some idea of who and what constitute arts and culture in the city. On the other hand, their perception of arts and culture might be a Boy Scout troop located in their district, or maybe an after-school program which, although worthy of public support, isn't exactly providing insight and training in the arts. Of course the large cultural institutions like the Philadelphia Orchestra, the Philadelphia Museum of Art and numerous others of the established cultural elite all received large disbursements of these monies. Typically, in this municipal climate of cultural conservatism compounded by crony politics, little if any city funding trickled down to smaller organizations like Relâche. When Wilson Goode was elected mayor, this changed by virtue of the work of a man named Oliver Franklin, who would establish and become the first Director of the Office of Arts and Culture.

Oliver Franklin—no relation—an insider on the Wilson Goode team became interested in Relâche. I think he was drawn to our "renegade" reputation as an organization willing to take chances and risks. Oliver and I met on several occasions, usually at one of the trendier bars in downtown Philadelphia where, it is safe to say, one needed to be seen if one were to get things done in this administration. Somehow despite our very different personalities and styles, we hit if off from the very start. So, I found myself in an unusual situation: I had become something of an insider myself, much to the chagrin of other arts organization directors in Philadelphia.

I used this newfound status to refine my concept into "Wilson Goode's New Music America Festival." Oliver Franklin and his colleague, the smart and savvy acting City Representative Barbara Fenhagen, understood immediately that a festival like New Music America could have a positive impact on the city and its disparate communities as they worked to change the image of Philadelphia from a more conservative one to a more dynamic and, well, hipper one. And they liked the potential media attention that the festival would bring to the city. So we arranged a meeting.

I walked into the meeting prepared to pitch the idea. Included in my arsenal was an outline of the festival identifying all of the potential partners I had begun pulling together including National Public Radio and the Office of Cultural Affairs for the Province of Quebec, among others. I was prepared to explain how a substantial city subsidy would attract corporate, government and private monies to the cause. I wasn't prepared for what happened next.

I was no more than two minutes into my pitch when Oliver interrupted asking, "How much do you want?"

"How much? Well, one hundred fifty thousand would do," I responded.

One hundred thousand," Oliver countered. "Plus access to various agencies in city government, like the printing office. And it doesn't have to be billed as Mayor Goode's New Music America. You can name it whatever you want as long as Philadelphia is in the title."

"How about New Music America nineteen eighty seven - Philadelphia," I asked.

"Fine," he replied.

I looked at Barbara Fenhagen who then looked at Oliver and they both began laughing.

"You look shocked." Barbara said. "You probably figured we would be a tough sell."

"Well, yeah, I guess so," I said.

"This is exactly the kind of thing we want to do. Something different. Something that has the potential to shake things up a bit in this city," Barbara responded.

"Yo," I said quietly while shaking my head, the equivalent in "Philly-speak" of "Hey, let's do it!"

"Okay," Oliver said. "We'll prepare the paperwork. The grant will be made to Relâche over a two-year period. The first check for $50,000 should arrive in about two months."

"Yo," I said again, quietly and to nobody in particular.

The City Representative's office was on the 16th floor of the Municipal Services Building with a panoramic view of the city. When I stepped out of her office I felt like I had stepped into the clouds, like Marcello Mastroiani in *Fellini's 8 ½* when, in the opening sequence, he floats serenely above lines of bumper-to-bumper autos, the wind whistling in his ears. I felt good and knew I could pull this thing off now. With substantial matching money from the city I was in an excellent position to secure major grants from foundations like the Pew Charitable Trusts, The William Penn Foundation and the NEA, as well as other public and private agencies. But first I had to build a staff, one that could help shape the festival while at the same time continue to present a series of concerts by the Relâche Ensemble in Philadelphia.

The team I assembled was excellent, hard-working, dedicated, creative thinkers who at times were extreme pains-in-the-ass. I did not seek out individuals who "specialized" in a given area, preferring instead to enlist those who I shared some part of my professional life with and understood the broad concepts I was reaching for and would not leave me in the lurch for a better job somewhere else. My long-time friends Arthur Sabatini and Merilyn Jackson joined me to form a nucleus.

Arthur is a brilliant writer-thinker-theorist-professor who at that time taught part-time at Drexel University and the Philadelphia College of Performing Arts, wrote book reviews for the Philadelphia Inquirer, and read...and read... and talked. Two years later he would enter a doctoral program at NYU, eventually receiving a Ph.D. in Performance Studies and begin an academic career on the faculty at Arizona State University West in Phoenix.

He and I had developed a close personal and professional friendship beginning in 1975 when a mutual friend—poet and writer Maralyn Lois Polak—introduced us as potential handball partners. Our handball lives took different paths but our interests in what can only be called "the arts" kept us on the same path and cemented our friendship, one that has endured to this day. When I met Arthur I also met Merilyn Jackson. They lived together in a house on South Front Street just below Fitzwater Street.

During the early years of our relationship Merilyn owned two cheese specialty shops, one on South Street, the other on Germantown Avenue in Chestnut Hill. After selling them she worked as a free-lance pastry chef providing desserts to several high-end restaurants in Philadelphia. Her culinary skills provided support as she and Arthur pursued lives that were never easy to categorize or pigeonhole. She wrote poetry and worked on a novel. She became active in the Polish-American community forming, with a group of other Polish-Americans and Polish immigrants—intellectuals, scholars, writers —"The Committee in Support of Solidarity" that provided financial and material aid to clandestine organizations and individuals in Poland who were then living under martial law. Later on she began writing dance reviews and criticism for newspapers and magazines, fulfilling a life-long interest to write about dance in America.

Their home in the Queen Village neighborhood thrived with activity and served as the unofficial gathering place for artists, writers and other assorted miscreants from Philadelphia and beyond. Many visitors to their house were internationally recognized writers and composers who mingled with younger folks just beginning their careers. I recall walking into their home and stumbling over a guy sitting in a low chair in conversation with a group of people. I excused myself then did a double take when I realized it was the notable Mexican writer Carlos Fuentes, then teaching at Princeton. He had just lectured at Penn and was hanging out at Arthur and Merilyn's house, just another wayward soul finding solace and companionship at their Front Street Salon.

L.R. Laurel Wyckoff, Arthur Sabatini, Merilyn Jackson, Joseph Franklin. Photograph by Kaye Pyle

Merilyn began to pick up free-lance jobs writing about food or cultural happenings around town and observed how arts and culture organizations in the city were less than effective at having their stories told and events promoted via the network of print and electronic media. I had been disillusioned for some time in the way Relâche was portrayed in the media and vowed to change this condition especially since New Music America '87 was now a reality. With a similar perspective on the need to help create a more informed arts and culture climate in Philadelphia, we joined forces.

Arthur organized and managed a series of lectures and panel discussions titled "Talking Music" that offered opportunities for the public to discuss meaningful issues with prominent composers, writers and teachers as they talked on a variety of topics. Among those featured on the series were Lou Harrison, Roger Reynolds, RoseLee Goldberg, Jerome Rothenberg, Douglas Kahn and Linda Montano. He edited the festival catalogue and commissioned essays from five different composers. He collected and edited all copy pertaining to the festival. Merilyn directed promotions for all events with assistance from several student interns. Laurel Wyckoff joined the administrative staff while continuing to play flute in the Relâche Ensemble. Along with administrative assistant Jon Mire she presided over festival scheduling and travel and accommodations for over 200 guest artists. DMK Productions—David Michael Kenney and his crew—was hired as production coordinator, and Joanne Hoffman served as principal graphic designer. Drew Keegan was hired to sell advertisements and solicit sponsors for special events which would propel the festival beyond the fringe.

On January 1, 1986 the New Music America '87 festival opened an office in the existing Relâche office located in West Philadelphia at 40th and Pine Streets. With the new team in place we began a two-year program to organize, produce and present the festival and organize, produce and present an ongoing concert series and manage regional tours for the Relâche Ensemble. Tina Davidson continued working with Relâche but did not participate in New Music America '87 activities. Other personnel were added as events dictated. The first priority was, of course, fundraising.

With an initial grant of $100,000 from the City of Philadelphia the Pew Charitable Trusts matched it. At that time John Killacky and the late Ella King Torrey were the principal contributions officers for arts programs. Each was familiar with New Music America's history and gave their wholehearted support to our efforts. The William Penn Foundation, second to Pew in overall arts support for city organizations awarded a large grant as did other smaller regional foundations. Following lengthy meetings both the Pennsylvania Council on the Arts and The National Endowment for the Arts awarded large single grants drawn from their distinct divisions such as Music, Performance, Media, Visual Arts and Radio. (The 1987 NEA grant affirmed their ongoing support for the New Music America concept.) Drew Keegan began to solicit major advertisers and business sponsors ensuring that we would be able to create a detailed glossy festival booklet and accompanying promotional flyers and programs. We successfully negotiated with radio station WNYC-FM in New York City to be the official radio component to the festival. Steve

Cellum, a member of the New Music Alliance, produced an eight-part series featuring performances and interviews taken from festival events.

We strengthened our position by forming professional alliances with numerous arts and cultural organizations in the city, thereby providing us an opportunity to program across disciplines and gain access to their audiences and supporters. Among the many arts organizations in Philadelphia to collaborate with the festival was the Fairmount Park Art Association which sponsored a parallel conference called "Public Art In America '87"; The American Music Theater Festival which presented Michael Nyman's *The Man Who Mistook His Wife For A Hat* and *Revelation In The Courthouse Park* by Harry Partch, both productions part of AMTF's regular season that were scheduled during the festival week. And, of course, there was The Yellow Springs Institute for Arts and Humanities.

I had hoped that Yellow Springs would host a performance or series of performances as part of the festival. Since the institute was located 20 miles away from downtown Philadelphia accessible only by car or chartered bus this was not a practical idea. John Clauser, the institute's director, wisely suggested another role: Yellow Springs would be the location of panel meetings to evaluate proposals submitted by prospective participants.

In early 1986 the New Music America '87 staff put a call out to artists worldwide for proposals to include solo performances, ensemble and orchestral works, site-specific and installation works, video and interactive computer works. We received a total of 212 proposals, some quite extraordinary, some quite ordinary and others quite bad. Laurel Wyckoff and Jon Mire organized them into categories, labeled them and attached all supporting material like audio and videotapes, scores, biographies and other documents that would eventually be circulated to panel members. I organized a pre-screening committee of staff and professional confidants to sort through the hundreds of proposals eliminating those that were clearly not competitive and categorizing those exemplary and/or unique ones for further evaluation. I then organized three separate panels that would meet at the Yellow Springs Institute in September of 1986, one year prior to the festival. For a one week period peer-panels of artists and producer-presenters sorted through the proposals, listened to recorded tapes and records and viewed videotapes to determine the quality of the work and recommend potential artists for the festival. By the end of the week the panel had made their recommendations to me.

With recommendations in hand and in consultation with staff members and members of the Relâche Ensemble I began the selection process to determine which of the two principal venues would be best suited for a particular artist's work. Would their music be better served in the Painted Bride Art Center with 200 portable chairs in a black-box venue or in the Philadelphia Maritime Museum Theatre with 500 fixed seats and proscenium stage? If a specific solo, instrumental ensemble or orchestral work by a composer were selected who would perform it? Relâche as the resident instrumental ensemble would be the obvious choice for many works. But what about those requiring a more "traditional" chamber group, like a string quartet, or a small chamber orchestra? Fortunately the majority of works being considered featured the composer as performer-soloist and/or leader of his own small ensemble— duo, trio or quartet, for example, so the choice was pre-determined. Which "alternative venue" in the city would be better suited for a specific work and, once identified, would this venue be available either through a city agency or private concern? With these questions in mind and a body of works that would eventually give shape to the festival we began putting all of the pieces together.

Located just blocks apart in the Olde City section of Philadelphia, the Philadelphia Maritime Museum Theatre and the Painted Bride Art Center were the principal performance venues for the festival. At the time the Philadelphia Maritime Museum and Theatre were owned by the City of Philadelphia so we did not have to pay rental fees for festival events. The Painted Bride Art Center graciously donated their facility to the festival. The combined savings were considerable. To ensure that both venues would have superb sound production for all festival events, I consulted with composer-performer-writer Pauline Oliveros who had been lobbying everyone within the New Music community to provide a better quality of sound enhancement at events.

Pauline was a founding member of the Good Sound Foundation (GSF) formed by a group of composers and engineers of Berkley, California in alliance with the John Meyer Studios, manufacturers of high-end audio speakers. Their mission was to design temporary and permanent remedial sonic environments for live performance by utilizing evolving computer and electronic software and hardware to project a clear "good" sound. Their premise was that no performance space, regardless of its design characteristics, is a complete acoustic success. There are always sound problems due to a variety of causes. Through the use of digital signal processing and installation of compatible hardware they maintained that sonic deficiencies in any space can be "corrected."

During a conversation at the New Music America Los Angeles Festival Pauline suggested I meet with the other members of GSF to learn more about their ideas and applications. "It's about time that we all had some good sound for a change," she said more than once to anyone who would listen. "Having a New Music America festival showcase the ideas of GSF will help both the festival's image and enhance the foundation's reputation for future endeavors," she continued. I was intrigued. I arranged a meeting in California that coincided with GSF providing sound enhancement for a performance in a theatre at Mills College in Oakland, California.

To celebrate composer Lou Harrison's seventieth birthday Mills College presented a concert of his works featuring soloists and ensembles in a variety of works to give broad representation of Lou's stylistic diversity and world music influences. I distinctly remember the clarity and separation of each instrument in the Bay Area Gamelan as they played a new work by Lou and the glistening interpretation of his *Varied Trio* as played by the Abel-Steinberg-Winant Trio. The sound quality on these and others on the program was remarkable. Meeting the following day with GSF members they described in detail and praxis how their concepts were applied to the performances. And they instilled in me a new awareness for sound enhancement technology, suggesting new ways to listen, what to listen for and how to make simple equipment adjustments to arrive at an even unencumbered ensemble sound. It was a revelation. I decided to engage GSF as the principal sound enhancement consultant for New Music America '87.

The GSF team of Loren Rush, Alan Johnson, Bob Hodis and Richard Zvonar arrived in Philadelphia early to assess the Port of History Museum Theatre and Painted Bride Art Center. Each venue required different treatment to "correct" acoustical deficiencies. For example, the Port of History Theatre was originally designed to showcase regional symphony and chamber orchestras. The sound from the stage was fairly even but dull. For small ensembles and soloists using a variety of computer and electronic sound systems the sound was very uneven throughout the auditorium. The Painted Bride Art Center was essentially a black box theater constructed inside the shell of an old manufacturing plant. It had many hard flat surfaces causing the sound literally to bounce around and throughout the space. As you can imagine the overall sound was "boomy" with slap echoes prominent. The uneven quality of sound was exacerbated considerably when using sound manipulation equipment or mixing recorded sound to real-time sound.

The first step in correcting these perceived acoustical problems is to electronically measure each space to determine what adjustments should be made. Using digital technologies the GSF team created a "simulation" of the ideal sound space wherein a variety of performance situations could occur. Essentially they designed a virtual sound space with ideal acoustical characteristics drawn from the actual space we'd use. Through the process of transduction, the original sound source, whether a musical instrument or voice or MIDI keyboard or computer generated or altered sound, passes through a microphone to controlling devices such as equalizers, filters and amplifiers. The processed sound is then projected back as the virtual space gives way to the actual physical space. Overall sound quality is even, free of distortion and as true to the original sound source as possible. The results of their work in the Port of History Auditorium Theatre and Painted Bride Art Center were truly extraordinary. Artists and audiences alike expressed their satisfaction and even amazement of the sound experiences they had at performances throughout the festival. It was indeed a festival with "good sound."

New Music America '87 officially opened on Friday, October 2nd with a gala reception at the Philadelphia Maritime Museum followed by an opening-night concert in the Museum's Theatre. *Music For Marcel Duchamp* for prepared piano by John Cage, played by Relâche pianist John Dulik, was a perfect opening night work honoring two seminal figures of 20th century art in the city where many of Duchamp's works reside. The Philadelphia Museum of Art owns several of his major works and the Relâche Ensemble has performed many of John Cage's music as part of exhibitions presented by the museum that related to Duchamp, his friends and collaborators. Next on the program: four works comprising a project titled *The Expatriates* curated by composer-pianist and expatriate Stephen Montague featuring American composers then living in England. The concert concluded with a rousing set by the Philadelphia-based jazz saxophonist and composer Odean Pope and his Saxophone Choir.

For the next 10 days Philadelphia was the focus for New Music in America with 85 composer-performers featured, 13 performing ensembles in residence and numerous related events rounding out the festival. From Fairmount Park in West Philadelphia to Penn's Landing along the Delaware River the city pulsed with New Music. Some of the music required careful

Poster for New Music America '87 designed by Joanne Hoffman

attention to detail while others rocked. Some of the music celebrated the work of master artists while others revealed emerging talent.

At one time I was standing on the bow of a weathered tugboat while it motored down-river into increasingly choppier swells, I peered into a dark gray sky sporadically illuminated with splotches of yellow light, the after-glow of lightning streaks in the distance, thunder claps rolling off echoing towards the farmlands of South Jersey. To my right was Philadelphia's distinctive skyline looming over the Port of Philadelphia.

Once the single largest fresh-water port in North America, the Philadelphia riverfront was quiet these days except for commercial development to house and entertain those urban warriors who can afford to spend $4,000 each month for a "room with a riverfront view" or dine at reasonably good restaurants at unreasonably high prices. To my left the New Jersey shore of the Delaware River held, in its muddy grip, the City of Camden, one of America's most blighted and inefficient cities. My view that day of Camden was of the newly minted Walt Whitman Park which skirted the riverfront, a pedestrian walk leading to a construction site of the future New Jersey Aquarium. Positioned at equal distances along each shore were eight large ship's horns facing one another across the murky Delaware River like ancient sentinels watching over the ghosts of a once proud bustling riverscape. That day the river was not happy; movement on board the tugboat confirmed it.

As the tugboat bobbed and pitched in the water the boat's captain-pilot assured me the storm would probably pass. If we waited an hour or so, he said, the skies would clear so Alvin Curran's piece titled *Maritime Rites* could begin. I spoke by radio with associates on both sides of the river; some suggested we wait out the storm, while others lobbied hard that we postpone it. The composer, Alvin Curran, was among those who wanted to wait it out. I however was not at all comfortable with the current conditions.

I had heard over the radio that the storm would arrive in about an hour and the rain would be constant and fairly severe. The next day, Sunday, would be clear and sunny. If we waited and attempted to perform the piece there was a possibility of heavy rain and lightning damaging the equipment on shore, not to mention putting all the performers and technical personnel at risk. Clearly I leaned towards postponing the performance. If we did postpone it we would likely lose the coverage by radio and television stations waiting on shore for the performance. And the tugboat captain-pilot informed me we might lose some of the participating ships docked in and around the harbor. The situation was resolved when the festival's production coordinator David-Michael Kenney called on the phone with a reminder that should anything go wrong the festival was liable for damages. Although Relâche had adequate insurance coverage it was not worth the risk. I informed everyone that we would postpone the performance until the next day at Noon.

Sunday, October 4th was one of those golden early fall days with temperatures in the mid-50s and a cool wind skimming over the Delaware River. Finally, Alvin Curran's *Maritime Rites* was about to launch. And with it the unofficial opening of New Music America '87.

Composer and performer of instrumental, electronic and environmental music, Alvin Curran has created a number of *Maritime Rites* on riverways throughout Europe and the United States, including a gorgeous realization along the Chesapeake Bay in nearby Delaware and Maryland. After hearing that version I arranged with the Philadelphia Maritime Museum to co-commission a similar work from Alvin to celebrate the historic Port of Philadelphia and serve as the opening work for New Music America '87—Philadelphia.

The *Maritime Rites*, as described by Alvin in the festival catalogue: "...8 – 12 ships' foghorns are installed at strategic locations on the Philadelphia and Camden sides of the Delaware River at Penn's Landing within a one-mile area. These horns are pitched and activated by musicians reading from a score and a computer program activated by the composer. The tones generated by these horns sustain for relatively long durations, mixing with one another to create a rich musical texture. Simultaneously three barges with small groups of musicians tack back and forth across the Delaware River their amplified sounds interacting with the ships' horns to fill the river and the shore."

As the piece unfolded against a cloudless sunny sky each of the ships' horns sounded their distinctive tone cluster on cue from Alvin while one barge of brass players floated up and down the river performing a selection of tunes with maritime themes. In addition to the eight ships' horns the tugboat and four other ships that were in port that day eagerly agreed to sound their horns on cue, adding to the mix. I probably had the best seat of anyone. From the bow of the tugboat I surveyed the entire scene, listening to the sounds blending and weaving in and around one another as the random harmonies rippled along with the River's current as it flowed south towards the Atlantic Ocean. At the conclusion of the piece, as the sound of the ships' horns decayed, the barge carrying the brass players floated by one last time playing *My Bonny Lies Over The Ocean*. It was a perfect ending for the piece and a perfect beginning for the festival. As the tugboat pulled into its slip on the Philadelphia side of the river I saw Alvin surrounded by a crowd of observers congratulating him, like a ballplayer who had just hit a game-winning home run. He had.

David-Michael Kenney whispered to Guy Klucevsek as he ushered him back on stage to a raucous standing ovation at a downtown Philadelphia night club, "Better get an agent." Guy looked at him, puzzled and asked, "An agent, why?" "Cause you have a hit on your hands," David told him, smiling. Startled at the suggestion but smiling back confidently, Guy shook his head, as if he hadn't realized what had just happened.

Before moving to Brooklyn and eventually Staten Island, Guy Klucevsek spent several years living in southern New Jersey not far from downtown Philadelphia. During those years he performed with the Philadelphia Composers' Forum as a guest before joining the Relâche Ensemble a year or so after it was formed. Guy remained with Relâche for the next 10 years as he simultaneously pursued a downtown New York presence and distinctive solo performance, recording and composing career. During his tenure with Relâche he was one of the ensemble leaders. Everyone in the ensemble respected his acute musical sensitivities and easy-going disposition. He composed innovative works for the ensemble, earning a role as one of the group's more productive composers. Over the years his back-and-forth visits from New York to Philadelphia for rehearsals and concerts forged a close, enduring friendship between us.

When New Music America '87 was taking shape I wanted Guy to have a special role, both as a performer and composer. A year or so before the festival Guy called to tell me about a project he had just launched, one he was going to name "Polka From The Fringe."

Growing up as a member of a Slovenian family in Western Pennsylvania's coal-mining country in the late 1950s, Guy was influenced by the music of Frankie Yankovic and other local polka bands and accordionists. In high school he formed his own polka band playing polkas he transcribed from radio broadcasts at weddings, parties and clubs, eventually writing several. After entering college, polkas lost their identity for Guy as he tenaciously pursued "serious" composition studies while developing a repertoire for the accordion that would earn respect—for the instrument and himself—from jaded faculty and students. This self-induced lapse of listening to, and playing, polka music lasted until 1980 when he discovered the Tex-Mex music of

Flaco Jimenez and the Louisiana Cajun musician Nathan Abshire.

Each of these musical genres are, interestingly, rooted in polka forms and have earned a loyal following among constituent populations as well as scholarly respect for their important folkloric contributions to American "roots music." The more he listened to these and other polka music styles, the more seriously Guy began re-discover or re-explore the polka. In 1986 he invited a group of composer-friends to, essentially, put all inhibitions aside and write a polka for him, preferably for solo accordion or accordion with tape or accordion with simple, easy-to-create accessories or props. "Re-think the polka. What is a polka? What do you listen for in a polka?" These are several of the challenges he gave to the composers. The result: 32 different polkas, all initially three minutes long, from a variety of composers as widely divergent as one can imagine. From William Duckworth to Lois V Vierk, from Fred Frith to Aaron J. Kernis, the polkas covered a genre-bending array of musical madness and elegance. *Polka From The Fringe* received its world premiere at the festival.

Rather than simulate a club environment for the performance we scheduled it for a trendy, respectably seedy after-hours dance club in Old City Philadelphia named "Revival," long-since gone, a casualty to the gentrification and galleryfrication of that historic section east of center-city near the Delaware River waterfront. At that time Revival attracted a mixed crowd of emerging and seasoned artists, and art students, along with the usual suburban-bound wannabes and curiosity seekers. We had hoped that by placing *Polka From The Fringe* in Revival and promoting it as a "downtown New York" event, we would draw not only the visiting festival attendees but the local crowd as well. To this day I'm not certain who was there or from where they came but it was packed, wall-to-wall with folks looking for a good party. Guy did not disappoint.

Thirty-two polkas—performed in two 45-minute sets, one more outrageous, or touching, than the previous, performed in a manner Guy never before revealed to his friends—was one of the true highlights of New Music America '87. His singing the lyrics to David Mahler's *The Twenty-Second Street Accordion Band* after he had ripped off his starched white shirt and folded it in pleated sections to "play" it is a sight that I don't think any of us in attendance that night will ever forget. It was Guy's night and as memorable a New Music America event as any during the festival's 11-year history.

Polka From The Fringe has been one of Guy's more successful projects.

Following the premiere performance and subsequent solo concerts elsewhere he arranged the polkas for a group of friends and musicians based in New York who became the "Ain't Nothing But A Polka Band." They toured throughout the United States, Europe and Japan over the next couple of years and recorded 28 of the polkas for "eva records," then based in Tokyo. Guy never did look for an agent.

Guy Klucevsek. Photograph by Steve Speliotis

For most of the performance of *Polka From The Fringe* I stood at the bar surrounded by a group of large guys from Montana who took turns pouring shots of whiskey for me to drink. Essentially, it was a test to see if I could keep up with them. This was a problem since I cannot stand the taste of straight whiskey and never developed the rhythm of drinking shots of anything alcoholic as a means of bonding with my *macho* friends. I prefer sipping a good dark stout or *Cuba Libre* when out and about. At all other times I rely on wines to temper my meals and lighten my moods. These guys were insistent and a bit annoying since I was hooked up to David-Michael Kenney's communications system so I could be in touch with him and others in the production crew at anytime during the festival. Fortunately there were no emergencies that night, mainly because *Polka From The Fringe* was the only thing happening.

The large guys plying me with whiskey were members of installation artist Patrick Zentz' entourage, Montana ranchers a long way from the desolation and sub-zero temperatures of the High Plains, taking full advantage of Philadelphia and the festival's nightlife.

Pat Zentz is an extraordinary artist and great guy, someone I got to know well during the three years I lived in Montana in the late 1990s. His friends were good guys as well but a bit out-of-control during their Philadelphia visit. Take the evening I was working with David-Michael Kenney at the Painted Bride Art Center preparing for a concert and he handed the phone to me—one of his production guys was on the other end, agitated. "Hey, Joseph, we might have some trouble over here," Bobby said, the "over here" being the Port of History Theatre.

What kind of trouble?" I asked.

Well, some guys claim to have a festival pass but forgot them and want to get into the theatre anyway. What shall I do?" he asked.

Who are they?" I asked.

Don't know. They're not from around here, I think they're from one of those rectangular states out there."

I laughed. "Oh yeah, the guys from Montana. Let me talk to them."

It seems they had found a happy hour in some bar nearby and were feeling pretty good about things, not used to being told they can't go someplace, pass or no pass. I asked them to settle down and listen to the music. They did and there were no problems. The "rectangular state" reference made its way around the festival, much to everyone's amusement.

The author at a time he was being tested by the guys from Montana.

Each weekday at 8:30 AM, then again at 11:15 AM and finally at 4:30 PM "Crank" was in full motion, its six bass drums tapping out an arrhythmic tattoo...*boom..boomboom...boom*, resonating in the cavernous lobby of the newly-renovated Curtis Center on Independence Square in downtown Philadelphia, in full throttle, the result of the "march of the secretaries." I'll explain.

Crank is the creation of Patrick Zentz. Like many of his large scale works *Crank* is a mechanical structure designed to translate environmental forces like, for example, the changes in wind velocity or temperature levels on the surface of a structure. These natural conditions are collected, then through a variety of translation processes, activate a mechanical response in a structure or instrument located at a distance from the environmental source. Many of Patrick's works are the result of his having grown up in eastern Montana, living and working on a ranch where weather conditions are extreme and fluctuate dramatically. Patrick has created works and installed them in creeks or in the middle of a desolate field where wind, water and sunlight are translated into mechanical action, *Crank* is similarly designed except for a critical difference: it is meant to be installed in an urban environment.

The six bass drums—all hand made from luminous pinewood—are attached by wooden arms to a large wood and steel crank that moves a series of pulleys to activate a piano hammer that is attached to the end of the wood arm and fixed just in front of the bass drum. An electric motor turns the crank when activated by a series of photoelectric cells located at the base of the crank. As traffic flows by disturbing or breaking the photoelectric beam solenoid switches are triggered setting the piano hammers in motion and striking the drums. The heavier the traffic flow the more frequent the beating of the drums. So, during the "march of the secretaries," *Crank* is cranking out some interesting rhythmic patterns. At other times during the day when the traffic flow is less, *Crank* stands alone in the middle of the brightly-lit atrium, in silent anticipation, waiting to sing once again.

Crank was commissioned by the Washington Project for the Arts in Washington, D.C. and installed there for a period of time. I first saw it at the Yellow Springs Institute where it was on display for two weeks while Patrick and his long-time friend and collaborator Dennis Voss were in residence. At that time they were both doing performance works based on their shared Montana experiences. Often these performances were part of their installations. In this case though *Crank* worked as a solo act in one of the gallery spaces at Yellow Springs. After meeting Patrick and Dennis, Arthur Sabatini and I immediately decided to invite Patrick on the festival. But there were logistical complications.

Their residency at Yellow Springs was during July. New Music America '87 was in October. So *Crank* had to be stored someplace in the area for two-and-a-half months since the cost of shipping the thing back-and-forth to

Montana and Philadelphia was prohibitive. And *Crank* is very heavy. Fortunately one of Patrick's Montana friends was originally from the Norristown, Pennsylvania area and had relatives living on a farm nearby so he arranged for us to store *Crank* in their empty barn until we were able to install it at the Curtis Center in late September.

Although it took a considerable effort to move *Crank* from its storage facility to downtown Philadelphia, it was well worth it. Along with the other sonic installations on the festival program, *Crank* was a popular destination for the curious and playful, in addition to the apprehensive secretaries.

I'm not certain how active *Crank* has been since the festival. I've often wondered if any of the secretaries who drove *Crank* crazy during their early morning and late afternoon strolls through the Curtis Center in 1987 remember his songs, especially if they've walked by any other installations that Pat Zentz has installed at airports, convention centers and other public venues throughout the United States. I do know that Pat Zentz continues making large interactive works even more striking then *Crank*. Because of his success he no longer works his ranch in Laurel, Montana, instead, devoting all his time to creating art works

When we accepted David Mahler's proposal for a piece using baseball imagery I suggested that we stage the performance on a baseball diamond in Fairmount Park. Intrigued with the prospect of realizing his work on an actual ball field and not in an indoor performance space, David agreed although with reservation. After I suggested we have a back-up plan to move the performance indoors in case it rained he felt much better. So did trombonist Stuart Dempster, who would be performing the piece.

Dempster's Fantasy On An American Theme is a collaboration between two close friends, both of whom have used the tape recorder as a musical instrument in the design and realization of a number of musical works. And they are avid baseball fans who often use baseball terminology, strategies and metaphors in their individual and collaborative projects. David and I share backgrounds as players, although my interest in the game has long since diminished, a casualty to the corporate culture that dominates the sport. David on the other hand remains active, playing senior league ball in Seattle where he has resided for 25 years. Unlike me he retains a boyish fascination with baseball, conversing easily about current major league teams and reminiscing about players and teams who excelled in a very different era, before corporate America soiled the game with their selfish promotions and spawned owners with an eye only on the bottom line. I'm not certain how much baseball Stuart Dempster played as a young guy but I am certain that he has followed the game closely over the years and is as knowledgeable about current trends and players as is David. Clearly this shared interest and enthusiasm for baseball gives them insight in creating works based on imagery and a legion of richly embroidered metaphors that no other team sport has created.

The production team for New Music America '87 loved the idea of designing a performance scene at an outdoor venue. Production coordinator David Michael Kenney was especially enthusiastic since he too was a former ball player and current fan, as were several members of his team. In collaboration with the sound engineers they designed a set with speakers placed on each base and behind home plate.

Stuart was to stand on the pitcher's mound with a microphone to record his trombone playing and commenting on the *mise en scene* before him. While Stuart was performing David would be recording him on a reel-to-reel tape recorder that would eventually reveal the secret to Stuart's seemingly random noise-to-noise playing. After Stuart finished, David would rotate the tape reels so that the take-up reel becomes the source tape; essentially playing back the material that had been recorded just moments before. What is revealed is the song "Take Me Out To The Ballgame." Stuart had just played the song backwards. David is a master at using the reel-to-reel tape recorder as a solo instrument, manipulating the recording speeds, reversing the reels to untangle what appears to be spoken gibberish only to reveal a coherent text. These and other techniques he employs in a number of early performance works which have proved popular at New Music events.

With the set ready and everyone in place we were poised to present *Dempster's Fantasy On An American Theme* on one of the baseball diamonds at Belmont Plateau in Fairmount Park, the site of the afternoon events. But there was a problem: it was clouding up with a forecast for rain.

After consulting with everyone, David decided we should revert to our back-up plan and move the set indoors in a section of Memorial Hall that was reserved for just this purpose. Although most of us were disappointed, we backed David's decision, fully understanding his concerns. It remained cloudy but did not rain that day.

Wearing an antique baseball cap and gray flannel jersey, Stuart played *Dempster's Fantasy On An American Theme* on his trombone with just the right amount of virtuosity and foolishness, coaxing natural and extended sounds from the instrument as easily as Hank Aaron used to roll his wrists and propel a baseball over the left field stands in old Connie Mack Stadium in North Philadelphia. And David rotated the reels on the tape recorder with a gleam in his eye and a bemused look on his face that teased the audience just right. When the tape played back Stuart's trombone singing "Take me out to the ball game, take me out to the crowd..." in muffled yet easily discerned tones everyone laughed, knowingly of course. It was a great piece but just think how it might have been if it had been played outside on the diamond. Hank would have approved.

There were times in my career as a presenter of New Music events when even I questioned my motives. One of those concerned a quartet of young musicians named Borbetomagus. These four guys might have passed for a member of a high school chess club except, that is, when they took to the stage. There, at times, they looked like they might be posing for an X-rated promotional photo: one of the two saxophonists leaning backwards his knees bent while steadying his pose; the other saxophonist standing on a chair in front straddling him, their tenor saxophones joined at their bells appearing as one large instrument uniting the two human figures. And they are both blowing their brains out! Behind the caterwauling saxophone screeching an electric guitarist and bass guitarist are laying down thick slabs of sound, not so much as an accompaniment but as a complement to the overall loud improvisational sound texture. And was it ever loud! Deafening actually.
So loud in fact that just about everyone in the theatre cleared out, except for one or two hardy (or foolish) souls and me. *Borbetomagus*. I have no idea what their name means. They were, without a doubt, among the more controversial artists to perform on New Music America '87.

During the panel selection process when their tape was played one of the panel members, Bob Wisdom, tapped to become artistic director at the Institute for Contemporary Art in London, was overly enthusiastic about the group. I remember Bob saying, "Joseph, you got to put these guys on the festival. They'll really shake things up." Another panel member, Walter Bodreau, the eccentric brilliant conductor and saxophonist from Montreal jumped up saying, "Wow. If these guys can keep up this intensity for a half hour, you have to have them. They are definitely crazy." No question about it. They were. I did. They did. Shake things up, that is.

We programmed their set to conclude the first full week of the festival's evening concerts at the Port of History Theatre. Prior to their assault to the senses, the other artists on the concert were pretty, well, sedate: pianist Geri Allen, who at that time had not fully emerged on the national scene, opened the concert playing an extended solo work beautifully displaying her brilliant technique and swinging style, then choreographer-tap dancer Anita Feldman with contact microphones located strategically on the dance floor to record and process the sound of her tapping feet performed a new work with music by Larry Polanski. Finally, Borbetomagus took the stage.

Even though I had heard the sound check earlier in the day I—along with everyone else in the theatre—was not prepared for Borbetomagus' intense sonic display. I cannot remember ever before hearing anything that loud on a concert stage, including Glen Branca's guitar orchestra that had both endeared yet enraged audiences with their loud just-intoned performances. Compared to Borbetomagus, Glen's "guitar-armies" band sounded like a string quartet! No, these guys were in their own uniquely sonic world.

Knowing they would be controversial I made certain that I—the person responsible for putting them on stage—was visible; I sat about halfway back in the center of the theatre with Laurel Wyckoff and Arthur Sabatini. As Borbetomagus' performance gained momentum and loudness, people started leaving, first a few at a time then in large numbers. By the time Borbetogamus finished their set there were about eight people left in the theatre, several ecstatic over the performance. As the sound began to ebb into silence I remember someone yelling, "Yeah! Yeah!" The applause was barely below the threshold of sound.

Outside a large group of veteran New Music artists and enthusiasts congregated, waiting, I thought, for me to make an appearance. As I walked outside Joe Celli asked, Want a drink?"

Sometime in mid 1985 or early 1986 I was listening to radio station WRTI-FM late at night. Then WRTI-FM was owned and operated exclusively by Temple University. Their programming format consisted almost exclusively of jazz, with a special Saturday night Salsa show. The student and volunteer disc jockeys were sometimes a bit uneven, raw at times but their presentations were getting better, the result of a new station manager who had been hired with a mandate to smooth things out and provide professional guidance to the student-volunteers. The late night programs tended to play extended works and those which might not fit into a straight-ahead format. It was on one of these shows I first heard George Russell's *African*

Game. It knocked me out! The next day I went out and bought the album and listened to it time and again. Wow!

I had long been a fan of George Russell. Along with other composer-arrangers of big band or large ensemble works like Duke Ellington/Billy Strayhorn, Gil Evans, Quincy Jones, Sun Ra, Bill Holman, Charles Mingus and Stan Kenton, George's music really caught my ear. He is an important link to the evolution of jazz; active with Dizzy Gillespie in the mid-1940's during the advent of be-bop, then in the mid-1950s when hard-bop and post-bop styles appeared. By then he had developed a mature, sophisticated musical language with adventurous harmonies which swung with the fire and intensity of bop. Like other great composer-arrangers he knew how to draw daring inventive solos from his players, giving them just the right amount of artistic freedom within his elegant formal designs. In 1956 he recorded a landmark album as part of RCA Victor's series "The Jazz Workshop." This recording, titled "Jazz Workshop; The George Russell Smalltet," is an extraordinary statement with great arrangements of original tunes played by superb soloists and ensemble players. Hearing this recording sometime in the late 1960s gave me insight into the inner workings of a collaborative music ensemble and affirmed—for me—a desire to pursue studies of musical composition.

George eventually settled in Europe where he remained for some years an important figure in the musical cultures there. When he returned to the United States to take a teaching position at the New England Conservatory of Music in Boston he continued writing and leading his band with most concert appearances at festivals in Europe. For reasons I have never been able to fully understand, George Russell has never been well known in America. This despite a musical style that's always embraced easily accepted and understood musical constructs like rhythm and song. His music always has a groove, often downright "funky" with easily identifiable tunes. I think even jazz aficionados armed with an educated ear and discerning viewpoint sometimes do not listen carefully to George's music. There is a tendency perhaps for some to listen *too* carefully to the musics' inner logic when, in reality, its sophistication resides in the actual groove or song itself. This is partially George's doing since he has created an image for himself as a musical theorist. His ongoing work in this regard, *The Lydian-Chromatic Concept of Tonal Organization*, to me doesn't give insight to his music as much as it presents a barrier to it. I feel George's great gift is creating small musical ideas allowing for a variety of interpretations—with the right mix of interpreters—which will yield a larger alluring cohesive musical work. And *African Game* works for me at this level of audition. I decided upon a second or third hearing that I wanted to program this piece and feature George Russell on the festival.

On the back of the record jacket it mentioned George Russell was managed and booked by Outward Visions in New York City. I called the phone number and talked with a man named Marty Khan who, along with his wife, Helene Cann, is a founding director of Outward Visions. I introduced myself to Marty and asked if we could meet in New York to discuss George's participation on the festival. We scheduled a meeting in the offices of the Nikolais-Louis Dance Theatre where Marty and Helene were working to reorganize the company at a time when the Nikolais-Louis Dance Theatre was experiencing severe organizational and financial difficulties. When I learned our meeting would be at the company's office I was stunned.

The Alwin Nikolais-Murray Louis Dance Company had played a critical role in my development as an artist. Years before as an undergraduate at the Philadelphia Musical Academy I studied theatre arts and movement with Ray Broussard, formerly one of the seven original members of the Nikolais Dance Company in 1954. Ray had become a filmmaker and teacher, his methodologies formed from his long association with Nikolais, especially Nikolais' unique use of lighting and costumes to highlight his kinetic fast-paced dance movements that formed a distinctive and revolutionary style of dance-theatre. Nikolais composed the music for all of his dance-theatre works using electronic instruments to create sounds on magnetic tape. He purchased one of the original Moog Synthesizers from its creator, Robert Moog, becoming a prolific and innovative composer of "electronic music."

My composition teacher, Andrew Rudin also studied with Robert Moog and was among the Moog Synthesizer's earliest proponents. He was then the director of the electronic music studio at the Philadelphia Musical Academy, one of the reasons I decided to study there. Andrew and Ray grew up together in Beaumont, Texas and remained friends as each of their careers developed in New York and Philadelphia. They correctly concluded that most composers who wrote music for dance and theatre did not have much of an understanding of these disciplines nor did they understand the language of dance and theatre. Accordingly they created a series of courses designed for composers that would integrate movement, stage design, costume creation, lighting and music as a means to better prepare a composer to work in these media. Their inspiration was Alwin Nikolais and Murray Louis,

Nikolais' partner and principal dancer. The course was a revelation for me as was discovering the art of Alwin Nikolais and his Dance Theatre.

So here I was poised to meet this guy Marty Khan to discuss how I might engage George Russell, another artist who was an influence on my development, in the Nikolais-Louis office. The "coincidence" was too good to be true.

From our first meeting in the summer of 1986 Marty Khan and I felt an immediate kinship, a trust that mutual interests will yield future projects. He is one of the few people I know who shares many of the same interests and values as I do, who lives a life of an "outcat" in America, who believes a man's word is good. Sure, the formal agreements are necessary, but we both knew that an exchange of information and ideas is sealed with a handshake and eye contact that affirms the word. That initial trust we felt at our first meeting has forged a long friendship and resulted in several collaborative projects. And it began with our mutual respect and interest in George Russell and his music.

Marty and I agreed to a fee for George and his Living Time Orchestra to perform *African Game* at the festival. But given the relatively large number of musicians in the ensemble the fee was a bit too high. To ensure his appearance I asked the Mellon Jazz Festival to help sponsor the concert. During those years the former Mellon Bank sponsored a two-week jazz festival in Philadelphia based on a model presented in large cities throughout the United States. Mellon hired Festival Productions based in New York City to manage the event. I had previously met several of the producers at Festival Productions and felt comfortable approaching them. They too respected George Russell's contributions to jazz and readily agreed to co-sponsor his performance. It was billed simply as "The Mellon Jazz Festival at NMA '87 Presents George Russell."

Scheduled for the second day of the festival, *African Game* soared. George and His Living Time Orchestra were in great form that night. I felt especially proud that I was responsible for presenting George Russell in a venue with a superb technical crew to help showcase his ensemble and music in a manner befitting someone of his stature. His presence added immeasurably to the overall artistic success of New Music America '87.

The late Annson Kenney once said, "Always, Joseph, Relâche has a point of view." This sentiment was apparent during New Music America '87, an event which left a sonic trace on the city for years after. Between 1988 and 1998 I adhered even more closely to a "point of view" by discovering and creating New Musical projects for the Relâche Ensemble and developing partnerships with area organizations to present work by visiting new and world music artists and dancers from throughout the world. That "point of view" also eventually led me away from the New Music Alliance. After New Music America '87, I focused my energy on the Relâche Ensemble's plans and participation at the Miami festival. Relâche had been invited to be one of the resident ensembles.

The author and Laurel Wyckoff at the closing festivities of New Music America '87

The 1988 New Music America Festival was held in Miami, Florida during the pre-Christmas days of December, a time when many performers and New Music enthusiasts from cold cities in North America headed south to warm, tropical, sultry and colorful Miami. One of the concert venues was located on Biscayne Bay directly across from a sprawling mega-shopping mall with stores, boutiques and food stands located throughout the waterfront plaza. An outdoor performance space with a sheltered stage was located at the edge of a pavilion facing away from the glistening waters of the bay. Standing behind the audience—who were facing the water—was a tall green one-dimensional wooden Christmas tree. At noon each day the wooden Christmas tree would sing. Well, almost.

Positioned from bottom to top on scaffolding attached to the front face of the tree—basses on the bottom, sopranos on the top, of course—a choir sang seasonal songs and Christmas carols for the shoppers who cruised the Mall. But there was a problem: New Music America had scheduled concerts for 1 PM on the outdoor stage each weekday of the festival. The dress and technical rehearsals were scheduled for 11 AM. While the performing musicians from the festival were setting up, checking levels and running through their parts, the Singing Christmas Tree began caroling at noon. Needless to say this enraged the festival musicians who, in turn, enraged the choir singing from the Singing Christmas Tree. Few people were exhibiting holiday cheer along Biscayne Bay during those days.

Simply no way the Singing Christmas Tree could compete with Scott Johnson's amplified ensemble as they rehearsed sections from his score to the film about Patty Hearst. And The Singing Christmas Tree greatly disturbed members of the Relâche Ensemble as they tried to negotiate new works by Stephen Montague and Scott Lindroth, both requiring careful instrumental nuance to support the vocal lines. To add yet more problems for the performers on the ground, in and out of the Christmas tree, overhead large jetliners were taking off including, if memory serves, the daily departure of the Concorde; the sonic thrust from their huge engines shaking everything on the ground below their flight paths directly over Biscayne Bay. Despite these interferences, each of the concerts went off as scheduled but many of the musicians on the festival felt that their music had been placed in a seriously compromised context.

Surely the choir in The Singing Christmas Tree felt equally compromised. Even when the departing jets' engines were not shaking The Singing Christmas Tree to its fey roots, the air around Biscayne Bay was filled with other dissonances. However, a few blocks away at the Gusman Center for the Performing Arts located downtown not too far from Biscayne Bay, a different kind of dissonance was playing itself out. Or perhaps resolving itself.

Relâche—along with the Kronos Quartet—was one of the resident ensembles on the festival. Accordingly the group was busy throughout the festival with a variety of rehearsals and performances. Joseph Celli and Mary Luft, festival producers, had received funds from the Pew Charitable Trusts Cultural Program to support Relâche's residency in Miami and commission four new works for Relâche to premiere. Together Joe and I selected Scott Lindroth, Mary Ellen Childs, Stephen Montague and James Tenney to receive the commissions.

With respect to the other three composers—all of them friends and highly esteemed by everyone in Relâche—I was especially eager to have Jim Tenney write a piece for Relâche. Jim is one of the most influential and innovative composers in America and both Joe Celli and I were in total agreement that he should have an important role on the festival. In earlier discussions Jim had confided to me he liked the sound of the Relâche Ensemble and had some ideas how he might use that sound to develop a new work challenging the musicians' interpretive skills in unique ways while creating a musical work which continued his exploration of harmonic functionality. Indeed he did. The result is titled *Critical Band* and to my mind it is one of the finest and most important works Relâche has ever performed and recorded.

Critical Band is, essentially, an experiment in tuning as a means of achieving a pure dominant harmony. The piece is scored for woodwinds, accordion or a drone-like instrument, piano and vibraphone. From the original program notes Jim Tenney explains, "A critical bandwidth is a frequency range within which complex acoustical stimuli evoke auditory responses very different from those evoked by stimuli separated by a larger interval (in the same register). For example, two simple sinusoidal tones separated by an interval much smaller than the critical bandwidth are not heard as two tones at all, but rather as a single tone, with beats which produce a sensation of roughness, at a subjective loudness which is correlated with the sum of their individual amplitudes."

The performance of *Critical Band* evolves from the normal process of the ensemble's tuning to A-440. Continuing from Jim's program notes, "After establishing a continuous unison on A (its continuity enhanced by a tape-delay system that re-cycles the collected instrumental sounds back into the auditorium), the players begin to expand the range of sounding pitches *geometrically*, above and below the central pitch. Each successive interval in a given direction is exactly twice the size of the preceding interval in that direction. Although these incremental intervals are always in strictly *harmonic* proportions (i.e., they can be represented by fairly low-integer frequency ratios), they are too small to be recognized as such (or even be heard as *intervals*) during the first half of the piece, in which the total pitch-range never exceeds the limits of the critical band (which, in this register, extends a major 2nd above and below the mid-point). Only after the expansion process has exceeded the critical bandwidth do the pitch relations begin to be heard as *harmonic*."

A piece like *Critical Band* is difficult to realize. Each player must concentrate totally on their roles as they incrementally tune each interval. It requires a somewhat different type of ensemble cooperation: each instrumental part is fiercely intimate yet communal, never losing its identity in the overall structure of the piece. In addition the sonic character of the space that it's being performed in must be highly resonant or it must be electronically enhanced to ensure that the sound appears to float throughout the space.

The success of any performance of *Critical Band* is incumbent on the sound engineers' abilities to distinguish between the acoustic and electronically enhanced components of the work. Their roles are critical: they must collect the evolving ensemble sound via an analog tape-delay system then carefully mix it with the previously recorded ones to create a seamless sonic tapestry to bathe the auditorium in sound. It's a difficult work fraught with potential problems both physical and structural. But when successfully realized it has a powerful effect as the pure dominant harmony is released from a dissonant texture that has accumulated for some 16 minutes. The climax is almost physical, or metaphysical as the sound virtually explodes throughout the space.

During the final dress rehearsal for *Critical Band* on the afternoon of its evening premiere just as the first complete run-through ended and the sound slowly faded, I noticed someone standing in the aisle, head down, listening intently to the barely audible decay.

It was John Cage. In the midst of rehearsal hubbub, I had nearly forgotten he was in the auditorium.

John was a featured composer on the festival. A new work of his titled *Five Stone Wind* was also being premiered that evening; he had just finished the final rehearsal with solo percussionist James Pugliesi before the Relâche Ensemble took the stage. I had greeted him at the end of his dress rehearsal and he asked my permission to listen in on the rehearsal. Needless to say I was honored beyond belief that he would ask my permission to listen in. We were all honored that he wanted to listen and I, of course, invited him to do so. As the sound faded John came over to me and asked what piece we were playing. "A new work by James Tenney," I answered. "It's titled *Critical Band*." He smiled and looked up at the ensemble then back at me and said softly, "That is the most beautiful piece of music I have ever heard." I smiled, thanking him, saying, I'll tell Jim."

Jim Tenney and John Cage had been conducting a long correspondence concerning their mutual interpretation or understanding of "harmony"; Jim being an articulate advocate of its architectonic role in musical praxis while John Cage countered that it was an artificial means of organizing primal material and was not a natural consequence of the musical gesture. Following the successful performance of *Critical Band*, Jim and John renewed their correspondence. As Jim later told me, smiling as he recalled the moment, John's letter congratulated him ending with the words, "If that's harmony, then I'm all for it." Unable to attend the premiere performance of *Critical Band* in Miami, James Tenney heard it for the first time in Philadelphia a few months later when Relâche performed and recorded it for release on a CD titled "Relâche On Edge" on Mode Records. *Critical Band* remained in Relâche's repertoire until the mid-1990s when several changes in personnel—and instruments—within the core ensemble made a successful realization of the piece difficult.

New Music America Miami marked the end of my tenure with the New Music Alliance, which, as I have indicated earlier, had begun to unravel a bit. It was time for a change, something many of the veteran New Music Alliance board members agreed on. Prior to arriving in Miami I decided to make public my resignation from the New Music Alliance board. Unfortunately I did not have the opportunity.

Prior to the official New Music Alliance meetings in Miami a group of folks, some current members and some not began organizing among themselves to re-think the concept of the festivals. Their position was that the festivals had become too big and institutionalized and needed to be smaller, less expensive to produce and more community based. I agreed only that the concept of the festivals had become a bit too institutionalized. I didn't agree with any of their other positions. In fact I advocated for even larger more expensive festivals, featuring not only music by American artists, but also representative works by European, Canadian, Japanese and Latin American artists. And I chaffed at the innuendo that past festivals, especially New Music America '87 were not community based. I felt that the previous nine festivals had been successful in building a broad context for presenting New Music while embracing and enriching the local communities where it was presented. Those successes, I felt strongly, should be developed even further to expand the festival in future years.

Most of the veteran New Music Alliance board members agreed but, like me, felt that it was time to move on, time for another generation to take the work we had done and propel the concept of a New Music festival forward into a new realm. What they did was halt the momentum we had created and threw the concept back into the margins of America's consciousness, in direct opposition to our wanting to escape from those very margins.

Accordingly, a new board was elected, replacing the then-current board members. This new group would advocate for a diminution of the festivals' format, creating a network of producer-presenters who would host smaller and shorter "festivals," some of them over the course of one weekend, some isolated performances scheduled within the context of ongoing concert seasons. "New Music America" would change to "New Music Across America." But before that could happen New Music America festivals were scheduled for New York and Montreal, their large-scale formats having been decided already. "New Music Across America" would have to wait two years.

In 1989 the Brooklyn Academy of Music produced New Music America, the tenth anniversary edition at venues throughout Manhattan and Brooklyn. I do not remember much about those performances. By being in New York City I never really got a feeling that a festival was taking place. Throughout the year many of the same people appeared there anyway so it was much different than attending a performance or event in a city that does not normally have a varied New Music presence. The Montreal festival in 1990 was, I'm told, a well-produced event that differed little from ongoing European music festivals. At the time the Canadian government provided substantial financial support for artistic endeavors so the festival was secure in terms of its professional production values. And Montreal is a great city. But I did not attend the festival. By 1990 I had lost the enthusiasm for the festival and felt that it had run its course.

Although I did not realize it at the time, I was about to experience a phenomenon familiar to most operatives in the field of New Music: burnout. Since the holidays were coming up I decided to get away for a while and fled to

New Mexico and the surrounding high desert regions of the American southwest. I spent a month there before returning to Philadelphia to continue directing the Relâche Ensemble's concerts in Philadelphia. In between concerts and planning sessions I traveled to Europe whenever possible, finding solace and new friends while developing new projects.

"New Music Across America" had a one-year run and then it disappeared.

In the years since my involvement with New Music America I have often commented that our efforts were admirable but ultimately we failed in our goal to create a large, informed, dedicated and supportive audience for New Musical works in the United States. As I was to experience first-hand in the following decade, audiences for New Music must be developed—slowly and carefully—on a local basis. Or to paraphrase the late speaker of the U.S. House of Representatives, Tip O'Neill, "All art is local."

In response to a question about the nature
of his music Thelonious Monk said,
"I put it down. You got to pick it up."

MUSIC IN MOTION

I met Michael Cerveris in 1990 while he was on the faculty of Duke University. He had heard about Relâche from a network of friends and was impressed with our efforts to create broader contexts for New Music performance. After several telephone conversations in which we discussed issues of mutual interest, mainly how to forge closer relationships among artists and their communities, Michael inquired if the Relâche Ensemble was interested in participating in a residency program he was organizing at Duke. Of course I was, so we began to explore the exact nature of the residency. After several planning talks he then informed me that he was leaving Duke to create a new program at Arizona State University West in Phoenix and would I be interested in talking about a new position there. Intrigued, I agreed to talk with him on an upcoming trip he planned to New York City.

It was not at all clear just what kind of program Michael envisioned for the new campus in Phoenix other than its being devoted to interdisciplinary performances and related studies. When we met to talk about the program it was evident that I was not the person he needed on staff since essentially he would be responsible to do many of the things that I do best: organizing events and residencies, managing a program or several related programs, administering a new entity, etc. What he really needed was people to create and teach courses for academic credit. I introduced him to Arthur Sabatini whom Michael eventually hired as one of the initial faculty members for the Interdisciplinary Arts And Performance Studies department at the university. The program launched in 1991 with the implied understanding that I would work with Michael to develop some new projects as the program evolved.

With Arthur and Merilyn Jackson and Michael Cerveris all moving to Phoenix I now had an even larger network of friends and relatives in Arizona to visit and collaborate with. One of the first things Michael did was schedule a residency for the Relâche Ensemble for February 1993. I stayed in Phoenix for an extra week after the ensemble's residency and scheduled a meeting with Michael to explore several potential projects. That meeting with Michael proved to be a decisive one.

Overall—at that time—things were going pretty well for Relâche. Fundraising for activities in Philadelphia was at an all-time high, audiences were as supportive as one could expect, touring was picking up a bit with a major European tour in the works, there was plenty of New Music to be performed and recorded; yet something was wrong. I felt that all of us in the New Music community were spinning our collective wheels. For every good idea, every innovative project that was launched and every successful new work presented to the public, we seemed to be taking strides backwards in terms of building new audiences and financial support.

In the aftermath of the New Music America festivals where producer-presenters around the country made huge efforts to enlarge the audience for New Music, we were still struggling to reach beyond a dedicated core audience, one that I was convinced would respond to new works if presented in a non-threatening way without sacrificing the artistic integrity of the music. Lacking this expanded audience, I felt it would be harder and harder to raise project and operations money from foundations and government agencies that were beginning to pressure all of the performing arts to become more inclusive of American society in general, a position I essentially agreed with. I shared these and other concerns with Michael as we sat by poolside at his home in Glendale, a suburb of Phoenix.

He too was concerned with audience development for new works, not only music but dance and theater as well, especially in Phoenix, a rapidly growing city without a solid informed audience base for the performing arts beyond the traditional fare that was available or well beyond the presenting series at Arizona State University that was essentially funded, or subsidized, by a combination of major foundation grants and income from high-impact events like tractor pulls in the football stadium. Our goals, Michael's and mine, seemed similar: audience development through education and exposure to living artists. A plan began to take shape, although it was far from clear just what this shape would be. Michael and I agreed to stay in touch as the idea came into focus with the intention that his program at Arizona State University West would have a prominent role in the project. Shortly after returning to Philadelphia I began to visualize a project directed at audience development and the creation of new musical works.

Back home I consulted with Arthur Stidfole who had recently joined the Relâche staff. A graduate of the Eastman School of Music and University of Illinois, Arthur was an accomplished bassoonist who had acquired administrative skills by working directly with a variety of performing, producing and presenting organizations mainly in New York City and San Francisco. When we met in the mid-1980s he had just returned from a residency in Japan with his then-wife, the composer Lois Vierk. The Relâche Ensemble was performing a work by Lois so she and Arthur came down from New York City to attend the concert. He then worked with the Pauline Oliveros Foundation, which in turn led him to the Good Sound Foundation where he eventually became their executive director, a position that led him somewhat indirectly to Relâche.

Divorced from Lois, disillusioned with certain aspects of the non-profit arts world, eager to become affiliated once again with a New Music performing and producing organization and interested in moving to Philadelphia, Arthur joined Relâche as development director in 1992. With knowledge of audio-acoustic sound enhancement systems from his past association with the innovative engineers and designers at the Good Sound Foundation, Arthur assisted Relâche's production team to ensure that the quality of sound at each Relâche concert in Philadelphia remained at the highest level possible, this in addition to expanding the fundraising base for Relâche. Essentially, Arthur and I spoke the same language, had many of the same friends in the New Music worlds and many of the same interests artistically and personally. We became good friends and allies as we pursued various projects, including the nascent one that was then just forming in my mind. When I returned from Phoenix I outlined my concept for a national residency program to address an issue that all of us in the New Music community faced: audience development. And audience development begins with audience awareness.

Our objective to develop a better-educated, more aware audience was limited of course to the music that Relâche and other similar New Music ensembles championed. Members of those ensembles are exceptionally well trained skilled musicians, graduates of select music schools and university music departments. But they differ from their counterparts who focus entirely on "classical music" by playing in a variety of ensembles and bands. Their knowledge of and enthusiasm for music is perhaps less specialized and more democratic. The same can be said of composers whose music is likely to become part of the repertoire of New Music ensembles. In addition to their training in Euro-American musical forms they tend to be conversant with world music, popular music and jazz. Unfortunately the general audience is not aware of these factors having been indoctrinated in the mystique of the "great composer," and indeed in the mystique of the "great performer" as well.

Popular mythology celebrates an image of the great composer: the Romantic tortured genius, isolated from the real world holed up in a room with reams of soiled music sheets stacked nearby, evidence of having "composed" a "great work," a symphony or concerto. Throughout the process of creating this great work they have made all or many of the decisions for the players in order to produce the sound that the composer has in his/her head, or so they thought. Instructions often include how a woodwind player is to finger or a string player is to bow their individual or group parts. What happens when the instruction is wrong or when a player has a better method to achieve the same or better result? Often the player will play a passage according to their unique system of production, regardless of the composer's instructions. And what happens when a group of musicians can improvise from a set of instructions or musical parameters resulting in a more coherent musical idea than the one the composer "composed"? Who has the final say in matters like this? Of course the composer does, mainly because their name is going on the work and they are being paid to compose it

Meanwhile, the audience is expected to genuflect at the altar of the composer, either accepting or dismissing the work as having achieved a level of authority or failure according to their comparative knowledge of Western classical music. But what about music which does not conform to Western ideals of form and structure? Are those works any less successful? And what about musical works which employ electronic and computer instruments and sources of sound production and/or instruments from non-Western cultures that utilize different tuning properties than conventional musical instruments? And why has classical music theory and praxis dominated pedagogical procedures in the United States from the beginning of the union? In developing our plan, Arthur and I determined to pose some of these questions to musicians and audiences alike.

We formulated a plan which would de-mystify the creative process among musicians and their audience by constructing situations whereby everyone could participate in the process of creation; where performers and composers, and composer-performers, would share information to develop a new collaborative work. The plan was simple in theory but complicated in praxis: five geographical regions in the United States targeted with a principal city in each region serving as the hub for a network of participating organizations which would share resources and activities. We identified Philadelphia, Minneapolis, Seattle, Phoenix and Orlando as the principal hub cities. In each of these cities we named a producing-presenting organization to serve as home base or be the principal partner or host site. In Seattle it was Cornish College of the Arts; in Minneapolis, the Walker Art Center; in Phoenix, Arizona State University West; in Philadelphia, the Fleisher Art Memorial; in Florida, Atlantic Center for the Arts or the Orlando Museum of Art. Each host site—in consultation with the project directors— would host a New Music ensemble selected from a list of five participating groups: the Relâche Ensemble, Present Music from Milwaukee, the California E.A.R. Unit from Los Angeles, the New Performance Group from Seattle, and Zeitgeist from St. Paul. The host site would schedule three one-week residencies each year at intervals three months apart. The host site and participating ensemble would select two composers to collaborate with the ensemble to develop a New Musical work.

The composers and ensemble would visit the host city, develop a working relationship with one another, agree to develop a new work collaboratively and agree to do all of this in the context of public outreach activities that would be scheduled by the host site and their aligned community partners. The overarching goal would be to focus on the process of creating a new work and not necessarily on the *product*, or, *completion* of a new work. A principal aim of the project was to give audiences an opportunity to observe and become a part of the creative process. In this way, we reasoned, the audience would feel a sense of authorship; they would be empowered to better support the efforts of New Music artists. Following the year's residency, the host site would select a new ensemble and collaborating composers and begin anew building on the audience base that had been developed during the previous year.

Each composer would spend a certain amount of time at the beginning of the residency consulting with each member of the ensemble to determine their playing styles, techniques they used to create a certain sound, their strengths and relative weaknesses. The composer would then begin sketching out phrases or complete sections. Together they would decide what was working and what is not. Much of these activities would be conducted in an open rehearsal format where those in attendance would be asked their opinions, advice or suggestions. At the conclusion of the first weeklong residency, the composer would begin to construct a work, consulting via email or phone with the players. The second residency week, two to three months following the first, would expand on the material thus far developed and continue the process. During the final residency week the ensemble would give a performance of the completed work or work-in-progress along with several other works from their respective repertoires. Throughout all of the residency sessions the host site would arrange television and radio interviews with the musicians and schedule outreach activities in schools throughout the region. Overall we would have developed regional hubs of activity with resultant information shared among all participants.

Other components of the project would be documentation and production of material created during the residencies. We envisioned producing and distributing a series of CDs containing musical works from the residencies along with descriptions of each work and the procedures used in its creation. A radio series would be produced in conjunction with National Public Radio to showcase the music developed in the residencies and interview the collaborating musicians and audience members.

As the plan unfolded Arthur and I identified potential funding sources, limiting our list to those foundations which had invested in New Music endeavors and expressed an intention to continue funding projects addressing issues relevant to the field of New Music. As a principal source we had only to look down the street to the Pew Charitable Trusts.

Over the preceding five years I had developed a professional connection with Marian Godfrey, Director of Cultural Programs at Pew and, at that time, one of the leading funding sources for the creation of new performance works throughout America. Marian and the principal program officers at Pew had been extremely supportive of Relâche. I usually had access to them when considering a new project and often mixed socially with Marian and others to explore ideas or discuss the current state of the performing arts. Informally, I presented Marian with the evolving idea for a national program to strengthen audience development efforts. Several hours later Marian said she liked the concept and would be interested in supporting it. She asked me how much I had budgeted. "Three Million bucks over a six year period," I answered. "You're crazy," she said. "That's not the issue, Marian. Of course I'm crazy to remain with this New Music business, but something has to be done to improve the current situation, and three million isn't much over a six year period," I responded. "Okay," she said, "go back and re-work the concept, but you must bring those numbers down to one and a half or two million dollars. If the board of trustees approves the proposal, Pew would provide about half of it. The rest you'll need to raise elsewhere." But, she cautioned that Relâche was not a big enough organization to apply for that amount of money. In order for Pew to look seriously at my proposal I would have to form a partnership with another arts organization with an operating budget of at least 1.5 million dollars per year, since Relâche's operating budget at that time was around $750,000 per year. I thanked her and set about reconfiguring the concept and finding a dancing partner.

Over the next several months Arthur Stidfole and I narrowed the goals of the project somewhat, reducing the radio and CD production components, and paring down administrative and artists' fees and travel-accommodations expenses to arrive at a projected budget of $1.9 million. Further, we divided the project into two three-year segments with appropriate reporting periods and benchmarks identified at the end of years one and two so that Pew could evaluate the progress of the project and determine if they were going to continue funding it for years four, five and six. We determined our initial request to Pew would be for $500,000 toward operating expenses for the first three-year period. Marian Godfrey thought that was a reasonable figure and again urged me about the necessity and importance of finding a fiscal partner, one with an impeccable record of artistic and fiscal achievement. Before presenting this version to Pew in the form of a formal proposal we had to form two separate partnerships: one to manage the project, and one to match potential funds from Pew.

Our first goal was to find a fiscal partner. By virtue of our long association with the Yellow Springs Institute, they were the first ones we approached with the idea. But their operating budget was not quite large enough and with a pending capital campaign being considered to expand their physical facilities we decided it wasn't the right time. I then began researching residency programs that I was familiar with and the Atlantic Center for the Arts (ACA) jumped to the top of my list.

Just a few years prior I had been approached by their then-program director to determine if Relâche was interested in being part of an artists' residency at their facility in New Smyrna Beach, Florida. After affirming my interest, I never heard back from them. I sent a letter outlining the project to ACA and about a dozen other artists' residency operations. The response was a thundering silence. After three months of failed phone calls or letters I was just about to give the project up, another casualty in the dysfunctional world of New Music in America. Then sometime in January 1993 I got a call from ACA, a guy named Dennis Szakas, their development director. He had fished my letter out of the program director's desk where it had been buried. After reading it Dennis realized this was just the type of project ACA wished to become involved with: a project which transcended their traditional artist-in-residence programs and created potentially new funding sources for their operations. We scheduled a meeting at ACA in the wilds of central Florida. For old time's sake, I decided to take the train.

I arrived at the AMTRAK station in Sanford, Florida somewhat equidistant between Orlando and New Smyrna Beach. Stepping onto the platform after an overnight ride from Philadelphia, the exact same smells of vanilla and mildew I remembered from my first trip to Florida in 1964 curled around me as I found my way to a rental car facility. After a short drive around Orlando I headed south to New Smyrna Beach.

New Smyrna Beach is a quiet conservative community populated by a combination of local residents who live there year-round and part-time residents from Orlando and points north with vacation homes near the beach. There really isn't very much to the place other than a series of beautiful white sand beaches for lounging and swimming, beachfront restaurants and bars and the usual trinket shops. Just ten miles south the Canaveral Wildlife Refuge offers a rugged coastline with meandering sand dunes dividing the only accessible road and the ocean; it is a distinct contrast to the well manicured tourist friendly beaches just to the north. If you were to follow the ocean south from Canaveral you'd come upon the old Cape Canaveral and the John F. Kennedy Space Center, still an awesome sight. From the beaches of New Smyrna and Canaveral you have an almost perfect view of the space shuttle launches active throughout the 1990s. Four miles inland at the north end of New Smyrna is the Atlantic Center for the Arts.

Founded in 1979 by the late sculptor and environmentalist Doris Leeper and located in a densely forested area just off US Highway 1, the Atlantic Center for the Arts has grown into one of the most respected artists' residency facilities in the United States. Master artists from all disciplines are invited to spend up to three weeks in residence there, having been selected by a national advisory committee. This committee consisted of senior artists, arts professionals and educators whose choices often reflected their conservative mainstream ideals. The result was too often a residency without any tension or controversy. And they were conducted in complete isolation from the public. When I first entered the site I saw a sign that read, "No Trespassing Beyond This Point – Artists At Work." Collaborations were rare and if attempted at all were not coordinated with a clear program plan to guide them. To help pay for the residencies other lesser known or novice artists apply to work with the master artists during the residency. These associate artists pay for the privilege of sharing the residency time with an appropriate master artist.

When I arrived in 1992, ACA had just begun planning for a major capital campaign that would eventually expand the facility from five multipurpose buildings to eleven including painters' and sculptors' studios, a research library, a rehearsal and recording studio and a black-box theatre. I was there during a time of transition. With the planned expansion going ahead on schedule, funds needed to be raised. Energy from the board and staff was directed toward the capital campaign. The residency programs—the very heart and soul of the organization—appeared to have lost their immediacy. Something was amiss at ACA but it was hard to figure out just what. The staff was cordial, cooperative, professional and competent. But they appeared to be going through the motions of administering residencies that were assigned by an advisory board. Among the staff there was no passion, no *esprit de corps;* there was no leadership. This became crystal clear to me when I eventually met the then executive director Ted Potter.

After outlining my concept and presenting—in great detail—how I envisioned the project working, he dismissed my ideas, preferring to feel that the artist, when working on a new piece, should remain isolated from the public until that new work was unveiled. Regardless of our difference, Ted and I needed each other, and he knew I had the potential of bringing money to ACA from sources they had not been able to gain access to.

With Pew already in line to become the principal funding source and with the potential of other large foundations coming on board, ACA envisioned substantial new money flowing through their books thereby building future relationships with these prestigious foundations. And (I think) Potter trusted young Dennis Szakas, his protégé. Dennis desperately wanted to change the residency format and felt strongly that without this change he, as development director, would not be able to generate new funding sources. So reluctantly Potter signed on.

We now searched for a second funding source, and this led me to a guy called Michael Dalakian. Certainly not your average arts guy, Michael Dalakian was a tough looking character bred in the streets of Newark, New Jersey. Built like a middleweight boxer, which he was at one time, he approached funding projects like a boxer sizing up his opponent in the early rounds of a match or looking for a tell-tale sign of weakness in a Poker adversary. At that time, Michael was an "independent consultant." Previously he had worked for a director of a prominent philanthropic foundation and knew many of the senior funding officers in New York City. I was intrigued with Michael because he was so different from the average arts professional. He walked with a swagger and talked like the guys I grew up with in North Philadelphia. I guess he and I were closer in spirit than even I was willing to admit. In any case we appeared to hit it off from the beginning.

Since retiring, Howard Klein, former director of programs for the Rockefeller Foundation, had become a well connected consultant to many prominent arts philanthropists and foundations; his signature on a proposal often put it over the top, or at least got the attention of important people with deep pockets and handy check books. One of his clients was the Lila Wallace-Reader's Digest Fund, now simply known as Wallace Funds. They had just completed a re-organization and were poised to bankroll large-scale arts projects throughout the United States. Arthur Stidfole knew Klein, having met with him while working in New York City. He suggested we prepare a letter outlining our project. If Howard liked the project, we asked that he recommend it to the Wallace Funds for consideration. We sent the letter then waited about a month for his response, which never came. Instead Dalakian called me to praise the project and inform me that he could convince Klein to recommend the project to the Wallace Funds. I assume Klein sent our letter along to Michael for his opinion. In return Dalakian wanted a defined role as the project developed. I agreed and suggested something like "Development Advisor," which he accepted. So now there were four of us spearheading the project. Dennis Szackas had, by this time, left ACA to take a position with the Jewish Museum in New York City.

After several exchanges to clarify certain points in our outline, Howard Klein recommended that the Wallace Funds consider our project for funding, the details to be worked out between my office and a program associate at the Wallace Funds. Klein advised me to call a man named Rory MacPherson, then a program associate and now Senior Program Officer at Wallace Funds.

MacPherson had been given a mandate by the foundation's culture program director to develop, nurture and fund arts projects that brought working artists and their audience closer together, continuing the funds' interests in audience development. Even though our project did not fit neatly into other projects they were then funding, MacPherson liked the idea, especially since he was a musician and supportive of music projects among New Music artists in New York City. During our negotiations with Rory we determined that the Wallace Funds would consider allocating $360,000 over the first three years of the project and, like Pew, evaluate its success to determine if they would continue funding it over the next three years. With this commitment in hand we sought a meeting with the Rockefeller Foundation to hopefully secure the balance of $140,000 needed to match the funds projected by Pew and Wallace funds.

Among the most prominent philanthropies in America, the Rockefeller Foundation dispensed large sums of monies for arts programs throughout the world. At that time they were especially interested in helping artists from the United States travel abroad to collaborate with artists from other countries. They were equally interested in supporting projects that brought artists from other countries to the United States to collaborate with American artists. Historically the bulk of their funds went to projects that embraced the "southern hemisphere," most notably Mexico and South America. Somehow the Caribbean Islands fit into this demarcated hemisphere as well. I saw an immediate connection with Rockefeller since our plans envisioned a component of the project being conducted in parts of the United States with strong Latino or Chicano cultures, one based on successful efforts that Relâche had developed in Philadelphia in tandem with Latino community organizations. Since Phoenix has a large Chicano presence and Philadelphia a strong Latino presence, we determined that those cities would share in our effort to invite composers from Mexico, Puerto Rico and Venezuela to the residencies scheduled in Phoenix and Philadelphia. An important alliance was created with Pima County Community College in Tucson and Arizona State University West in Phoenix to strengthen our position in Arizona. Rockefeller liked the idea and agreed to yearly grants of $50,000 to be evaluated each year to determine if they would renew their commitment. They did, contributing a total of $150,000 over the first three years. We now had a total of $1.1 million tentatively committed to the project over a three-year period. All we needed now was a name for the project and time to prepare the formal grant requests.

Finding a name was relatively simple. Merilyn Jackson in Phoenix was writing articles for local newspapers there on arts events and was preparing a piece about upcoming events at Arizona State University West, then viewed obliquely by the local population as a place where "oddballs" gathered. Merilyn's article was intended to portray the new facility as not only a place where prominent artists visit but also where new works would be presented. And the school wished to develop strong community ties. Accordingly their programs contained community outreach activities along with performances of works-in-progress, the result of ongoing residencies by visiting artists and ensembles. During a phone conversation with her I described the concept of our project, taking care to explain how easily it fit into the school's aim to engage the community in all aspects of creating and developing a new work. During our talk she remarked, "This is Music in Motion." Perfect! I decided to use that name for our project. We now set about to craft separate proposals to Pew, Rockefeller and Wallace Funds

Arthur Stidfole and I spent hours discussing the concept, talking with potential collaborators, getting their commitments to the project and sketching out the costs to pull it off. To facilitate matters we divided the cities between us with Arthur taking responsibility for Minneapolis and Philadelphia while I took on Seattle, Orlando/Atlantic Center for the Arts (they were the principal residency site in tandem with the Orlando Art Museum) and Phoenix-Tucson. The plan called for us to manage the host sites in these cities, determine the projected costs to host residencies and travel-accommodations for the participating artists. When all of the data was collected and tentative dates identified in each city we developed a project plan and budget. I had my old friend the writer and poet, Maralyn Lois Polak, edit the text so it provided a clear rationale for why we believed a project like this was essential to the future of New Music in America. Or at least we wished to clearly present a way of correcting the existing situation which, by all accounts, was not a healthy one. And we wished to state our case for the importance of the variable ensemble in American musical culture and a potential new role for the composer. After several months of consultation and re-writes we completed the plan and adapted it to three different grant proposals according to the format required by the three members of the funding partnership. Eventually Pew, Wallace Funds and Rockefeller approved the proposals. Arthur and I scheduled our activities for the six-month planning period built into the plan. Everything appeared to be going well.

We scheduled the six-month planning period for April – September 1993, with the residencies to begin in October. After dedicating two productive months—April and May—to working out details and negotiating fees and administrative costs for each host site and beginning the process of selecting participating artists I left for Japan on a two month residency, having been awarded a grant from the Asian Cultural Council in New York City. I was to spend the time in Tokyo, Osaka, Kobe, and Kyoto and then a week in Singapore exploring potential exchange programs between United States and Japanese composers and learning about new developments in Japanese music. The trip was a complete success. I returned to Philadelphia in July to prepare for both the initial Music in Motion residencies and Relâche's new season.

During my absence Ted Potter had resigned his position at Atlantic Center for the Arts. Suzanne Fetscher, the assistant director, was named interim executive director while the board of directors conducted a search for a permanent director.

I had only met Suzanne one time at an early planning meeting before I left for Japan. We hit it off quite well and I sensed in her an inquisitive manner, quite eager to learn about New Music—her background was in the visual arts—a thoroughly pleasant personality and an unquestionably honest way of doing business. She and I were to develop a close professional relationship over the next six years and proved to be one of the most reliable business partners I have ever had. When we launched Music in Motion in October 1993 she was acting executive director at ACA. Within the year she had been hired as the new executive director, committed to Music in Motion as one of ACA's most important projects. And she faced a pending capital campaign which would transform ACA into a world class residency site. After a year of planning and hard work we were off and running with Music in Motion. Until, that is, Arthur Stidfole informed me he was leaving Relâche and Music in Motion.

Arthur and his future wife, Kathryn Bauer, had reached one of those points in life where a change was necessary. Each of them had spent years in the arts—Kathryn had been trained in Theatre and was then working as a stage manager for the Wilma Theatre in Philadelphia—and, like most of us at the time had very little in the bank to show for it. They decided that they would return to graduate school and earn degrees in nursing, having correctly concluded there would never be a problem finding work anyplace they chose to live. Years later their decision has proved to be the right one; they currently live in Placerville, California near the Foothills of the Sierra Nevada Mountains while working in Sacramento and San Francisco in well paying jobs while enjoying their abundant leisure time. Arthur assured me he would wrap up all loose ends pertaining to Music in Motion and Relâche before entering school. I decided that I would manage all of the partnerships while contracting with someone in each participating city to handle the localized details.

The first phase of Music in Motion went pretty much according to plan, although each host organization was quite different in terms of how much support services they could provide for the project, and how effective those were. The Walker Art Center, for instance, has a dedicated administrative-program staff, but in relation to other departments there, it is relatively small. With so many events scheduled throughout the year, Music in Motion residencies were sometimes squeezed into times and places which were not always effective. Walker collaborated with the American Composers Alliance whose very mission is to nurture composers, performers and develop an audience for New Musical works. Their efforts were instrumental in creating outreach activities while Walker provided a professional and warm performance venue. In Seattle the Cornish College of the Arts was effective in developing awareness for the project within their multi-disciplined departments but had little experience in creating community alliances other than with local high schools. Since they did not have a production department or community outreach director the job of organizing and scheduling activities was taken over by Paul Taub, flutist for the New Performance Group. As a busy performer, producer and teacher, his time was limited but without him there would have been virtually no activities outside of Cornish. In Philadelphia the Fleisher Art Memorial simply did not have the experience or the staff to schedule and manage the types of multi-disciplinary community activities I sought. After the first year we mutually decided the Painted Bride Art Center would be a better partner in years two and three. In Phoenix at Arizona State University West Michael Cerveris and his staff worked closely with me to develop alliances throughout the city. In addition we were able to bring Tucson into the fold by partnering with Pima County Community College. At that time, Carol Williams was just beginning to develop a presenting program there and immediately connected to the mission of Music in Motion. Atlantic Center for the Arts proved to be the most effective of all host sites, although at times it was difficult for me to encourage some of the staff to think a little differently about outreach activities and change some of their established approaches to artists' residencies. As a principal partner with ACA the Orlando Museum of Art was a great host whose staff was extremely helpful in developing an identity for the project in Orlando. Within each residency the participating ensembles and composers had varying degrees of success in discovering ways to collaborate on new works.

Not every composer "got" what was important to the success of the project, their willingness to suspend—for a brief time—their need to satisfactorily *complete* a new work. I spent much too much time explaining this to folks, that we as artists develop working contexts so the public can find their way into the creative process. This is the key: yes, the *process* not the product. And yet that pathway itself could, paradoxically, reveal failed compositional efforts or, more accurately, unfulfilled experiments, which ran counter to the grain of many composers. Despite my efforts, almost all of the 30 composers who participated in Phase One of Music in Motion completed a new work. That was okay because most of them required considerable post-project revisions to become part of the repertoire.

Conversely, all the participating ensembles "got it." They understood implicitly how important it was to become part of the process of creation, allowing the audience to have a say in how a new work is developed *with* them, not *for* them. Except for the Relâche Ensemble, none of the other groups had participated in similar residency situations. Several had a little experience working with composers during the early stages of creating a new work, but nothing to compare with the extended situation created by Music in Motion. As part of the arrangement each ensemble agreed to perform works created in residencies other than their own thereby enhancing each repertoire. In many cases the works required adjustments, changes in instrumentation and, sometimes, personnel. Each of the groups informed me time and again how the experience helped them become better group performers, and in some instances, a *real* ensemble. What really helped was having an opportunity to stay in touch both electronically and in-person over the course of a one-year period, to continually experiment and explore new techniques of sound production, ensemble balance and internal relationships; to learn to play better together!

Over a three-year period of intense activities in five cities Music in Motion nurtured many unusual situations, some touching and some a bit off base. There were few dull moments. For me, there were many high points.

One of the more successful public outreach activities at ACA was with a group of senior citizens who attended on numerous days during the duration of the project, and in doing so, got to know many of the performers and composers. Retired from successful careers in business and education, these folks were insightful and thoughtful in their interactions with the musicians. At one of the middle-year residencies with Guy Klucevsek and Present Music, Guy and the ensemble played a section of the work they were developing. Following one run-through of a fairly lengthy section, a woman asked Guy what the title is or would be. Guy didn't yet know and asked the woman if she had an idea. She did. The woman, a Holocaust survivor, described how the music reminded her of an event or perhaps a series of events, even a mood she experienced as a child in a concentration camp in Poland. She suggested the title be "Tesknota," meaning—in Polish—a powerful longing.

Composer Mary Ellen Childs arrived at ACA with a plan to have the members of the Relâche Ensemble bow a marimba; each musician—bow in hand—would learn the technique of bowing the bars of the instrument, a popular yet often ineffective method used by contemporary composers to create a shrill, overtone-rich sound. But that technique was developed on the vibraphone using a bow on aluminum alloy bars. The marimba keys are made from rosewood or a synthetic material called Kelon; there is no way a sound will result from placing a bow at the edge of a key and bowing up and down. After numerous failed attempts—one in front of a group of high school music students fairly dumfounded by the idea—Mary Ellen gave up and proceeded to write a beautiful piece for Relâche, the second of three she would write for the ensemble, each player in their more comfortable roles as instrumentalists.

Composer Kyle Gann proposed a complex compositional scheme for the Relâche Ensemble based on a scale containing 21 notes to the octave with equally complex metric signatures that changed from measure to measure with, for example, a signature of 11/27. After a week of working together to tune each chord in this scheme, everyone concluded that the ensemble could negotiate the meters but could not successfully tune. As someone in the ensemble commented, "We sound like a junior high school band." Kyle agreed. He abandoned the tuning system, kept the metrical concept and proceeded to develop most of a work that became *Astrological Studies*, a piece successfully performed numerous times by the Relâche Ensemble in the succeeding years.

Chinary Ung was in Philadelphia with the New Performance Group at the time trying to find a way to approximate the sound of a chanting Buddhist monk using the instruments in the ensemble, but nothing was working out. Then cellist Walter Gray suggested he chant the part. Chinary was surprised and a bit skeptical until Walter opened his mouth and let loose a deep rich bass chant, while continuing to play his cello. It worked! Later at the final residency a special event with an extraordinary group of Cambodian musicians and dancers, Chinary led the ensemble through his new piece and then brought everyone together for an improvisation, combining the Western instruments with indigenous Cambodian strings, flutes and percussion. Chinary left Cambodia for New York in the early years of the Pol Pot genocides, arriving in Philadelphia to teach at the University of Pennsylvania in the mid 1980s. He has a wry sense of humor and loves to tell stories about his life in America, especially about the cultural differences he encountered when he first arrived. While in Philadelphia he and his new wife lived in an old working class section of northeast Philadelphia called Torresdale. The only Asian in the neighborhood, Chinary was a distinctive sight. One night a neighbor asked, "Chinary, what's the difference between a Cambodian and a Chinese?" "Cambodians," the composer replied, "have a mole on their chins." Chinary had a mole on his chin.

At the conclusion of Year Three or Phase One of the project the staff at ACA and I prepared a detailed report for each of the principal funding agencies. After analyzing the report we submitted to Pew, they agreed to continue to provide funds for the next three years but not at the level of the previous three. They suggested we cut the number of participating ensembles and host sites and cities from five to three. One of the ensembles —The New

Performance Group—were having personnel problems and eventually disbanded, so the choice of which ensembles would remain with the project was made a little easier. The Painted Bride Art Center in Philadelphia and Walker Art Center in Minneapolis had taken on too many other projects and felt they could not continue hosting residencies. So, again, the choice of which cities would remain with the project was made somewhat easier. After meeting with Pew and getting their commitment, and since we had achieved almost all of the goals set forth in the initial plan, we figured Lila Wallace Funds and Rockefeller would follow Pew's lead and continue funding the program. If only it were that easy.

Mexican composers Arturo Marquez and Eduardo Soto Millan with the author in Tucson, Arizona at Music in Motion residency

I scheduled a meeting with Rory MacPherson at the Wallace Funds office to go over our report and determine if they were going to continue funding the project. This meeting proved just how frustrating the business of arts funding can be.

Essentially, Rory was impressed with the results of the project; he acknowledged that we had indeed accomplished just about every goal we set. A total of 30 new works was created in a collaborative manner while new audiences were created through repeated visits and numerous outreach activities. Substantial media coverage resulted in newspaper and magazine articles, radio and television interviews and features appeared in most of the participating cities. And a solid network of ensembles, composers and producer-presenters had been created and, most importantly perhaps, proved that new musical works can be developed through carefully planned collaborations among all concerned. After congratulating me for the project's success Rory then informed me the Wallace Funds could not continue to support the project. The board of trustees decided to change their funding priorities and Music in Motion no longer fit these new priorities. So, I asked Rory, "What are these priorities, what is the board looking for?" "Technology and the arts," he replied, without elaborating further. "Well, Rory, how about if I come forward with a technology component to add to the formula we've already developed," I responded. Surprised, he looked at me and agreed to review a proposal. "Give me a few weeks and I'll have something ready," I said.

I always wondered why Rory appeared surprised at my reaction. Having worked with me over the previous three years, he should have known that I was not about to slink away from our meeting—and Music in Motion—with a meek, "Thanks for helping with this project." Frankly, this was a disturbing development. Unlike other large projects being funded by major foundations in America—many of them good, well-intentioned ones but unfortunately not particularly well-managed, their results often less than what they might have been if they had been better organized—Music in Motion was well organized and well managed and deserved continued funding. I was determined to hang on to this important funding source. And that's when Mark Weber came into the picture.

Mark Weber is a composer and, at that time, 1996, a fledgling web artist. Like many composers of his generation—he was 30 when we met—Mark is fluent in the evolving usage of music and technology, especially MIDI, which stands for Music Instrument Digital Interface, a data communications protocol describing a means for music systems and equipment to exchange information and control systems. Unlike many young composers who embrace technologies at a high level of discourse, Mark's musical sensibilities are grounded in jazz; this is what attracted me to his work.

Originally from suburban Philadelphia, Mark had been living in New York, first in Rochester where he attended the Eastman School of Music and then in New York City after graduate studies with the legendary trombonist, composer-arranger Bob Brookmeyer at the Manhattan School of Music. He returned to Philadelphia with his wife and young son to teach and establish a career as a composer-arranger. After attending a Relâche concert he approached Laurel Wyckoff and asked if he could submit a tape of his work to Relâche. Laurel always encouraged young composers to make themselves known to Relâche, which Mark did by sending me several cassette tapes of his music.

I received many unsolicited tapes and scores during those years and tried my best to give them a careful listening to and review. Sometimes, overscheduled as I was, I just didn't have the time and asked one or more of the ensemble members of Relâche to give a listen. Mark's tapes sat on my desk with a bunch of other ones for several months until one day I scooped them up and packed them into my car so I could listen while driving to Erie, Pennsylvania, a five-hour drive. I vaguely remember that the first couple of tapes I listened to that day were rather unimpressive, several containing music well crafted and performed, but they just did not fit the Relâche sound. I was starting to lose my enthusiasm when I slipped Mark's tape into the tape player. It got my attention.

Every piece on the tape was well written, orchestrated and performed, all expressing a joyous spirit that was evident from the opening of each work. Although influenced by jazz and, to a lesser degree, the music of Phillip Glass, Mark's music had if not a unique quality, then the potential to evolve into something higher, were he to work closely with the caliber of musicians in the Relâche Ensemble. When I returned, I set up a meeting. Mark's knowledge and enthusiasm for his work reminded me of a younger version of me. He had no pretense whatsoever about who he was and the kind of music he liked; he was informed about current musical trends and personalities and passionate in his likes and dislikes. I could just sense he was reaching for something else not evident in his music or in our initial conversations. He had just been awarded a grant from the Pennsylvania Council on the Arts and I suggested that he write a new piece for Relâche as part of the award. Perfect! This gave us all a chance to develop a relationship, build alliances with the players in the ensemble and hopefully gain a new work for the repertoire. And the piece, funded by a grant, would not cost Relâche anything other than the musicians' time. Everything worked out as planned. Mark made a new piece premiering in Philadelphia on the following season's schedule. He and the players formed a relationship and, most importantly, he and I formed a friendship. After getting to know him better I decided to offer him a future role with Relâche as managing director.

After 18 years as the artistic and executive director of Relâche while concurrently directing Music in Motion I had decided it was time to begin a transition to new and hopefully younger management. I had been looking around for someone to bring into the organization who could be trained to take over the day-to-day operations so I could concentrate exclusively on the artistic direction of the Relâche Ensemble, Music in Motion and other future projects. Of all the prospects I met during that time, Mark stood out. As a literate musician-composer with plenty of good common sense he appeared to be a perfect choice. After considering the offer Mark declined. He was not attracted to a job as managing director, preferring to continue to write music and hopefully develop some projects of his own design. Although disappointed, I fully understood his position. I then asked him if he had some ideas for new projects we might initiate.

A few weeks later he presented four different proposals to me for projects that would either celebrate the music and legacy of a specific composer or a themed event aimed at attracting a much younger, and much sought after, audience. Though the first three proposals were good enough, they really did not get my attention. The fourth one, however, did.

He proposed that we develop a live and interactive Virtual Concert using new technologies and Internet tools to build a presence on the evolving World Wide Web and stream audio over the Internet. His idea was to use existing technologies to build a new form of composition celebrating participants' logging on to the new website and exchanging musical information with the composer, in this initial case, with Mark Weber himself. Although, as he said at the time, there's abundant information currently available on the Internet and in just a few years there would be so much more, there wasn't very much real artistic content. I agreed with him and proceeded to explain in detail how his concept might fold into the existing residency models which had been developed by Music in Motion. Essentially we had an opportunity to apply Mark's idea to create virtual residencies that would align with the existing real-time residencies to enhance the goals of Music in Motion, specifically to create an enlarged and better-informed audience for New Music. Mark gave me the angle I was looking for: bring Relâche into the globally linked world of the Internet and, most importantly, reconfigure Music in Motion to embrace new interactive technologies. We set about working on a plan and proposal for Music in Motion – The Virtualconcert.

Initially we determined that three of the original cities—Phoenix, Seattle and Orlando/ACA—would host year-long residencies with one of the participating ensembles and one, rather than two, composers selected for their combined compositional and technological skills. The overall scheme of the residencies would be the same as those from Phase One: the ensemble and composer would spend one week in residence three times a year collaborating on a new musical work while conducting as many of their activities as is appropriate before the public. Each composer would be responsible to create and manage an interactive website to enable those who log onto the site to participate in the ongoing creation of a new work using interactive computer tools designed by the composer. In essence, as the new work evolved, its structure, overall shape, etc., could be determined from input by numerous individuals who participated in the virtual residency. The collaborating ensemble still would work directly with the composer throughout the process, performing sections of the evolving work before the public during the real-time residencies. Each session of the real-time residency would be recorded digitally then placed on the composers' website so those who log on could follow the progress of the work. In addition, Mark Weber would create a Music in Motion – The Virtualconcert website to serve as a gateway into the project and link to each participating composers' website as well as other relevant New Music project links. At the conclusion of the yearlong residency a concert featuring the new work plus others from each ensemble's repertoire would be presented by the host site and webcast via streaming audio over the internet. The plan was developed into proposals that went to all the funding partners.

Critical to the project was matching the funds that Pew had committed. It was very frustrating to me to have to prove—once again—the merits of the project, especially after Wallace Funds had expressed their satisfaction over the results of Phase One only to back out of Phase Two. Ultimately though, that probably worked to our advantage.

Rory MacPherson had developed an interest and knowledge of interactive computer technologies and was intrigued with the potential of using the Internet to change the way music was not only distributed but also created. When he read our proposal, he understood it implicitly, and was able to award a grant of $100,000 for the project but only for one year with the funds coming during the second year of Phase Two or the fifth year of the overall project. We now knew that The Virtualconcert would happen but were unsure of how to make it happen with a budget far less than Phase One. We realized also that in order to get the project up and running we needed at least a year of research and development, especially for Mark who would become the artistic director for the project. We decided that year four, or the first year of Phase Two would be a transition year. Only the Relâche Ensemble, which by this time had formed a close relationship with ACA, would conduct a yearlong residency at New Smyrna Beach.

During that year Mark and I met with the remaining participating ensembles and host sites to determine who would continue in the newly configured project. To ensure continuity we formed a national advisory committee consisting of eight New Music specialists with expertise in technology and artists' residencies to provide an assessment or overview of our plan. This transition year proved invaluable, giving Mark and me the time to really explore how his plan would actually work, and it gave me an opportunity to discuss—in detail—the philosophy and practical aspects of the entire project with the advisory committee. As we worked out these details the Relâche Ensemble and composer William Ortiz from Puerto Rico participated in a residency which essentially held to the models of the previous three years' residencies at ACA.

We decided two ensembles would continue with the project: the Relâche Ensemble and the California E.A.R. Unit. Zeitgeist and Present Music were experiencing changes in personnel and neither had fully integrated technologies into their performances, so the decision to go with Relâche and the E.A.R. Unit was the correct one. Relâche and the E.A.R. Unit each had worked with composers versed in interactive technologies and were prepared to enter into the kind of residency situations we envisioned. We now had to decide which of the remaining three host sites would continue with the project.

With the opening of five new buildings including a well-equipped music and technology studio, ACA was committed to develop programs to support evolving interactive technologies. It was clear that they would remain as one of the two host sites. Faced with critical changes in his program and under pressure from the university to cut back on his financial commitments,

Michael Cerveris at Arizona State University West decided not to continue with the project. This left Seattle as the most logical city to serve as host.

During Phase One, Cornish College of the Arts dropped out for a variety of reasons. I found this odd especially since the Seattle area is the home of Microsoft and other software developers. During Phase One, an organization named Jack Straw Foundation had become a principal partner with Cornish and they definitely were seeking close ties with the powerful technology industry. When the Virtualconcert concept began to take shape the executive director of Jack Straw Foundation, Joan Rabinowitz, leaped at the opportunity for her city to become the host site.

Jack Straw Foundation is a media center that serves artists from throughout the Pacific Northwest. Initially their mission was to support broadcast and recording projects while offering residencies and public outreach programs. With the need to support new interactive media projects that area artists were developing, they adapted their mission to embrace not only radio and recording projects but also inter-media ones as well as purchasing new equipment and constructing a new performance gallery. We now had two host sites to partner with Relâche and the California E.A.R. Unit: ACA and Jack Straw Foundation.

In addition to his role as artistic director for the Virtualconcert, Mark Weber was selected as one of two composers for the first year's residency at ACA with the Relâche Ensemble. The California E.A.R. Unit was in residence at Jack Straw Foundation, collaborating with composer Rand Steiger. With plans now firm for the Virtualconcert and with the blessing of Pew and the Wallace Funds, we approached the Rockefeller Foundation to seek their continued support. Like the Wallace Funds they had recently become interested in supporting new media projects, specifically those that use the Internet to create artistic content and develop ways to disseminate information and programs. After Mark and I made a presentation to their program staff they agreed to continue funding the project at $50,000 per year. We were now set to launch Music in Motion – The Virtualconcert, the first residencies set for October 1998.

Mark Weber's concept for his website and new piece was based on integrating new software applications or plug-ins that had just appeared on the market using them as tools to aid in the development of his new work titled *Disconnect*. An application named "Beatnik" had just been launched that enabled the internet user to access MIDI files imbedded into a website. Mark

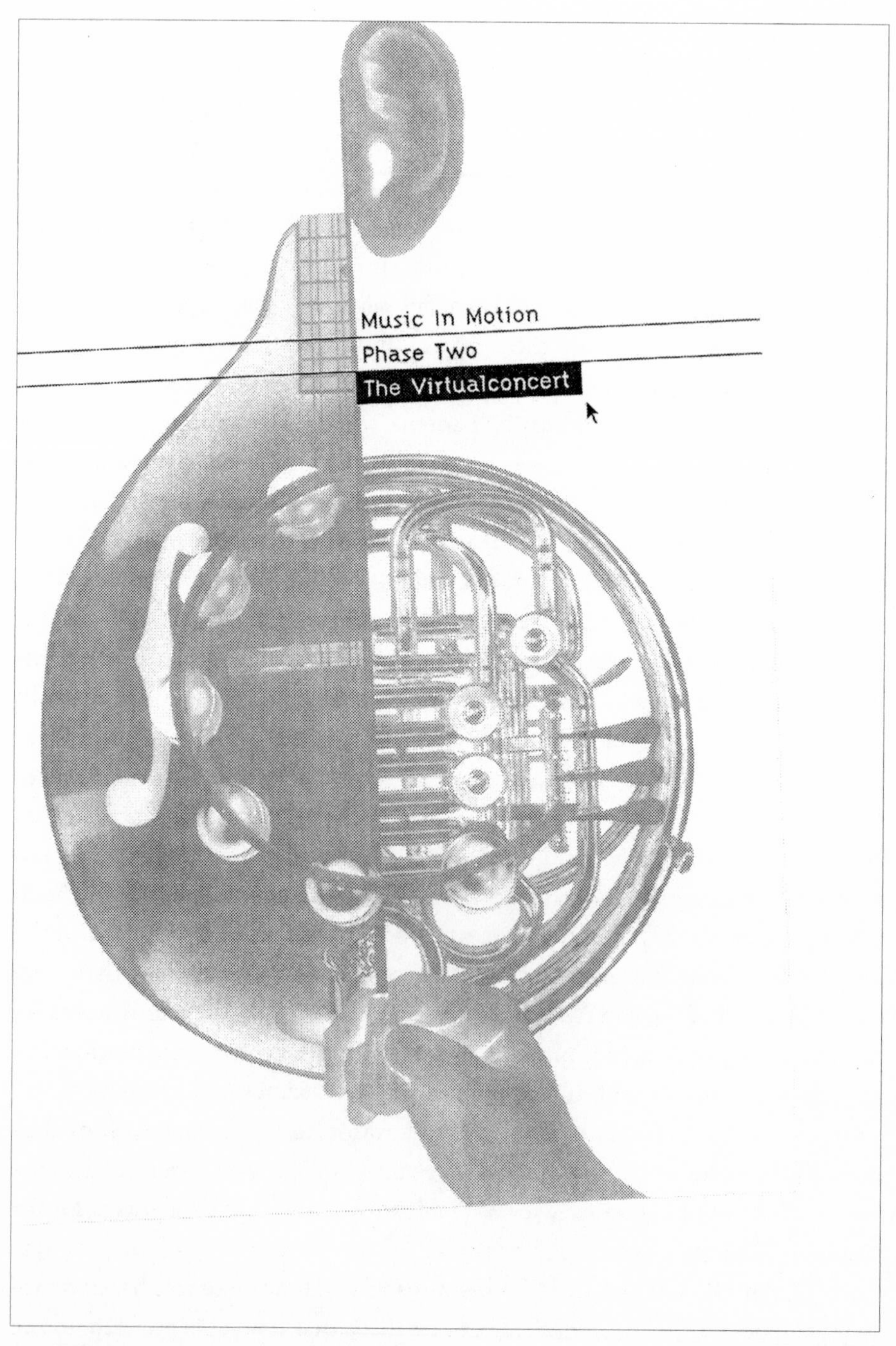

Music in Motion – The Virtualconcert Flyer

used Beatnik to trigger a file, each containing primary musical materials such as a set of rhythmic patterns, simple musical motives stated in one measure or whole phrases played over several measures. These were played by MIDI instruments configured to sound like one of the musical instruments used in the Relâche Ensemble (i.e. flute or oboe) and accessed via a colored button set in a graphic interface on the website. After accessing the website and navigating to the interface, a click of the mouse would trigger one of the files, for example, one of the rhythmic patterns. Buttons labeled with the name of each instrument were placed horizontally across the page (screen), and embedded behind the button was a MIDI file sounding a pattern set in 3/4 time. The first row contained buttons for a drum set that served as the musical underpinning over which the other instruments could be added. After establishing the pattern in 3/4 time on the MIDI drums one could then add one of the other instruments playing a beat pattern in 3/4 time or change it to play in 4/4 or 5/4 time so that the overall musical construct would be in sub-divided groups of three against four, or three against five or four against five. Another graphic interface displayed similar colored buttons that controlled each motive and phrase that was assigned to a specific instrument. By using these controlling devices, computer-users could experiment with Mark's musical ideas, altering them so that a phrase played by the saxophone could be transposed and shifted to the oboe. Or the user could create his own musical phrase and send it to Mark via a MIDI file with suggestions as to how it might fit into the overall scheme of the evolving work. Mark would then decide to use the file or discard it, always responding to the person who sent it, thereby expanding the user mailing list. As the materials became more developed Mark sent them via email to each of the musicians in Relâche. Later on as Mark developed more facility with the tools, the musical work and website became more sophisticated and interactive.

During the first real-time residency at ACA Mark distributed the instrumental parts to the players so they could begin the process of putting them together in coherent sections, trying this and trying that, searching for material to serve as building blocks for the eventual work. Each session was recorded via DAT tape then imported into the website to be accessed via the then relatively new Real Audio Player as streaming audio. This procedure gave new meaning to the concept of outreach. In all instances when Relâche and Mark conducted an outreach program at ACA, the Orlando Museum of Art or Rollins College in Winter Park, those in the audience had an opportunity to gain a deeper understanding of the ongoing process of composition by accessing the website prior to the outreach session and then afterwards. It became a fully participatory experience, one that was especially successful at the Orlando Museum of Art.

Over the previous four years of Music in Motion a dedicated core audience had evolved in central Florida, centered at ACA and Orlando, a fairly conservative city with an affluent population powered by the entertainment and tourism industries. The Orlando Museum of Art has benefited from this affluence by establishing an attractive and well endowed visual arts museum. Their director immediately saw the wisdom of collaborating with ACA and Music in Motion – The Virtualconcert, knowing that the program would bring new people to the museum. Among the most enthusiastic attendees to these events were artists and technicians who worked for the Disney Company in various creative capacities.

These folks were eager to meet other artists, especially those who used technology; they connected directly with us and helped to build an enthusiastic audience. Mark and I were able to secure technical support through in-kind services from several prominent technology businesses in Central Florida who provided additional hardware for the outreach events at the Orlando Museum of Art. A company in Daytona Beach—Datapex—was especially helpful. They provided their server—free of charge—and a technician to help manage it, an expense that would have cost $15,000 over two years. For the final presentation at the museum we positioned laptop computers throughout the space so everyone who attended the concert could spend time prior to the performance accessing data that had been collected on the website over the past year. And it gave those cautionary souls who remained intimidated by computer language and usage an opportunity to experience first-hand tools and applications that would eventually become part of their everyday lives.

Overall, Mark's piece, *Disconnect*, worked. His initial concept to use newly created computer tools and applications to build a musical composition while sharing the content with internet users proved workable. Certain other aspects of the experience proved not as successful but valuable nevertheless as the project became more expansive.

Each of the other collaborations over the two years of the Virtualconcert had varying degrees of success: at ACA with Panaiotis and the Relâche Ensemble and at and Jack Straw Foundation with Rand Steiger and the California E.A.R. Unit and Jovino Santos Neto and Musician's Accord. For the final year the California E.A.R. Unit was replaced by Musician's Accord, based in New York City, due to scheduling conflicts with the E.A.R. Unit in Europe. The working relationships between composers and ensembles varied as well as did those of the composers to the overall concept of the project as perceived by Mark Weber. In several instances Mark worked directly with the composers to realize the objectives of creating a convincing website to support their compositional ideas.

Music in Motion – The Virtualconcert achieved its goals to integrate existing and new technologies into the process of musical composition and reach out to new audiences through the use of the Internet. Overall the initial concept that resulted in the creation of Music in Motion and then Music in Motion – The Virtualconcert was a positive exercise in the ongoing quest among composers and performers of new musical works to expand their audience base by combining talents to develop new works while daring to place their strengths and weaknesses before the public. Equally important were the relationships which developed within specific communities as the host organizations connected directly with partnering organizations in their respective cities. Services linking the artists—the composers and performers—with the community have included lecture-demonstrations, open rehearsals, special concerts, related courses, special demonstrations in schools and colleges and expanded interviews in newspapers and on radio and television. Audiences have been directly involved in observing and, in some instances, participating in the process of developing a new musical work, thereby gaining a sense of ownership.

Did Music in Motion – The Virtualconcert develop new adherents to and supporters of new American music? Yes, but not at the levels *really* necessary to lift the music from the margins of America's consciousness and place it in a position where it is listened to and understood in broader cultural contexts. Some of the participants in the project were more successful than others, while some have reverted back to their usual way of producing-presenting New Music, which means, well, less than spectacularly. I believe the effort we made to insist on collaborations among participating artists was the right one but I do not think it has had the kind of impact that I initially envisioned it would have. It was, after all, a grand experiment and often experiments take time to determine their effectiveness.

About that time, I again heard Larry Tso, his soft uninflected voice echoing off of the red rocks of Canyon de Chelly in Arizona. This time though Larry's voice emerged through a scrim of memory: images of the high Southwestern dessert that often haunt my daydreams, usually when I'm operating at overload as I was in the summer of 1997. It was, I decided, the time to make another pilgrimage to Canyon de Chelly, my first visit in five years.

Laurel and I planned to spend the entire month of August in New Mexico and Arizona with at least one week or more on the road traveling around the Four Corners region and camping for a few days outside Canyon de Chelly. When we arrived at the canyon I inquired at the visitor's center if Larry Tso were available to lead us on a tour, this time much deeper into the canyon. No one could find him so we hired another Navajo man to guide us. Much more talkative than Larry Tso but without his sense of poetry, Robert guided us into the canyon along barren dirt roads to Spider Rock, one of the most sacred sites in the canyon.

Spider Rock stands alone jutting straight up from the canyon floor reaching for the sky; two chambers forming a "V for Victory" sign—or is it a "peace sign?" This is the place where, according to Navajo lore, Spider Woman originated before traveling the land to teach Navajo women how to weave, leaving a loose thread somewhere in the woven piece to allow the weaver's spirit to emerge. We arrived at the base of the rock in early afternoon the sun at full staff and stood there in silence, not a sound anywhere except the scraping of my boots on the hard rock surface. We sat for a long while looking up at Spider Rock, wondering if Spider Woman were sending a message down to us from her sacred perch, a code to be deciphered through the silence to link us back to the eon time and ghosts of ancestors who traveled through the canyon, ancestors we might have had and yet had no knowledge of. If she sent a message to me on that day I have no proof of having received it, but I did receive something there that day to force a radical change in my life.

After arriving back at our campsite just outside the south rim of the canyon I informed Laurel that it was time to move on from Relâche, to move away from Philadelphia to the west, preferably New Mexico. At the end of the camping and hiking part of our trip we drove back to Corrales, New Mexico where her parents live and began searching the Internet for potential jobs. All this while continuing to direct Music in Motion – The Virtualconcert and preparing for a full season with Relâche in Philadelphia. Although I had made a firm decision to leave it was far from clear just when it would happen, probably at the conclusion of the upcoming performance season. Little did we realize that I would be gone by the end of the year.

Back in Corrales while searching the Internet we found a job description for "Artistic Director, Helena Presents" in Helena, Montana, an organization I knew a little about. Noticing that the job listing had just expired I called them to see if they were interested in receiving a late application. I distinctly remember that call: the person who answered the phone was unaware there was currently a job search underway to hire an artistic director. In retrospect that should have been a clue to me that something was amiss. I left my name and number and within hours I received a call back from the head of the search committee, also a member of their board of directors. Yes, they were interested in having me apply for the position, which I promptly did. We returned to Philadelphia and dived into the new season.

By mid-September I heard back from the head of the search committee who informed me that they were interested in conducting a formal telephone interview. The interview went well and I was invited to interview in person with the search committee. I traveled to Montana to visit the center, spending two days getting to know the organization, most importantly, the staff. The interview and visit went very well and I was subsequently offered the position which I accepted after weighing the consequences of leaving an organization which had only had one executive and artistic director—me. I prepared to announce my departure at an upcoming board of directors meeting.

The previous year I had hired a managing director, a woman named Colette Dominguez who had previously worked for HBO in New York. Originally from Manchester, Great Britain, the daughter of a Jamaican father and English mother, she had lived in Bermuda and the Virgin Islands before coming to the U.S. Married to guitarist and web designer Abel Dominguez, she was an excellent choice to take over the administrative direction of Relâche, which she did upon being offered the position. I suggested to the ensemble members that they form an artistic advisory committee to select and program the music they felt they wanted to play and work closely with Colette to guide the organization in possibly a new direction. Everyone appeared to like this idea so I felt better about leaving. I resigned from Relâche effective November 1, 1997 and prepared to leave Philadelphia, the only city I had ever called home.

When I accepted the position with Helena Presents - The Myrna Loy Center I informed their board of directors that I would continue to direct

Music in Motion - The Virtualconcert. This required that I spend a certain amount of time at ACA in Florida and at Jack Straw Foundation in Seattle. These visits were in addition to trips that were essential to my position of artistic director for Helena Presents.

As Laurel and I began the transition from Philadelphia to Montana I thought back to that August afternoon at Spider Rock in Canyon de Chelly wondering where Spider Woman left the loose thread in the archetypal weave she made for us that day and if her message was one of hope or caution. I think it was a cautionary one.

Now thou he's away from his warring and fighting,
He has gone to the place where naught can delight him,
He may sit now and tell of the sights he has seen Oh,
Why forlorn he does morn on the Isle of St. Helena.
—Anonymous Irish Folk Song

MONTANA

Seen through large picture windows of my house in Montana is an unobstructed, and breathtaking, 32-mile panoramic view of the Helena Valley and surrounding mountains facing due north. At dead center, the "Sleeping Giant" appears as a sentinel; a mountain named by the locals for its appearance: it resembles a man—though of course some insist it's a woman—lying supine, the profiled face sculpted by a formation of jagged rocks to form the forehead, nose, mouth and chin while its stomach arches upward in a heaving gesture. This much-loved figure was formed when the earth shifted then rocked the region in a devastating 1928 earthquake, altering the landscape until the next time the land is re-configured, jolted by the earth's interior movement, the result of unsettled mass residing on a major fault line running straight through the valley. On clear days this view is spectacular and affirms one of the many reasons I moved out West. On this day, however, the view is marred by smoke from the fires that rage outside.

Huge tracts of virginal land throughout Montana blazed for two months during the summer of 2000. The forested areas, populated with millions of fir, cedar and pine trees provide ample fuel for the forces of nature and the foibles of careless men and women. All summer Montana waits in cautious denial while the drought lengthens, the temperatures soaring to record highs. Dry lightning streaks the night sky, their supercharged fingers lashing out towards the parched, arid landscape, tempting to ignite proud fearful trees and assorted grass and brush. Locals and tourists alike gingerly hiked, camped and fished in the abundant public lands, but ever so careful not to tempt fate by mostly respecting the "No Burn" restrictions posted throughout the region. And then on July 25th it happened: the first of many fires erupt in a valley 10 miles north of Helena, the result of carelessness.

White-hot charcoal bricks, dumped in a driveway after a family barbecue, ignited the dry grass adjoining someone's home. The fire sprang to life within minutes. That day I was out running some errands and had pulled into one of many strip malls lining the city's streets, the mall facing the valley where gray-black smoke from the fire spiraled upwards, smearing the late afternoon turquoise sky. I watch in fascination, anticipating the sound of sirens from the trucks manned by the volunteer firemen who wait in tense anticipation to launch their well-rehearsed assault on the unpredictable, fierce, elegant beast. Finally I hear the sinuous, oscillating sounds as they sped from three directions to the fire.

Unlike the blare of a siren in the city, where its high-pitched frequencies are amplified by hard-edged structures built close together causing the sound to slam into your head with a piercing shriek, the sound in rural western areas is more musical; their signals seem to float on the shifting air currents which rise and fall amidst the mountains and valleys. I watch the fire from a distance, hoping the smoke will gradually turn all gray, signaling its death. It doesn't and becomes even darker as a small plume gradually widens and hovers over the valley like a winged dragon. I return to my house, eat dinner, forget about the fire and watch a favorite film that proves to be prescient: *Apocalypse Now.* During the night a second fire erupts 25 miles from the first one, this started by dry lightning and, unlike the first—now named the "Bucksnort Fire" burning in grasslands— this one burned in a heavily forested area just outside of Canyon Ferry Lake, one of the largest dammed, or is it damned, portions of the once mighty Missouri River and the darling of developers throughout the region. By the next morning both fires are burning out of control, threatening permanent and vacation homes as well as prime public and private lands. The siege had officially begun.

From the deck of my house I clearly saw the fires in action. They were now approaching crisis point. The Canyon Ferry fire was especially dramatic; I could see the flames shooting through the smoke, licking at the tops of trees as they consumed one tree after another, moving east, then north according to the direction and speed of the winds. Slowly the smoke from each fire began creeping in toward town, almost as if it were being viewed in time-lapse photography, their formations at first quite elegant then becoming ugly and threatening. Within days the smoke engulfed the city of Helena, blocking out the sun and rendering the entire area a monotonous steel gray color. The acrid smoke hung over everyone.

Domino-like, other fires broke out all over the state. The Bitterroot Valley, located 150 miles to the southwest of Helena, experienced a rash of big and small fires driving hundreds from their homes. A huge fire ignited 40 miles east of Helena joining others ablaze in the Elkhorn Mountains just 20 miles south of the city. Depending on the direction of the winds, the smoke from all these fires found its way to Helena, adding to the initial layers. Day after day the smoke hung in the air sometimes only 200 feet above the surface. The temperatures remained in the mid to upper nineties while the rain stayed away. People were warned of daily air pollution hazards and cautioned against outdoor activities. Eventually the governor closed down thousands upon thousands of acres of public lands, forcing most people indoors for long periods of time. The population was irritable, sad and depressed. This was not a good time to be in the wild and wooly West.

For the next six weeks as fires rampage throughout the state, the smoke-clouds hovered, sometimes receding for a few hours as the wind shifted to the north then south back toward the city. The sunsets during summer months in Montana are unusually spectacular with extraordinary cloud formations colored by golden yellow and magenta hues. During the summer of smoke the sunsets were obscured by a slowly moving battleship-grey scrim, the setting sun burned through the haze. The menacing red-orange ball that hung in the sky resembled photographs of the planet Mars. From my perch above the city I observe these shifting patterns of wind and smoke and glimmering views of the sun devolving into nighttime views without the thousands of stars that normally glisten in the black light, trying to find metaphors for a new life that had, indeed, incinerated my hopes and dreams. Helena, rather than becoming a Valhalla for me, had quickly become my Hades.

Where the preening great prairies of the high plains meet the massive Rocky Mountains at the Continental Divide, Helena, Montana lies east of the great Rocky Mountain Front. It's no accident Helena came into being where many of the great and not-so-great rivers in Western America join and decide their eventual fate: flow west to the Pacific Ocean or east to the Atlantic. From any point in downtown Helena one can view a series of mountain ranges, each with its own history and mythology: the Gates of the Mountains, where Lewis and Clark emerged on their trip up the Missouri River after months of traveling through endless stretches of flat lands across what is now Iowa, South Dakota and the "Wild and Scenic Missouri" of central Montana, to Mullan Pass, where pioneer and adventurer John Mullan built the first "superhighway" for commerce and passage to the Pacific Northwest. Helena, Montana's capitol, is a quiet city of 33,000 people, many of whom work for the state government in elected or appointed civil service jobs. It's a city that doesn't easily accept outsiders. A city that appears to be governed by the hypnotic rhythms of traffic lights which begin flashing at 7 PM on Friday, marking the start of a weekend exodus by the majority of its citizens to the surrounding forests, ski trails, lakes and rivers.

In 1864 gold was discovered at Last Chance Gulch, now the revered Main Street of the city and a two-block long walking mall that, sadly, doesn't feel the weight of too many feet these days. For 20 years Helena—initially named Last Chance Gulch—was one of the wealthiest cities in the United States, with an estimated yield of $3.6 billion worth of valuable minerals, from gold to copper. Chinese, Irish and other European immigrants extracted these ores from numerous mines in the hills surrounding the city. Along with a curious mixture of laborers, drifters, rabble-rousers and homesteaders who traveled from the east and west coasts in search of new lives, Helena gradually grew into a bustling city with a downtown section rivaling those many times its size. An enormous cache of natural resources created more millionaires per capita than any place in the country. The wealthiest bought and brought their particular vision of Europe to the mud-soaked streets of the wild American West. Small wooden homes housing large families stood in sharp contrast to grand mansions built by the new wealthy class complete with roomy carriage houses to accommodate the servants, cooks and nannies, who tended the families of the *nouveau riche*. Today many of those mansions are home to a different kind of ruling class: lawyers, medical doctors and building contractors. Few are descendants of the early residents, most arriving over the past 20 years or so from a variety of locations, seeking the benefits of a rural lifestyle and escaping the "horrors" of urban America.

Other large and small cities throughout the state offer amenities unique to the rural West. For example, Missoula, although an old ranching town at heart, is home to the University of Montana giving it a "bohemian" character unlike any other Montana city. Bozeman is populated by wealthy cattlemen and ranchers. Retired businessmen from the East joust with the Hollywood "elite" to see who can design and erect the biggest—and often ugliest—homes in the spectacular pastures of Paradise Valley. Great Falls is home to one of America's largest and still potent Air Force installations once controlling hundreds of armed missiles located strategically in deep silos within a 100-mile radius of the city. Now the city seems to exist in a sort of time warp, its citizens uncertain of their collective mission other than living out their lives as best they can. Billings, the largest city in the state, has grown from a sleepy western town built to support a wealth of farms and ranches located throughout the eastern Montana plains. In the 1970s Billings grew even more when oil was discovered creating a thriving industry and a new wealthy class of citizens. Those days are long gone but the residue of the wealth that oil brought to the city is evident: the Yellowstone Art Museum is the largest and best endowed in the state; the Alberta Bair Theater is the largest and most active performing arts venue in the state and there are nationally respected medical care facilities and research centers. Other parts of the state, unfortunately, have not fared as well.

At the end of the 20th century Montana ranked 49th in per capita income with the situation in decline. Agriculture and mining were once the life-blood for the proud people of Montana. Its farms provided vintage wheat to other states in the U.S., Asian countries and Russia. Its ranches nurtured prized cattle and sheep that were shipped to points throughout the world. But now family owned and operated ranches and farms cannot compete against the overwhelming power of corporate Ag-Business.

The mines that once supplied huge volumes of silver, copper and even gold have been depleted and, worse yet, poisoned with chemicals that have seeped into the treasured lands and rivers around the mining areas. The technological revolution that transformed parts of the United States in late 20th century bypassed Montana. Chambers of commerce and government agencies continually tried to lure major corporations to re-locate throughout the state but were rebuffed because of an overall lack of amenities for their employees. Tourism remained the number one industry in Montana, with each city marketing themselves according to their particular location or homespun virtues. In January 1998 I landed in this massive troubled state to assume my new job as artistic director of the Myrna Loy Center in Helena.

The Myrna Loy Center is a performing arts and film center named after the actress, Myrna Loy, who was born in nearby Radersberg, Montana and raised through her teens in Helena. The famous actor Gary Cooper was also reared in Helena. The Myrna Loy Center is located in a renovated county jail just a few blocks up the hill from Last Chance Gulch. A fine old building, it has two-foot thick gray walls made from vintage granite blocks drawn from a nearby quarry. The center houses a proscenium theatre, a film screening room, a small gallery to exhibit the works of local artists, a concession stand, box office and administrative offices. Throughout the building there are photos of Myrna in various film roles that she created: Myrna and William Powell in the *Thin Man*; Myrna and Clark Gable standing side-by-side striving to appear infatuated when they actually detested one another; and my personal favorite: Myrna in her classic broad-brimmed hat sitting atop boxer-actor Primo Carnero's huge hand as he stands inside a boxing ring seemingly readying himself to shot-put Myrna into the bleachers. In stark contrast to this faded Hollywood gloss, other inhabitants of the old jail lurk about: ghosts.

I was told by several locals that they will never step foot in the Myrna Loy Center, not because of the film and performance fare, but because of ghosts of prisoners past. When the building was renovated in 1991-92 several walls were left in their retired state containing graffiti penned by prisoners. It's sort of eerie, especially in the staff bathroom where one wall is inscribed, "Careful of the swinging doors," and "This really is Hell!" Other than these contacts I never encountered any of the infamous ghosts of long-gone prisoners. I had enough to keep me occupied during my tenure there.

The Myrna Loy Center was created by a well-intended individual to bring unique performance and film works to a city that seemed not really interested in the notion of discovery through the arts. The product appealed to a small yet dedicated clientele of local artists and their friends who gave whatever time and money they could afford to help realize the mission. A hard-working, effective and woefully underpaid staff developed programs often without overall institutional support. By creating alliances with individuals and organizations throughout the area that shared their interest in arts education and cultural enlightenment, the staff was able to build a reputation as a driving force within arts presenting and education, not only throughout the region but nationally.

For The Myrna Loy Center to present works that have limited appeal it had to subsidize those performances. Most of this subsidy was in the form of grants awarded by major national philanthropic foundations, the state arts council and the National Endowment for the Arts. In the early 1990s the NEA directed as much funding as possible to rural American arts facilities, selecting those that developed innovative programs to empower its region to support a combination of traditional and new artistic works. These funds were then used to match other gifts from major national foundations like the Rockefeller Foundation and Wallace Funds. When this money began to dry up, the Myrna Loy Center found itself with a severe lack of money to support not only their programming goals but the overall administration costs.

Large, multi-year awards were restricted to programs and specific educational and audience building projects, with the intention that other regional foundations would provide matching funds along with "earned income" to sustain daily administrative operations. This income would then be matched by local contributions from individuals and businesses in the community, a formula that can work quite well when the organization is located in a large and relatively sophisticated market. There are, however, few regional foundations located throughout the High Plains that can match the large grants awarded from national agencies and foundations. This forces an organization like the Myrna Loy Center to rely almost entirely on federal funding and grants from large national foundations. Unless organizations like the Myrna Loy Center have strong, visionary board leadership to develop ongoing income streams, then they may fail once the national funding strategies change. These strategies did change and the Myrna Loy Center faced many challenges.

When I arrived in Helena the board of directors consisted of well meaning individuals who were, essentially, friends of the founding director or friends of each other. Many were devoted to the Myrna Loy Center and its mission. A few attended all of the events they could possibly attend at the center. Some never attended anything. None were wealthy or connected to the wealthier members of the community. None seemed to understood the current trends that informed how arts organizations strategically align themselves with federal and state agencies, local and national corporations and community organizations to develop partnerships and alliances so that critical issues could be presented and discussed in a collaborative environment. They were never asked to give or raise money, organize fundraising events or develop plans to elevate the organization's image in the community at-large. Most critically they were not trained to be board members of an arts organization and therefore did not have strong leadership. And they did not raise money. To remedy this I took it upon myself to develope a marketing strategy to broaden the appeal of the Myrna Loy Center in the region.

I set out to change the image of the Myrna Loy Center within the community and reach out to those who, for whatever reasons, viewed the center as "weird," the operative word I heard in my travels around the city. The existing arts education programs, although exemplary, were viewed as focusing only on elementary and secondary students throughout the area. This despite the fact that a huge effort was made to reach out to other segments of the adult community, specifically senior citizens, Native Americans, Montana artists and professional educators. Unfortunately, little effort had been made to embrace the largest percentage of Helena's residents: government employees. By appealing to these and other folks who felt disenfranchised by the center, we might have been able to expand the audience as well as solicit individual contributions and memberships from them. I tried to empower the board to be more pro-active in the community. One of the tasks I assigned them was to introduce me and other staff members to influential citizens who, in turn, might schedule meetings and related events to better inform people of the role the Myrna Loy Center plays in the community. While this appeared to me a simple request, it proved problematic. After repeated requests and pleas I determined that this community board of directors did not know very many people in the community and certainly did not know those influential citizens, especially ones with "deep pockets."

I then suggested we create a series of fundraising events aimed at the folks in Helena who were interested in wine, food, travel, literature, etc. These events might bring people together in a convivial atmosphere to meet, learn about one another and discuss issues of interest. As a wine enthusiast and consumer I was friendly with the two wine merchants in town, neither of whom had ever met one another before. We developed a plan to host a wine tasting, featuring expensive wines they would purchase from their distributors at a price well below the usual cost. We then enlisted the services of a new restaurateur who had recently opened the only trattoria in town. He readily agreed to provide food for a multi-course dinner—at a minimal cost—to accompany the wine tasting. I suggested to the board that we charge $100 for a couple and $75 for an individual to attend and aim for 100 people, generating around $8,000. After expenses the Myrna Loy Center would have about $6,000 in revenue. It seemed like a good deal to me but not to the board.

They felt that the admission/contribution prices were too high, that folks in Helena would not pay $100 or $75 for a wine tasting to benefit the Myna Loy Center. To save money someone suggested that the board provide food. My plan was not moving ahead. The board did not act on my proposal and the tasting was never held. Some on the board perceived my effort as somewhat effete, that I was misrepresenting the image of the Myrna Loy Center.

Shortly after this failed attempt to raise funds, another opportunity popped up. I received an unsolicited gift that could easily have generated a large sum of contributed income. An anonymous donor gave the Myrna Loy Center a work of art by one of Montana's most celebrated artists, Deborah Butterfield. Ms. Butterfield's works are based on the image of the horse. Elegant and often highly "abstract" her sculpted pieces can be found in museums and private collections worldwide. The donated work is one of her earliest: a relatively small piece depicting a pony grazing, its body, hair and other features made from various wires commonly used on ranches throughout the west. Several styles of barbed wire, for example are used in its construction. The donor wishing to assist both the Myrna Loy Center and another art center in Bozeman, Montana which was also having financial problems, entrusted the sale of the work to the Myrna Loy Center which would, in turn, deliver one-third of the revenue from the sale to the other organization and retain two-thirds. If handled properly the Myrna Loy Center stood to receive $20,000, which would be used—as per the donor's wish—to establish a fund to present the works of Montana performing artists. To me, this gift was truly wondrous; everyone wins, the Myrna Loy Center, the other arts center and selected performers throughout the state. I asked the board of directors for their help but received none.

Eventually, with the help of Peter Held, director of the Holter Museum in Helena, we sold the work through a highly respected gallery in Seattle, but for a lower price than we hoped for. The gallery represents Deborah Butterfield and the owner felt certain that this early work would be attractive to collectors of her work. He was correct. After the gallery took their commission the Myrna Loy Center received $10,000 to be used to support Montana performing artists.

Things continued to decline for me—especially relations with the board. There was just no way I could continue without the support I felt was needed: a board with active fundraising capabilities and a sharing of my artistic vision.

It was clear to me that it was time to move on. I submitted my resignation and formed a consulting company named Metadesign Associates. I had made a number of contacts in Montana and concluded that my experiences could help organizations statewide. I was hired by several organizations to help with fundraising and programming, giving me time to search for a new position while Laurel continued to build the programs she inherited at the Montana Arts Council. The remaining eighteen months we lived there gave us ample opportunity to explore the state and enjoy some of the most spectacular land in the United States. But living in Montana was still a struggle.

The tempestuous fires that scorched hundreds of thousands of acres of western land during the summer of 2000 rekindled in new and old residents alike a respect for nature's way. Forest fires are a natural phenomenon, at least those caused by lightning, not by carelessness. Fires replenish the land by clearing dead or dying trees to make way for new ones. As older pine trees become consumed by the flames, their discarded cones release new seeds that replenish the land with seedlings. Within a generation the seedlings will become mature trees to nurture the land and await their eventual demise and transformation.

Like those pine trees, I too had experienced a transformation that could only have come about by dramatically changing my life. By exchanging the high-amp intensity of city life for the low-key reflection of rural life I discovered that the differences between the two lifestyles are fairly transparent. Other than the ways in which the physical beauty of places like Montana informs people's behavior, people really aren't that much different from place to place. They will, in general, do whatever it takes to "win," at any cost; the differences are in style.

Those three years I lived in Montana were strange ones indeed. The cultural differences I experienced were too great for someone reared in an urban environment to find acceptance in rural regions of the United States. When I left Philadelphia I was angry. I had tired of "fighting the good fight" for recognition and financial stability, tired of leading a performing arts organization that had achieved high visibility throughout the United States and abroad yet faced indifference at home. In retrospect when compared to the short time in Montana my life in Philadelphia was a joy, a series of challenges and discoveries that might only have been experienced from having grown up in a neighborhood beneath the rumble of the Frankford Elevated train and not in the shadow of a mountain called The Sleeping Giant.

LOUISIANA

For many years radio station WRTI-FM, owned and operated by Temple University, valiantly endeavored to present "America's Classical Music—Jazz" to listeners in Philadelphia. They like most radio stations in the United States dedicated to a jazz format struggled against indifference and ignorance, but they hung in there until the mid-1990s when the university administration formed a partnership with radio station WFLN-FM, an independently owned classical music station that, like WRTI, was losing audience and sponsor support. The result of this partnership, known by the call letters WRTI-FM, is a radio hybrid with classical music in the morning and afternoon and jazz in the evening with Salsa on Saturday nights. Throughout this transition and new program format, Harrison Ridley Jr. remains a presence on-air, as he selects thousands of tunes from his vast personal record collection of "straight-ahead jazz," big band and vocal music and weaves them into intelligent reassuring programs, his distinctive voice flowing if not smoothly then soothingly across the wire.

Harrison is a passionate student of the jazz traditions and clearly enjoys sharing his knowledge of this music with his dedicated listeners. One of the charming things about Harrison is the way he sometimes tells his stories: steeped in history and rich with personal observations yet blessed with the occasional malapropism. One of my favorites is his way of announcing a timeless standard, "That was what a difference do a day make," the meaning clear and endearingly rendered.

When I lived in Montana there were no less than three excellent public radio stations I could tune into, and I certainly did. There was, however, little jazz other than a few nationally syndicated programs picked up by one of the stations. In Billings, Montana, their local public radio station hosted a two-hour jazz program every day, pretty daring for that region and certainly appreciated by those of us who love the music. But sadly there was nobody like Harrison Ridley Jr. to spin the discs and entertain with anecdotes and personal histories about the music, rendered in such a distinctive style.

I arrived in Baton Rouge, Louisiana in late July 2001, a huge weight lifted from my shoulders. The final eighteen months in Montana were lived inside a large bubble that burst only when we took off for a weekend of cross-country skiing or hiking in Yellowstone or Glacier Parks, or a long weekend trip to Seattle, or visiting friends in Missoula. The silence I heard every day in Helena was frightening and a bit devastating to a guy like me whose existence had been shaped by the sounds of a life lived fully, sometimes dangerously and loudly. Laurel and I landed in Louisiana almost by chance, although in reality our journey was conceptually—or curiously—well planned.

While still in Helena I began to plan how I might return to writing and radio; create—once again— my own organization; or expand an arts-management consulting business I had founded, but someplace else. I suggested to Laurel we begin looking for a position for her now that she had established impressive credentials in Pennsylvania as the director of a community music school and in Montana as the director of programs for the Montana Arts Council. One of the first listings we found was an executive director's position at the Louisiana Division of the Arts. Laurel sent off her application. Within a month she got a response. The person heading the search committee—a board member of the Louisiana Division of the Arts appointed by the governor—called to schedule a phone interview with Laurel, one that went very well; she was invited to formally interview for the job in Baton Rouge.

After interviewing with senior staff from the Lieutenant Governor's office and the search committee Laurel was asked to stay over an extra day in order to meet personally with the Lieutenant Governor, Kathleen Babineaux-Blanco which proved the deciding factor in the interview process. Laurel returned to Helena fully expecting to be offered the position of director, Division of the Arts for the State of Louisiana. When the call came two weeks later an offer was made not to direct the Division of the Arts but for a senior position in the Lieutenant Governor's cabinet overseeing the divisions of the Arts, Historic Preservation and Archeology. It turns out the interview process was actually to search for two positions and Laurel fit the profile for the senior one. She accepted and after giving notice to the Montana Arts Council we set in motion the process of once again selling a house and moving across country, only this time a move into America's Deep South.

Following an exploratory trip in June to find a new home in Baton Rouge, sell our house in Montana and pack our belongings, we drove to Louisiana, arriving on a Saturday in mid-July, the temperature pushing 100 degrees Fahrenheit with the humidity at around 90 percent. The landscape surrounding us was green and lush and wet. Since the moving van would not arrive with our furniture for another five days we had prepared to stay in our new house by buying a futon and cooking with utensils from our hiking and camping supplies. I had one small portable radio with me. On our first night in Baton Rouge we cooked succulent Louisiana shrimp and turned on the radio. The first voice I heard in this new land has remained with me. The voice was that of a man named Tabby Thomas.

Tabby Thomas is a veteran Blues musician from Baton Rouge who personifies an era when Blues artists were King in Louisiana and throughout the entire Mississippi Delta region. A large man who barely fits behind the wheel of his ancient Cadillac as he drives around the city, neatly dressed in suit and hat; the man has style. He owns a small blues club named "Tabby's Blues Box and Heritage Hall." Set amidst the remnants of downtown Baton Rouge "Tabby's" features blues artists from throughout the region including numerous performances by Tabby Thomas' Swamp Cats. Blues aficionados do not exactly flock to Tabby's but they do support his efforts to present pure Southern Blues in a room that has loads of character.

In addition to performing and promoting blues artists, Tabby also hosts a wonderful Blues show each Saturday on a small public radio station owned and operated by the Baton Rouge Magnet High School. Although a bit rough around the edges and prone to Tabby's repeating himself from week-to-week, it is a good little show. Clearly Tabby and his independent radio hosts could use some expertise at the production end, but that aside, Tabby's informed comments about the blues artists he has known and worked with are priceless. So is the way he expresses himself. And this, our first taste of Baton Rouge and of Tabby Thomas was precisely what we needed after three years living in the desolate High Plains.

As we sat in our new empty house on the floor eating shrimp that first night in Baton Rouge Tabby was in the radio studio playing music and reminiscing about the life of Blues men and women from his past. With personal references to Howlin Wolf, Muddy Waters, Clarence "Gatemouth" Brown, Louisiana Red and others, Tabby sort of paused, sighed and said in his gravelly baritone voice, "Guess I'm gettin' carried away thinkin' about my old friends. Times ain't what they used to be, it's hard tryin' to make a living singin' the Blues these days. And I done been around a long time. I guess you could say I'm in the twilight zone these days." Laurel and I looked at one another, laughed and in unison said, "Yeah, what a difference do a day make."

Once again we found ourselves living in a fairly large city, one only 75 miles equidistant between New Orleans and Lafayette in a region rich in cultural diversity and history. Baton Rouge, the state capitol, is much more conservative than other southern Louisiana cities, ruled as it is by the overwhelming presence of Louisiana State University and the bureaucracies of state government. City leaders have been working for years to turn the downtown areas around and bring people once again to the city's core along the shores of the still mighty Mississippi River after years of urban sprawl, white flight and the sad Malling of America that has virtually decimated the downtown section of the city. But, unfortunately, it's a city without a soul. We lived there, sure, but we spent all of spare time in New Orleans, having found a wonderful inexpensive weekend apartment to use as our staging ground to explore the ancient city. We met a number of artists, architects, writers and other folks who were either born in New Orleans or, like us, migrated there in search of a new life. These new friends embraced us and made certain that we felt welcome. We did feel welcome but we knew our stay in steamy Louisiana was temporary.

PHILADELPHIA REDUX

I went back to Philadelphia on September 14, 2001. My trips to Philadelphia and New York City had been planned well before the terrorist attacks and despite the national trauma and general apprehension to fly. I did not consider canceling the trip. I was on a mission to put closure to my Philadelphia life.

The Relâche Ensemble was to perform at the Philadelphia Ethical Society, site of many Relâche concerts I had produced. This was not simply another Relâche concert; it marked pianist John Dulik's final performance with the group. After 22 years John decided to "retire" from the music ensemble he had devoted so much time and energy to. Although he would continue to perform around the city he was cutting back a bit to devote more time to teach and roam around the farm he shares with his companion Sandra Foltzer in northern Pennsylvania.

John Dulik is *the* original member of Relâche. We met shortly after both of us returned to Philadelphia from military service, subsequently attending graduate school together at Temple University. Throughout his tenure with Relâche I think it is safe to say that he was a steadying influence on everyone who performed with the group. With impeccable musicianship, unerring artistic awareness and a friendly even-tempered disposition John gained the trust and respect of everyone who played alongside him. One word epitomizes him: steady. In addition to attending the weekend concert I was to have dinner with many of my old friends in Philadelphia and New York City. Accordingly I planned to drive to New York and spend a few days there.

John Dulik

The drive is one I have made hundreds of times: 92 miles from my former home in South Philadelphia to midtown Manhattan via the New Jersey Turnpike. It isn't a picturesque journey, although during Autumnal foliage the kaleidoscopic landscape alongside the highway blazes with colors of burnt sienna, orange-red and green-brown, an especially dramatic view when contrasted against a clear blue sky. On September 22, 2001 with a slight fall chill in the air I once again found myself on the same familiar stretch of road, only this time feelings of discovery were replaced with feelings of despair at what I knew I would see in New York City.

In past times this drive was one I have always enjoyed. As Philadelphia's uneven pleading skyline disappears from view, you enter a portion of New Jersey's lesser known areas, the Turnpike's swath of concrete set far from the ubiquitous tracts of suburban homes that seem to hide from view and thoughts. This approximately 40-mile stretch of land running alongside the vast reaches of McGuire Air Force Base on the east and the elegant picture-perfect campus of Princeton University on the west often reminded me of those moments before sleep, when the conscious self straddles the unconscious, anticipating a realm of dreams with magical images dancing in-and-out of view. I was passing from my all-too-evident conscious awareness of Philadelphia's low-key energy to New York's highly attenuated intensity of action and reaction. Although firmly in command of my senses as I negotiated the rough road of one of the country's oldest highways, my body tensed, preparing itself for the onslaught of images and signs that consciously signified New York City.

While driving due north past New Brunswick and the square glass facades of the New Jersey Turnpike Commission office buildings the landscape changes from semi-rural to industrial raw. Manufacturing plants sit next to warehouses with dozens of shipping bays dispensing goods into trailers for delivery across the country while petroleum refineries spew their toxic waste into the air just to keep those trucks on the road. Right about at this point, Exit 12 leading to Edison, New Jersey, your gaze penetrates the smoke and haze of industrial America to catch the first glimpse of perhaps the most famous skyline in the world. Although on this glorious early fall day something was missing. It took me a full minute to realize that the downtown Manhattan skyline, a vista I had relied on for years, a navigation point that psychically transported me from one life style to a dramatically different one, had changed. And irrevocably so.

As I continued heading towards Manhattan more and more of the cityscape appeared. Newark Airport just to the west of the Turnpike came into view, the airspace filled with commercial jets departing and arriving casting fleeting shadows as they pass directly overhead. Through the traffic in the air and on the road the Manhattan skyline was now in full view. My eyes scanned the view from midtown in the left-side of my periphery, seeking the Empire State Building as a beacon then slowly shift my eyes to the right-side periphery where I expected to see the sun glinting off of the World Trade Center towers, their size dominating the vista. But the Towers were not there. In their place was an ugly gray spiral of smoke reaching for the same thin air as those departing airplanes, its inverted pyramid-like shape smearing the crystal clear blue sky on its journey up and over the Atlantic Ocean. I felt sick to my stomach. And the constant mechanical sounds of cars and trucks sailing across the soiled concrete of the Turnpike contrasted sharply with the eerie dull quiet that settled inside the car.

Past Exits 15 and the closed Holland Tunnel I continue up the turnpike as it bends to the left before hooking back towards Manhattan bringing me closer to the city. The traffic was heavy on this day but it somehow felt different from previous trips; everyone it seemed was feeling the same as I was and driving with some hesitation or perhaps newfound courtesy for others. I couldn't help but feel that everyone's eyes were doing the same dance: from rear-view mirror glances to the road ahead to the skyline on the right, fixing those looks a bit too long perhaps, then beginning the sequence again. The exit for the Lincoln Tunnel came into view. Many cars, trucks and busses began the slow crawl to the toll booth before heading for the final stretch of road that leads to midtown Manhattan.

The road linking the Jersey Turnpike to the Lincoln Tunnel is approximately three miles. It slowly meanders under numerous pedestrian and auto overpasses and past movie complexes, cheap rent-by-the-hour motels complete with ceiling mirrors and in-room movies and other sediment of urban excess. Seldom does one make this part of the journey in less than 20 minutes, on a good day. On this day it was bumper-to-bumper and took about a half hour.

Suddenly the much-anticipated unobstructed view of the expansive New York skyline appeared, a dramatic sight stretching from uptown near the George Washington Bridge in the Bronx all the way downtown and across the bay into Staten Island, the sun glistening off choppy waters surrounding the island, the majestic Verrazano Narrows Bridge in the distance. It was a breathtaking vista marred this day by the gray smoke furling upward. From this distance and at this perspective the smoke's color and thickness was sickening beyond belief. I slowly inched closer to the toll booth then entered the tunnel lit by the harsh glare of high intensity mercury lights and hundreds of pairs of headlights guiding their masters to the playgrounds of New York City.

I emerged at the other end of the tunnel having slipped under the Hudson River, and headed directly for the Port Authority Parking Garage on 42nd Street that I have used for years to park my car before heading out onto the big bad streets of the city. Again, something seemed different. Over the course of the next two days I was to experience as close to first hand as I could the effect of the terrorist attacks on this proud city.

Although I never officially lived in New York City I know its geography and rhythms quite well. From my base in Philadelphia I built an international entity, a task made easier by my proximity to New York where major foundations and numerous composers and performers reside, where informed audiences wait in anticipation—and critical repose—for new concepts and ideas to take shape. To establish a reputation in the field of musical creation and performance one simply had to work in New York, whether one lived there or not. Over my many years residing in Philadelphia I averaged at least one visit to New York each week, more when Relâche performed there, often as a starting point in a tour throughout New York State.

Once in the city I usually navigated to my appointments via the subway and elevated trains, busses and ferries, all of which provide efficient and inexpensive passage to the city's five boroughs. And of course you walk, walking being among the many pleasures enticing resident and visitor alike. To successfully negotiate the public transportation system and the streets of New York, you adopt an attitude, a way of walking or standing or moving through a crowded concourse. For a Philly boy this was not difficult as the streets of that home city can prove equally demanding. But for others less experienced in urban ways and wiles, it could be problematic. Once you declare yourself and affirm your piece of concrete—however fleeting that ownership may be—you can find the flow and just go with it. One succumbs easily to the tempo. On this day however the movement through the streets appeared erratic.

I emerged from the parking garage near Times Square fully prepared for battle, anticipating the usual in-your-face attitude I had become so accustomed to over the years. But when I stepped onto 42nd Street and began walking toward the Seventh Avenue Subway it appeared that everyone was moving at a slower pace. Eyes normally fixed straight ahead in a "don't mess with me" kind of look were much less severe; soft glances or an acknowledgement, even smiles accompanied their slower movement through time and place. "Hey, how you doin' today," they seemed to be saying, a gesture of shared humanity. Entering the subway at Seventh Avenue I saw it was almost empty, rare on any day at any time. I took the Number 1 train heading downtown where I was to meet friends in Greenwich Village.

Like the people on the streets above the subway, everyone riding on the trains appeared to be in a daze. Once again, there were friendly looks and gestures of accommodation; nobody brushed by on their way in or out of the car with little regard for a "Pardon me." Today it was, "Excuse me, this is my stop. Thanks." The train seemed to float through the underground tunnels, their steel wheels skipping over the rails rather than mechanically grinding forward in a reckless ramble from stop-to-stop, wheels screeching through a glissando of high-pitched wails. Rather than getting off at 4th Street in the Village I decided to go further downtown, close to "Ground Zero," something I hadn't planned on doing. I felt a strong psychic attraction, something pulling or pushing me downtown.

I got off the train at the Canal Street Station and, as I've done many times in the past, headed toward the Leonard Street stairway. When I emerged from the station onto Sixth Avenue, the first thing I saw was a flatbed truck that had stopped at the intersection directly in front of me. There were five cars stacked on it, each a different shade of gray-black, their roofs crushed and mangled from the tons of concrete and steel that might have landed on them when the towers fell, their metal bodies seared from the fires. I stopped and just stared in disbelief. The truck moved on leaving a clear view of a hole where the towers once stood, acrid smoke rising from the fires still burning below ground. Through the haze an elegant web of water from the fire hoses appeared, their forced wet streams aimed from various points around the perimeter of the gaping hole, directed at flames smoldering and slowly consuming everything that had been rendered lifeless just ten days before. After observing the scene I began walking back uptown to the relative comfort of my friends and away from the sickening smell that permeated the air.

Walking north on Sixth Avenue I passed a fire station. The entire front of the building had become a shrine to the men from that unit who died in the collapse of the towers. Reliquaries of photographs of the dead or missing and drawings by school students from the neighborhood stood in silent anticipation alongside colored candles and boxes of food left by residents in deep mourning for times past, never to be recovered. Three blocks further on I passed a police station, more candles, boxes of food, stick-men drawings made with familiar Crayola colors posted next to rows of black-and-white photographs of more dead and missing men and women; the photos haunt, their smiling faces appear to float in-and-out of my memory. I continued up Sixth Avenue to Greenwich Village and the sanctuary of old friends.

I hadn't seen Eve Beglarian since late 1999, my last visit back to New York. One of the many innovative composers I have had the pleasure of working with during my career, we were looking forward to catching up on old times. We met at her apartment on Sixth Avenue at 10th Street. From just outside her entrance, looking south, one has a perfect view of downtown. She began detailing her experience when, on September 11th she stepped outside her door after hearing the scream of sirens cascading down the adjoining streets to see black smoke billowing from the north tower of the World Trade Center searing the blue sky, then a second explosion and more smoke and flames from the south tower. She watched in disbelief as the buildings cascaded down accompanied by a low rumble and a cloud of smoke that began moving towards her. She fled inside and for the next two weeks, amid the eerie quiet of Greenwich Village, began a recovery that will take months, if not years. Another friend was even closer to the destruction.

Abel is a guitarist and web designer. On September 11th he was in his office just a block from the World Trade Center when the planes hit. He stepped onto the street as part of a fairly orderly evacuation, not certain just what had happened, only that the occupants of his building were told to go home as quickly as possible. What he saw will remain with him forever: bodies falling out of the sky along with debris from the slowly weakening World Trade Center towers. He told me quietly what he saw, his eyes never moving from mine. Then silence. We never discussed it again.

The remainder of my visit to New York City was uneventful, with time spent on the phone attempting to arrange visits with other friends only to abandon those plans as travel in-and-around the city was complicated. When I finally began the drive back to Philadelphia I found myself coursing through the same pattern that defined my trip the day before, only this time my every action was in reverse order. Now it was the uneven, beckoning New York City skyline that receded in the distance.

As I eventually approached the familiar asymmetrical skyline of Philadelphia I felt an odd, paradoxical sensation: I was home, although I no longer lived there. But, I was home, at least temporarily with the images gleaned from two days in New York resonating deeply and sorrowfully in my soul. Nothing I saw on television, the Internet or in newspapers and magazines adequately prepared me for what I had seen on this return visit. I stood just blocks from the site of the destruction peering into that enormous hole and remembering a time back in 1970 when I watched workers lay the foundation of the first World Trade Center tower. I will never forget the contrasting images of birth and destruction, the memories of professional and personal achievement, the joy and discovery of new artistic works in theatres, galleries and concert halls that define my New York experiences throughout a productive life. And I will never forget this visit at a time when life in America has been dramatically changed.

The remainder of my visit to Philadelphia went according to plan. The Relâche Ensemble concert was beautifully performed, the new configuration of the group quite different from the one I left; the overall ensemble sound quite different, of course, but the spirit prevailed giving a glow to the music. John Dulik was—as usual—brilliant, his playing strong and decisive. Afterwards at a reception for John he and I reminisced a bit about our long professional association. I reminded him of a comment he made to me while we were visiting a Shinto Temple in Japan: "Who would have thought it, Joseph, from that little concert at the Painted Bride, to Tokyo. Way to go."

Did I gain a feeling of closure from this visit as I had hoped? It's hard to say given the circumstances and the sadness I felt, images of a violated New York City still visible in my mind's eye. In contrast the Relâche Ensemble concert was a joyous experience, an affirmation of my desire to be part of something that remains a unique component of 21st century musical life in Philadelphia.

On September 20, 2001, a cold Philadelphia wind catches me off balance just as I emerge from my friend Tony Creamer's car, a warning perhaps that my planned journey to my old neighborhood would chill the otherwise warm memories I had carried with me since leaving over three years previously. I park Tony's car on the corner of Tioga Street and Kensington Avenue just below the El and start walking along Kensington Avenue. The unseasonably cool air reminds me of frigid winter days when I stood on that very corner waiting for the SEPTA number 5 Bus, my nose numb to the cold.

My plan is to walk the streets I knew as a young boy starting from my old house on Pacific Street. I walk down Kensington Avenue hoping to see and hear the El overhead; I guess my timing's off, the El rumbles by just after I turn east on Pacific Street past boarded up houses and empty refuse-strewn lots. My boyhood friend Harry Musarino lived in one of these houses with his extended family while chickens, cats and dogs ran around in their junkyard backyard dodging a steady stream of leathered bikers who hung around with Harry's dad. I stopped at the intersection of Pacific and Glenwood Avenue and stand in the middle of Pacific looking toward Jasper Street remembering all the games of stick ball, half ball and wire ball I played within the confines of our street diamond. And I recall the feel of a white pimple ball in my hand before throwing it straight up to the sky trying to hit not one but several of the electrical wires strung overhead, a lattice-work weaving that appeared to bind the streets together in a sometimes uneasy community.

Wireball is one of the stranger street games we used to play, the goal being to hit a wire with the ball sending the ball zooming in another direction with dizzying spin so your opponent had a hard time catching the ball as it fell to earth. If he caught it, you're out. If he dropped it—or did not touch it—you were awarded a score according to the number of wires the ball did or did not singe.

Standing in the middle of the street lost in the memories of childhood I suddenly realized how quiet it was; there's nobody home!

All the houses on the south side were boarded up except for one, while those on the north side were in somewhat better condition: six of the ten occupied. My old house stood proud amidst the rubble, the green awnings that topped every window and front door appearing as inanimate sentinels fixed to ward off the ghosts that roamed throughout the neighborhood. As I walked down the street I grew apprehensive the closer I got to the stoop I had helped my mother scrub down with cleanser and bleach, the same stoop where matters of important domestic and international affairs were settled by the knights of the neighborhood in faded denim and soiled khakis. In the window at 1855 East Pacific Street there were two small American flags crossed above a small sign that read, "**NEVER FORGET**."

The wind picked up once more and carried a potent scent toward me, more than a little familiar, and not at all pleasant. As I approached Jasper Street a vacant lot stood where another of my boyhood friends had lived. The lot was filthy with garbage and assorted debris, the ground giving way to gravity and untold abuse over the years. The stench was stronger there and unmistakable: sewer gas. The sewer system had probably not been cleaned out for a long time. It had become overly ripe, its acrid odor mixed with mildew and rotting garbage. The air always smelled a bit foul when I grew up there, the result of numerous factories forcing gases and smoke into the air, but never that bad. I turned right and walked south on Jasper toward Tioga Street and the corner candy store and tap room that served as gathering places for many in the neighborhood. Both were boarded up, as were many of the houses along the street. As I approached the corner I hear recorded music, a distinct clave rhythm clicking along propelling the horns and conga drums beckoning the old Salsero ancestors to bring some of their warm perfumed Puerto Rican air into this decaying Philadelphia neighborhood. For the first time since I had begun this little journey I smile.

The music came from a small house on Tioga Street located directly next door to the Craftex Mill, long closed but miraculously still standing! The water tower on the building's roof had small trees and weeds sprouting from its carcass, somehow thriving while most everything else around it was dying. The music became clearer as I walked past the house and I think I recognized the sound of Orchestra Unica, one of the finest Salsa bands in Philadelphia, one that I had heard many times in my associations with the Latino community while I lived there. As I pass by I noticed the window of the house; more flags, this time, a small American flag crossed with a small Puerto Rican flag, over still another sign that reads, "**NEVER FORGET**."

CODA
NEW MEXICO

I returned to Louisiana to build a new life and support Laurel's effort to work in state government. After 2 ½ years and too many close encounters with seedy land developers, stuck-in-the-mud bureaucrats and visionless city leaders we decided to sell our house in Baton Rouge and move to New Mexico. We left in February 2004 with a plan to live with Laurel's parents in Corrales until we could establish ourselves in the community. It took only five months for both of us to find new positions and a home in what is obliquely referred to as the "People's Republic of Albuquerque," a section of the city just south of the University of New Mexico.

By the end of the summer I had been hired as the new executive director of Chamber Music Albuquerque, a long-time presenter of chamber music in the city. Although distanced from the post-classical world that I had been so much a part of, I nevertheless found myself challenged by the demands of directing an organization that had built its reputation on presenting traditional repertoire from the Euro-American classical music canon. But Chamber Music Albuquerque had established a regional reputation for excellence and fiscal responsibility. And they had a board of directors that understood their roles and their relationship to the executive director. This was a huge change from my experience in Montana. Shortly after taking the position Laurel was hired as the executive director of the New Mexico Association of Food Banks, a position far from her field of expertise but one that used her considerable administrative experience. We settled in to a new life in a growing city with an expanding network of friends and collaborators. We determined that, whenever possible, we would explore the region and visit many of the sites that had been seared into our memories on previous trips to New Mexico and the Four Corners region. And, of course, Canyon de Chelly beckoned.

I suppose we all have a place in this world—a building, wooded trail, river or ocean beach—that leavens the soul; a place where from time-to-time, we must escape to clear the mind and body from the daily tension of contemporary life. Clearly, for me, Canyon de Chelly is that place. We planned our first re-visit to Canyon de Chelly for April, 2005.

We arrived at the canyon on a beautiful early spring day to hike the White House Ruins, one of many sites built by the Anasazi people who inhabited the canyon during their brief dramatic history. This is the only hike that is permitted into the canyon without a Navajo guide and one that we had made many times in the past, arriving at the White House Ruins after a steep forty-five minute trek down a path that cuts through the rock and scrub of the canyon. Our previous hikes down this now well-trod path were exciting ones. At the bottom of the canyon, one follows the path as it leads to a sandy spew of land that hooks around one of the enormous rock walls that stands guard over the spirits of the White House ruins. After threading through the brush and slipping over a narrow rivulet—part of the Chinle Wash—one comes upon an orchard of cottonwood trees. Behind the trees are the ruins. Spreading out from both sides of the fading ancient brick dwellings are two flat red-rock walls. Beneath a crease in the rock that runs parallel to the ground about 30 feet above the floor of the canyon are rows of pictographs that once told elegant stories of the friends and foes of the Anasazi. The stories are still imbedded in the rock art, but these days viewing them is difficult due to the barbed wire fence that has been erected around the ruins and along the base of the rocky wings that reach for the tips of the old cottonwood trees. The pictographs had been defaced.

There wasn't a need to spend much time at the ruins. We viewed it through a prism of time that focused the images we had stored in our minds of the ruins from times past, disgusted at the actions of those who had violated the ancient land. Our trip back to the top of the canyon was subdued. That day, the mystique of Canyon de Chelly like air from a pricked tire was in danger of escaping from our minds and souls, until, thankfully, the following day.

The rains thundered in from the north that night, soaking the sacred land, adding its precious cargo to the already bloated Chinle Wash; a good omen at this time of the year given the long-standing drought that the region had been living through. In the morning the clouds hovered over the canyon, a misty gray scrim of repressed denuded water that shifted ever so slowly in the undulating currents of air that floated above and below the canyon. And it was cold: 40 degrees with a wind-chill factor like those Aquarian blasts of icy air that splattered into our faces as we navigated the urban canyons of Philadelphia or New York City. We decided to drive along the rim road and stop at designated overlook sites. Our goal was to circumnavigate as much of the canyon's rims as weather permitted. We began with a top-side view of White House Ruins and proceeded east along the rim of Canyon de Chelly on our approach to the point where Canyon de Chelly meets and collapses into Canyon del Muerto, just west of the magical pinnacle of Spider Rock. The gray clouds stayed their course, dampening everyone who navigated along the rim's edge. The wind shifted east then south just as we approached the overlook to Spider Rock. We parked our car in the overlook parking lot and walked out to the barricaded overlook site, the wind whipping the slowly falling rain into a frenzy of small tornado-like funnels of stinging water.

As we approached the overlook site, with its steel-girded railing where one could grasp the cold metal and peer down into the vast canyon, the sun broke through the undulating clouds. Like time-lapse photography the view brightened as the sun pierced the gray scrim and illuminated the canyon. Before us stood Spider Rock and just to the left the portal into Canyon del Muerto. The entire vista glittered like the mythical gold Alberich stole from the Rhinemaidens in Richard Wagner's opera *Das Rheingold*. Unlike Alberich our greed was not for the gold but for the ownership of the land that we now were a part of. That ownership was not literal, of course, but metaphorical. We stood looking at Spider Rock, that mystical point of remembrance hoping that Spider Woman would offer us the loose thread that would lead us into the inner life of the land that we were destined to reside in.

Finally, we were home.

Printed in the United States
68187LVS00007B/22